THE INNER NATURE OF
COLOR

STUDIES ON THE PHILOSOPHY
OF THE FOUR ELEMENTS

THE INNER NATURE OF

COLOR

STUDIES ON THE PHILOSOPHY
OF THE FOUR ELEMENTS

J. L. BENSON

SteinerBooks

2004

Copyright © J. L. Benson, 2004

Published by SteinerBooks
400 Main Street, Great Barrington, MA 01230
www.steinerbooks.org

Library of Congress Cataloging-in-Publication data

Benson, J. L. (Jack Leonard)
  The inner nature of color : studies on the philosophy of the four elements/
J. Leonard Benson.— 1st ed.
      p. cm.
  Includes bibliographical references.
  ISBN 0-88010-514-3
  1. Steiner, Rudolf, 1861-1925. 2. Color (Philosophy)—History.
3. Four elements (Philosophy)—History. 4. Anthroposophy. I. Title.
  B3333.Z7B46 2004
  111'.1--dc22

                                                    2003027282

                10 9 8 7 6 5 4 3 2 1

                Printed by McNaughton & Gunn, Inc.

All rights reserved under International and Pan-American
copyright conventions.

Printed by in the United States of America

Contents

Part 1

Part 2

* * *

PART ONE

Hymn to the Four Elements

Sirens

The waves are transfigured with fire-laden wonder,
They glitter in impact, in flame leap asunder
Here's shining and swaying, and spurting of light,
With forms all aglow in the track of the night,
And lapping of fire touches all things around:
Let Eros who wrought it be honoured and crowned!

Hail to the Ocean! Hail to the wave!
The flood with holy fire to lave!
Waters hail! All hail the fire!
The strange event hail we in choir!

All voices in concert

Hail light airs now floating free!
Hail earth's caves of mystery!
Held in honour evermore
Be the elemental four!

—Johann Wolfgang von Goethe,
Faust II, Act 2, "Klassische Walpurgisnacht"

Translated by Philip Wayne

PREFACE

THE INSPIRATION FOR THIS VOLUME arose in the course of a career devoted to understanding the visual arts—with no particular consideration of color—in the conventional academic way. Typical of that way was to regard art as something "out there" which can be dispassionately dissected and analyzed. That way, in fact, follows in principle the system of the physical sciences which does not differentiate the agent of observation, that is, the human being, as belonging to any realms other than that of the abstract laws believed to govern physical phenomena. Thus, the personality, private beliefs and experiences of the art historian are regarded as irrelevant to the main task of arranging and defining the "objects" of art under discussion.

At the same time, the beliefs and experiences of the artists who created the art objects are held to be worth considering if they can be documented. This double standard of research is so universal in all fields of the academic world and in all its numerous dependencies in government and public life, that anyone who would challenge it on the grounds that the "objectivity" achieved through this system does not do justice to the complex spirituality of the world will likely be put aside as not really making sense.

From almost the beginning of my career I immersed myself in the ideas of Rudolf Steiner and was thereby obliged to live in two different spheres, as it were, but was gradually able to let his ideas give a certain refulgence to my teaching (decidedly noticed by many students) and even to some minor phases of my research. Yet it was not until near the end of my official career that I began to realize that the temporal structure of the seemingly miraculous unfolding of Greek art (and culture) could be illuminated by the philosophy of the Four Elements. While the reality of the four elements had been experienced to some degree consciously prior to the Greeks, it was the particular mission of that people, under the inspiration of the Archangel Michael (according to Steiner), to conceptualize it in philosophical terms as the underpinning of the Intellectual Soul epoch (and beyond): 747 B.C–1413 A.D. Indeed, the very discipline of philosophy was "invented" to pursue the question of the underlying principle (element) by which the planet was formed. While universal agreement about a *system* of four elements did not emerge until Plato and Aristotle, their work was made possible by the efforts of a few brilliant predecessors, in particular Empedokles, who remain somewhat shadowy in our knowledge of history; but they were surely well enough known to the generation of Greeks following their own. The extraordinary personality of Empedokles gave rise to legends which lasted long enough to be known and interpreted by the poet Hölderlin.

In view of the situation described above, I conceived the task of creating an up-to-date history of Greek color theory and practice, which is inextricably intertwined with the philosophy of the Four Elements, using all the scholarly resources of the twentieth century. On the other hand I realized the necessity of preparing a separate treatise (which is *The Inner Nature of Color*) to relate the results of my research to the inexhaustibly fruitful spiritual research of Rudolf Steiner so as to try to contribute to a new understanding of the background out of which it arose. The fact that any intimate knowledge about the spirituality of the ancient world and, above all, its relation to the present has not only dropped out of the intellectual life of today but in some quarters is actually impugned, seems reason enough to offer this study for whatever use Anthroposophists or anyone else can make of it.

Therefore I have incorporated the most basic explanatory aspects of my academic study (*GCTFE*) in the form of short essays that do not presuppose a professional knowledge of Greek art and philosophy; furthermore, there are rather general discussions of the nature and meaning of color experience applicable to all phases of human life, culture and artistic creativity. These are followed by sections on purely esoteric considerations of the nature and meaning of color experiences, again applicable to all phases of life and perhaps of particular interest to practitioners of the visual arts. At the same time this presentation may offer (as suggested above) a way of understanding more consciously the historical foundations of Western culture which Rudolf Steiner constantly referred to in his works as the fourfold nature of our planet and of the human being.

INTRODUCTION:
THE COSMOLOGICAL NATURE OF COLOR

Why Cosmological?

For the unimpaired human being, color is the most constant, inescapable and omnipresent of the sense impressions. The world is simply always colored, even at night, even in outer space. Therefore, any systematic attempt at explaining the phenomenon of color necessarily presupposes a world view and thus has real cosmological implications, whether these are recognized and spelled out or not. By the same token, such an attempt is in itself a symptom of considerable intellectual sophistication. We find this precondition in Greece at the time Empedokles provided the culmination of the philosophical speculation which had been carried on by the so-called Ionian School. In a poem (or poems) he undertook to explain the nature of the world as consisting of the four elements called earth, water, air and fire, each one being the expression of a deity as the divine force behind its dynamic manifestation in the visible world.

There is written evidence that he and other thinkers of the time associated four colors: black, white, yellow and red with those elements, although the pairing off is not immediately clear. They also took black and white to be the primal colors, all remaining colors being mixtures of these two in some way. That is approximately the extent of what one can compare with the modern physics of color which, with some historical distortion, is generally referred to as Newtonian color theory.

Leaving aside Newton's own, not inconsiderable, cosmological speculations, which proved to hold little interest for those who accepted his physics, we find the irreducible core of his theory in the claim that all colors (excepting black and white which were not regarded as colors) are contained in light. A very real cosmological implication of this view—surely not foreseen by Newton himself nor articulated in the scientific tidal wave that followed upon his work—is that denial of a role to darkness in the genesis of colors devaluates darkness in all its other manifestations to a state of non-being. It may not be immediately apparent, but I believe it is inevitable, that acceptance of this hypothesis has come with a heavy philosophical price: it obfuscates the role of the tragic, the dark side of human existence. This might be apparent in the oft-heard reaction to tragic events: if there were a God, he would not have let this happen. The Greeks were under no such preconceptions about the role of divine powers, as Gertrud Kantorowicz and others have pointed out. That ancient people, perhaps more than any other, accepted the dark side of life as an integral part (rather than as a senseless interruption) of reality, just as they accepted darkness (black) as an integral part of color. It cannot, therefore, be surprising that it was they who invented the tragic drama as an artistic expression of the way human beings live, learn and die.

Even if one senses the importance of the gulf between the Greek and the modern orientation to color discussed above, it may seem an intellectually daunting task to try to use it as a basis for interpreting Greek painting. Thus it was not until, in the pursuit of my own avocation of painting, I became aware of the depth of the color theory (Farbenlehre) of J.W. Goethe (and began, as he recommended, to experiment with a prism), that I started to understand how that scanty tradition mentioned above can be focused, as it were, onto a fully intelligible image of reality out of which the Greeks seem to have worked.

Nevertheless, in order to pursue such a goal, which by its own terms has to be approached in an unusual way, I had literally to invent new methods and new concepts which may at first sight seem strange. But the operative question is, would these methods and concepts have seemed strange to the ancient Greeks themselves? While, of course, no answer to that question is possible, it at least suggests what I have tried to do, that is, expunge from consideration all of our own preconceptions (many of which might well seem outrageous by the standards of ancient peoples) and follow carefully what clues exist. Yet this does not need to be tantamount to abandoning the perspective we enjoy by being so far away from the ancient world in time.

Written documentation is not abundant and what exists is to a great extent incomplete or even fragmentary. The corpus of terracotta colored materials, especially pottery, offers many specimens for consideration, but there is a dearth of evidence in most other media, especially painting on panels and walls, at least until the later fourth century. From this evidence in its totality I succeeded in making certain inferences which came together in the form of various diagrams and charts. I strove for a *theoria* in the ideal sense of philosophical speculation which might lead directly to empathy with the philosophical and artistic concerns of creative Greeks; for the mere fact that philosophers and artists associated each of the elements with its own specific color bespeaks an objectivity which is totally foreign in our age of individualism and subjectivism. This factor, and all it implies, is surely the reason why ancient artists, in contrast to some contemporary artists, neither could nor would have explained why they used this or that color; they (and everybody) *knew* at some level why they did. If we are disappointed with the apparent vagueness of references to color in ancient poetry and even (in late times) treatises on color, that is surely to be explained on the basis of different cultural expectations.

My suggestion, therefore, is that readers not turn at once to my interpretation of the meaning of colors as this might apply to specific works of ancient or modern art, but rather at first give some attention to my systematic examination of the color qualities of each of the four elements (pp. 35-44) and to my discussion of the polaric nature of spectral phenomena (pp. 56-59). Since even scholars, let alone general readers, may not be accustomed to think in terms of the strict polarity which is implicit in much of Greek thought, it would be helpful if readers would consider carefully my fundamental concern for instances where the polarity principle should or can be invoked. I have provided various inducements to do this in the text, in these essays.

A Modern Approach to Four Elements Philosophy

So far I have discussed the relation of the canonical four colors to the four elements. But what about the elements themselves? What do the words earth, water, air and fire mean to the person of our era? Let me assume, for the moment, that these constituents are not registered as parts of a philosophical system but as figments of fifth-century lore. In that sense, at least, they do survive in modern consciousness and might justifiably be regarded as ghosts of once living concepts, their vitality having been dissipated. The reason is not too far to seek. Elite academic thought, as reflected by historians of ancient science, has a world view that is either unaware of, or else discounts, the dynamic quality of the microcosmic aspect (that concerning organisms) of Four Elements philosophy, an aspect that interacts at every level with the macrocosmic aspect (environment in the widest sense). Yet it is precisely this microcosmic aspect that has lived on just below the surface, as it were, of Western consciousness. This will be explained in detail in the following essay, but there is an easy way to form a preliminary impression of the dynamic interaction between the macrocosmic/microcosmic spheres. Instead of thinking about earth, water, air and fire as four substances, we can regard them as four principles basic to existence: the solid (nourishment), the liquid (irrigation), the gaseous (atmosphere), and warmth. If an organism (a microcosm) is deprived of all food, it will normally consume itself and starve; if totally deprived of liquids, it will dehydrate quickly and die; if deprived of air, it will normally suffocate in a very short time (the possibility that there are anaerobic microorganisms merely proves the rule); and if totally deprived of heat (as in technologically produced extreme refrigeration), it would die almost instantly. In an anthropocentric worldview like that of the Greeks, the relevance of reasoning of this kind (this particular reasoning is not being ascribed to them) would be at once apparent. It may perhaps also provide a starting point for an understanding of the basic, organic macrocosmic-microcosmic orientation of early peoples that led to the synthesis we know as the Four Elements Theory made by the fifth-century B.C. philosopher Empedokles.

Since we live in an age in which science (the equivalent of philosophy in ancient times), clothed in immense authority, undertakes to understand life as a system of chemical reactions steered by infinitely small microorganisms which have, from the human point of view, beneficent or hostile intentions (all of this in a universe which is openly regarded as baffling and the subject of constant new speculation), some readers may need some help in trying to grasp my detailed reasoning about actual qualities that can be associated with various levels of macrocosmic/microcosmic activity (summarized in Ills. 12-13). As this help I again refer to the following essay, which presents a systematic explanation of how I understand both the historical and the derivative philosophy of the four elements; further, I have elucidated that explanation with a single striking example of visual form (fig. 1) which shows how the views being developed here can be helpful in understanding the form and content of an early work of art.

1.

UNDERSTANDING THE FOUR ELEMENTS THEORY TODAY

THE IDEA OF MACROCOSMOS (WORLD) AND MICROCOSMOS (HUMAN BEING)

"And first he (Bacchus viewing the doors of the palace of Neptune) saw, depicted with a wealth of colour, the confused features of primeval chaos, with a representation of the four elements about their divers functions. Above was fire, sublimely independent of matter and, ever since Prometheus stole it, the source of life to all living things. After it, soaring lightly and invisibly, came air, that found its habitat more readily and left no corner of the world, however hot or cold, unfilled. Earth, disposed in hills and valleys, was clad in green swards and blossoming trees, whence the beasts that inhabited it derived their varied sustenance; while, scattered about the land mass, water was clearly to be perceived, not merely nourishing many a species of fish, but supplying the humidity essential to existence."

—Camoens, *The Lusiads* Canto VI (W.G. Atkinson translation.)

The Concept of a Fourfold World

There are overwhelming obstacles to assured understanding of Presocratic philosophy—the mental equivalent to Greek art in the generations from the High Archaic to the High Classical Periods. First, our knowledge of it depends entirely on fragments preserved by later, sometimes very much later, authors and their commentators. There is not even certainty in many cases that the preserved fragments were actually written by the philosophers with whose names they are associated and, in any case, the context is lost.[1] How disastrous that is need hardly be insisted upon. All this gives rise to an ample secondary literature interpreting, at a vast distance of time, a large body of fragments of ancient secondary literature.

Secondly, the potentiality for misinterpretation of the intent of words was already formidable in the last-mentioned fragments and is increased by an inverse ration in modern secondary literature; for any words we use for translation and interpretation are freighted with a ballast of associations accumulated over thousands of years[2] and—what is more problematic—filtered through minds which can hardly escape being affected by a skeptical, materialist-positivist world view. However much we may feel that the Presocratic philosophers form the first link in the chain leading to this view, it would have been historically impossible for them to have had anything like it. Their rather poetic musings on how divine forces actually operated physically in the world are reminiscent of the way Galileo and Descartes emerged from a religious cocoon while hoping to enhance the glory of God with their discoveries.

Yet in Greece there was no powerful church to restrain natural philosophers and public opinion was largely tolerant. To the outside world their ideas, if noticed at all, must have seemed as strange as the constantly changing style of the statues gracing temples and public places. In this milieu the Four Elements philosophy and contrapposto were in place by the middle of the fifth century (close dates are hard to come by[3]): on the one hand the first scientific method for a profound exploration of reality and, on the other, a formula (the Canon) for a profound understanding of the human body-mind interaction, a subject never previously brought to full consciousness. The two men responsible for this climax, Empedokles and Polykleitos, might be called midwives who delivered the two perhaps most revolutionary impulses that informed mature Greek culture and its ever widening influence.[4] Yet the Four Elements philosophy, though ultimately prevalent, was to some extent misunderstood and contested by contemporaries of Empedokles, whereas the contrapposto stance invented by Polykleitos (Plate 2, left) seems to have been immediately and instinctively grasped and became the touchstone for all later Greek sculpture (and beyond).

Although some generalizations about Presocratic philosophy can be made, there is no help for the verbal impediments to interpretation pointed out above. It has seemed to me therefore to be useful to consult the uncontaminated non-verbal record afforded by Greek art: at least theoretically and *grosso modo* a richer experience of the two categories should be attainable by allowing ideas derivable from the one to reflect onto the other and vice versa. That was the method pursued in my online book (see bibliography). Given that the current wisdom says that these are two unrelated aspects of Greek culture which should be kept apart, my results may seem unfamiliar to those who expect, after all, pure art historical analysis with perhaps a few references to what was going on in contemporary philosophy, or else a review of Presocratic philosophy with a few happy parallels from sculpture and painting. I did not fulfill either of those expectations, especially since others could do that better. My whole purpose in writing that book was to see whether it is feasible to pursue consistently the philosophical quality of Greek art and the artistic quality of Greek philosophy—both as vital aspects of "Greekness."

It is not within my competence to enter technically into the dispute as to how much Presocratic schools owe to influence from Oriental sources. The prevailing tendency, with notable exceptions, seems to be to deny this as much as possible,[5] whereas in regard to art the opposite tendency has long been characteristic of archaeologists. This question of the Greekness of Greek creativity, in whatever category, is obviously of profound significance for accuracy of historical interpretation. At the same time the hefty divergences of opinions about the same facts demonstrate that feeling and willing in individual coloration play no less a role in modern scholarship than they did in the sixth century B.C. In this light I present my opinion as to what was really different about the modality of thought introduced in Miletos and Ephesos, Samos and Croton from what had previously prevailed.

It will be well initially to set aside the well-worn formula: from mythical to rational thinking, the complexities of which G. S. Kirk[6] has graphically demonstrated. More generically, the Greek tendency was to pursue a line of creative endeavor tenaciously over generations, until the "right form" for it was attained, after which creativity expressed itself horizontally rather than vertically, in variants. Rhys Carpenter's[7] derivation of this judgment from the history of the architectural orders seems to me to throw light also on the history of figure style in Greek ceramics. While each of its stages, beginning with silhouette style in so-called Geometric pottery (8th century, B.C.), continuing with black figure in Corinthian and Attic pottery, and ending with Attic redfigure style, had its own rationale, collectively they represent an unceasing striving to find the most effective way of depicting in two dimensions the naked male form simultaneously being worked out in an unbroken series of three dimensional stone statues. It is not without interest that the development of redfigure is generally considered to have peaked in the first half of the fifth century when the final struggle to achieve what we call contrapposto in sculpture was taking place. Thereafter redfigure drifted into a more theatrical stance and was exploited, especially in Magna Graecia, rather than developed further in the original sense indicated above. To some extent this parallels the exploitation of the orders once they were finally crystallized.

The kind of formal order that emerged in Attic Geometric and Archaic vase painting has less tangible but certainly recognizable parallels in the literary endeavors of Hesiod—and then in the next stage in the parallel stream of Orphic inspiration: Pherykydes and Pythagoras, and then in the Ionian School. It is not difficult to see that each of these was searching for the "right" explanation of the experiential world, but their methods differed so greatly that to find a common denominator is not easy. Certainly what did *not* change from an earlier stratum of experience is that in all of these the foundation of existence was felt to be divine, even if traditional religious formulae could be put in doubt or even discarded.[8] It is exactly this which removes them furthest from our intellectually self-eviscerated age. To assert that Antiquity, no less than the Middle Ages, was an Age of Faith (even though, of course, the definition of faith has to be broadened accordingly) is not to help anyone understand that. But to visualize through art that, in the critical period we are considering, the "unbroken" world of the Archaic Greeks became the "broken" world of the Classical Greeks,[9] might help.

The Four Elements

The stones (sc. minerals) have a fixed condition
and the plants have their growth.
The dumb beasts have all that and their soul pictures as well
but the power of reasoning (is) peculiar to human-kind.

—Adapted from Chrysippos as quoted by Clement of Alexandria
(I. von Arnim, *Stoicorum Veterum Fragmenta*, no. 714 Leipzig 1903)

By the middle of the first millennium B.C. cumulative human experience with the basic structure of the earth and its denizens was evidently sufficiently extensive and inwardly absorbed that a "philosophy"—a rationalization—of that structure could be formulated. Based on well over a century of tentative ideas and speculation[10] about the elementary composition of the world, a literally classic theory of four equal and commensurate elements was formulated by Empedokles at the latest and taken up by Aristotle. They pointed out that earth, air, fire and water exist not only in recognizable isolation but also are constantly combined in nature to form innumerable inorganic and organic compounds, giving the basis for substances and beings that came to be summarily classified as mineral, plant, animal and man. The order is hierarchical with mineral having only one element (earth) and man having all four.

The elements were understood equally as substance or the processual activities associated with it (solidification, liquefaction, rarefaction and combustion)[11] and certain qualities were more or less arbitrarily associated with the four: hot, cold, wet, dry; and the four temperaments and perhaps more. The interdependence and commensurability of the microcosmic and macrocosmic forms of the elements under the influence of attraction and repulsion (love and strife) were fundamentally assumed. But I must stress that this summary is an *ideal* description of what was in ordinary life probably more felt and instinctive than articulated.

In the light of this specific schema we become aware that, by the time of its formulation, in art the division between man and god was still being drawn with self-evident precision. The consciousness of an earlier millennium about it is reflected in the well-known ritual vase from Warka[12] (Fig. 1). Earth—or the mineral realm—is represented or at least implied by the supporting base of the receptacle itself, above which the realm of water is depicted as a conventional design. Over that is a frieze depicting the realm of plants—which live from water into air—and then above the plants a frieze showing the realm of warm-blooded animals who also live from water and air into warmth through their blood and breath. Above this again is a taller frieze of men, servitors, who embody the sublimation of inward warmth to self-conscious activity in the service of the gods. Then towering over all this is a taller frieze depicting the goddess (or her priestess) toward whom all the activity and resources of the world flow. The divine world honored by the height of the frieze floats above the tangible world.

FIGURE 1

At this stage it must have been impossible to conceive of the four-fold world without divine overseers, as is equally evident in the art of the Pharaonic state, the First Babylonian Dynasty and in the Biblical account of the Hebraic theocracy. This is the conception inherited by Greece from the past and still vitally and visually alive in the pediments of Olympia. Yet what the Ionian philosophers as a whole achieved was the detachment of the concept of certain individual underlying elements from the total scheme so that these could be individually scrutinized and evaluated as to their qualities.

The process of intellectual inquiry thus initiated was *prima facie* specialized and one-sided, a tendency that appears to be reflected also in the concentration of Archaic sculptors on a narrowly defined schema of the human body—the youthful male or *kouros* type—as the key to unlock the psychosomatic riddle of the elementary human body. Other themes, even the female body, were neglected accordingly. This creation of philosophical inquiry and of a basic statue type of consummate perfection constitutes *ipso facto* a new stage of human self-consciousness that separates the Greeks from anything in the older civilizations, however much they may have taken materials from these.

It is again altogether in keeping with the Classical mentality that the discovery of substance *per se* at the price of onesidedness, should have been drawn back by Empedokles into a dynamically balanced philosophical system. He at least is the first thinker we know of who specifically proclaimed the commensurability of the *four* elements and their incessant interaction (this includes human thinking). Yet there is no reason to doubt that Empedokles and, in fact, most philosophers, continued to recognize the existence of a higher spiritual realm and the compatibility of the highest expression of the four elements: man himself, with it.[13] Nevertheless, consciousness henceforth began to be drawn subtly and inevitably to phenomena and processes of the visible world; in effect, the divine factor came to be relegated to an extraterrestrial sphere considered to be, as it were, a fifth element—*aither* in Aristotle's *De Caelo,* then *quinta essentia*—

obviously more subtle than warmth. As the quadripartite conception showed itself increasingly useful and versatile, the elimination of the divine factor from practical considerations (the quintessence becoming eventually the bailiwick of the alchemists) brought a certain freedom to downgrade or even ignore it.

In Hellenistic times a kind of pallid forerunner of modern "secular humanism" may have arisen; but Greek sculpture, drama and mainstream philosophy never totally lost a sense of spiritual realities, in whatever shading these might find expression. Paradoxically, from an early stage of its development onward, the Greek mind was also instinctively and creatively turned to the physicality of the world by the Four Elements theory, an explanation so deeply rational and fundamentally apposite to the human condition, that it could still today be profitably taken into account by the scientific establishment—which all too often remains in a maze of mathematical abstractions as it pursues power over nature.

The Four Members

At least two historians of ancient art have found it necessary in their analyses[14] of Greek sculpture to refer to various "levels" or "souls" inherent in the human make-up. And they did not do this theoretically or as a quaint theory of the past. However, since their use of this concept was not systematic—and could not have been without full-scale discussion of the Four Elements theory—I shall attempt to provide that systematic investigation here. The concept of souls is undoubtedly the least understood aspect of the parallel structuring of the macrocosm and microcosm, although hardly the least known. There are enough references to it in Plato and Aristotle to guarantee that, in some way, the total system existed in antiquity as experience and perhaps tradition. In fact, once it is grasped, indications of it—even fairly systematic ones—can be recognized in earlier cultures, particularly that of Egypt. Yet modern scholarship on the whole has not shown much interest in that subject.

There are gaps, sufficiently plentiful that one can proceed only by analogy and deduction. On the one hand we have in the *Timaeus* Plato's description of the earth as an organic World-Soul enveloped by a (physical) body. As Cornford[15] then put it: "The parallel of macrocosm and microcosm runs through the whole discourse... and the soul itself is a counterpart, in miniature, of the soul of the world." But for us too much is assumed to understand this easily. We also have the Empedoklean, Platonic and Aristotelian total commitment to the interweaving (*krasis*) of the four elements as the basis of all physical and organic reality. On the other hand, we have Aristotle's description in *De Anima* of the structure of the human being, whose parts bear a relationship to the processual spheres of the four elements. If not much else is spelled out, we can assume either that it was too obvious to need comment, or was discussed in lost writings, or—perhaps most likely of all—that the full systematic implications of the microcosmic-macrocosmic four elements theory lay beyond the particular interests of ancient philosophers. After this we find rather its traces, as a worldview taken totally for granted, in such things as medicine and alchemy, for centuries, even millennia, to come.

Stated in the most reduced terms, the system requires that the members of each living being correspond in quality to subsuming similar members of the living world organism in which they in fact exist and without which they would perish. This is, for example, most easily understandable in the case of the individual physical body, which cannot be conceived of without its mineral component—for there would be no skeleton or, in the lowest echelons, visible substance. The recurring fantasy in films about "invisible men" demonstrates, moreover, that in the modern artistic imagination, at least, the human being is not limited to physicality but is shot through with invisible processes on which sentience and consciousness rest. It is precisely these processual systems, of which only the *effect* can be observed, and without which the physical body becomes a corpse, that comprise the upper three levels or souls of

the four member system. The four-member system is most con-
cretely documented by Aristotle (although he tends to take the physical level for granted and thus does not actually speak of four).

Though at present the least regarded aspect of the Four Elements theory, the quadripartite articulation of the human being has
remained as the essential frame of reference of the western world
and still survives—largely unexamined and uncoordinated—in
our conceptual life as physical anthropology (study of skeletal systems, among other things), physiology (study of the vital systems,
particularly glandular), psychology (study of the emotional and
mental capacities, particularly as carried by the nervous system)
and ego. Since modern psychology has no concept of soul as such, it
overlaps into conclusions about the ego, which in the Greek system
corresponds to a separate fourth member, *nous,* the cogitative faculty, not present in animals. In effect, the crowning term of the
four—all derived from the Greek language and fossilized in our
time—should be philosophy. The latter, deprived of its former relation to peoples who understood themselves in fourfold terms, has
had no choice but to become increasingly abstract and peripheral
in human affairs.

Despite the present tattered condition of the system, it was used
in a dynamic correlative sense as late as the nineteenth century by
Ignaz Paul Troxler (Basel) and others for medical and philosophical
conclusions[16] and even later by Nikolai Hartmann (1882–1951) as
a framework for his philosophical system.[17] It has been used for the
interpretation of ancient Near Eastern art by Walter Andrae (see
note 12). To the historian's eye the full integration—or
re-integration—of this system by Rudolf Steiner (1861–1925) as
the basis of his cosmology indicates that the Four Elements theory
is still evolving.[18] To my knowledge Steiner, working closely with
concepts from Goethe's scientific work, is the only modern thinker
to give full weight to the macrocosmic aspect of the microcosmic
foursome. Above the physical body (which Aristotle dealt with *en
passant: de An.* 411[a]) he uses the term etheric body for Aristotle's

threptikon or nutritive soul, astral or sentient body for the *aesthe-tikon* or sensitive soul, and ego for *nous*. His subordinate parts of the *nous* are likewise documented in Aristotle (see my online study of Greek sculpture, Chapter I). The etheric body of an individual (plant, animal, man) regulating the vegetative, liquefying processes of life is dependent on the etheric body (roughly atmosphere) of the earth organism as a whole. The individual sentient body (of animal, man), seat of the feeling life, is correlative to the sentient body (a collective phenomenon, from the individual point of view) of the earth. The ego (of man alone) is related to a macrocosmic ego of divine nature.

All of this is, explicitly or implicitly, a Hellenic view[19] of human reality. It is probably safe to say that its existence, in varying degrees of explicitness and understanding, was never seriously challenged in principle until the intellectual effects of the nominalistic contro-versy of the Middle Ages began to condition the definition and practice of natural science. Even then it was too massive to be totally displaced, as noted above, and it has also had a succession of powerful defenders, e.g., Kepler and Goethe. Nevertheless, the nominalistic world picture that originated in medieval philosophy and culminated in the materialism of the 19th century has us all in its grip, despite our perhaps valiant efforts to escape it[20]—even though twentieth-century quantum physics and relativity theory have discredited much of it (in a manner, unfortunately, too abstruse and impersonal to penetrate or fructify public consciousness[21]). The natural sciences each pursue their own agenda to infinite particulars while the social sciences make what they can of the results of the elite sciences. Nor can ancient studies stay above this obtrusive intellectual turmoil. This is not said in a spirit of criticism of its practitioners but to explain why I am impelled to offer this study: it is my way of trying to make sense of the crisis[22] sketched out above.

NOTES

1. A clear overview of this situation in J. Burnet *Early Greek Philosophy* London 1930. For example p. 39: "All we can really be said to know of (Thales) comes from Herodotus."

2. Commentators sometimes consciously take account of this, e.g., B. Farrington 1961, 41, 55.

3. On the dates of Empedokles see M.R. Wright 1981, 3-6. Wright estimates the working period as 470s to 430s.

4. In this same sense their contemporary Sophokles presided over the perfecting of tragedy as the ultimate display of human affective life. This evaluation of the importance and universality of the work of Empedokles is not automatically given by his critics but I share it with S. Toulon and J. Goodfield, *The Architecture of Matter* New York 1962, 53-54. B. Farrington 1961, 58-59 also accorded a great significance to Empedokles, particularly for his demonstration of the "corporeality of viewless air." Farrington's discussion of this is almost panegyrical; it is, of course, quite true that that insight of the philosopher pointed far into the future and is one of the most modern of Greek scientific ideas. G.E.R. Lloyd *Early Greek Science: Thales to Aristotle* London 1970, 39-42 evaluated the Four Elements theory in the light of the modern conception of elements. S. Sambursky *The Physical World of the Greeks* Princeton 1987, 17-20, lays particular emphasis on Empedokles' discovery that "light propagates through space and requires time to do so"—another insight confirmed by modern science. Although academic critics show appreciation of this or that feature of the work of Empedokles, no one to my knowledge has treated him as a consummate artist of ideas which can literally be visualized in a picture—as I shall try to demonstrate in this study—as well as understood in a poem. In this respect he is *the* High Classical philosopher just as Plato is *the* Late Classical philosopher.

5. For a summary of the problem see M.L. West 1971, 115-170.

6. G.S. Kirk 1974, Ch. 12.

7. R. Carpenter *The Aesthetic Basis of Greek Art in the Fifth and Fourth Centuries B.C.* Bloomington 1959, Ch. IV.

8. This is defended specifically by Kirk 1974, 299-300. Herakleitos' use of Logos is interpreted by many writers as a spiritual symptom, not least by those who speak of an esoteric tradition, e.g., Wilhelm Kelber *Die Logoslehre von Heraklit bis Origines* Stuttgart 1958, *passim* but denied by West, 1971, 124. The arguments of Karl Schefold *Griechische Kunst als Religiösos Phänomen* Hamburg

1959 are directed specifically to a pervading sense of the divine in all Greek life and nowhere more specifically, on the basis of ornament, than on his p. 27. He is one of the few commentators to refer to developments in European culture since 1800 as skewing the contemporary view on this. Equally concerned with a primary engagement of Greek thought with suprapersonal forces is Friedrich Hiebel *Die Botschaft von Hellas* Bern 1953. Some commentators deal with this problem more in terms of the overriding concern of mid-century psychiatry which, absorbed with the human experience of anxiety, works with the dichotomy of rational and irrational: so E.R. Dodds 1951; J.J. Pollitt 1972, 3-8 on Order and Chaos.

9. These terms derive from Ernst Buschor, 1980, 6-9.

10. Cf. "Hot and Cold, Dry and Wet in Early Greek Thought" by G.E.R. Lloyd in *Studies in Pre-Socratic Philosophy Vol. I The Beginnings of Philosophy,* ed. David J. Farley and R. E. Allen New York 1970, 255-280. esp. 267-269 on possible origins of the Four Elements theory.

11. Cf. Herakleitos Frag. 126: "cold things grow hot, hot is cooled, wet is dried, dry becomes wet"; Aristotle, *de gen. Et* cor. B, ii,iii.

12. The abbreviated description of the piece by Henri Frankfort *The Art and Architecture of the Ancient Orient* Penguin 1954, 10 masks the totality of the conception. Earth, as the hard, lifeless mineral realm it appears to us, can hardly have been in the consciousness of this early epoch, for earth was felt to belong to the gods along with everything else, to be a part of them, as it were — hence more spiritual than physical in our sense. Even the earliest Greek philosophers who speculated on the four elements still had an awareness of the divine nature of each element. If we demand logical placement of earth in the composition of the Warka vase, we can find it only minimally in the consideration that the life-giving water of Mesopotamia in the lowest frieze flows on top of the earth element—not in a void. What the composition really pictures is the absorption of the artist in divine being, while the earth conditions that support life are present more as ancillaries. The spiritual approach of the Near Eastern artists to the depiction of mineral, plant, animal and man was thoroughly discussed by Walter Andrae in "Der Alte Orient" in *Handbuch der Archäologie* hrsg. v.W. Otto, Munich 1939, 754-780. M.L. West 1971, 31-41 discusses the so-called "five elements" and "three elements" recognized in early Iran and India. As all these served religious purposes rather than conceptual thinking a rigid consistency in number is not to be expected. The Egyptian fourfold schema of (physical body), Ka, Ba, and Akh: W.S. Smith *The Art and Architecture of Ancient Egypt* Penguin 1958, 9

perhaps more readily constitutes a doctrinal conception anterior to, but very similar to, the Greek version of the four members.

13. Precisely the same evaluation is given by W. Burkert *Greek Religion* Cambridge, Mass. 1985, 318. Cf. also M.W. Wright 1981, 76.

14. Buschor 1980, 18-20 and G. Kantorowicz *The Inner Nature of Greek Art* New Rochelle 1992, 17-18.

15. F.M. Cornford *Plato's Cosmology: The Timaios of Plato* London 1937, 6.

16. Peter Heusser, *Der Schweizer Arzt und Philosoph Ignaz Paul Vital Troxler* (1780-1866) *Seine Philosophie, Anthropologie und Medizintheorie* (Basel & Stuttgart 1984). Successor to Troxler is Friedrich Husemann, psychiatrist, who used Steiner's concept of a four-organ system in demonstrating the inner dynamics of the four elements in bodily-psychic functions as a basis for therapy: *Das Bild des Menschen als Grundlage der Heilkunst* Vol I 1940. Cf. also Ekkehard Meffert, *Carl Gustav Carus* Sein Leben, seine Anschauung von der Erde Stuttgart 1986. Carus is an important and creative 19th century thinker who viewed the earth as a living organism.

17. *Der Aufbau der Realen Welt* Grundriss der allgemeinen Kategorienlehre 3. ed. Berlin 1964, 173-183 (Kap. 20). Hartmann is the academic philosopher who most closely approached my viewpoint. His paper "Die Anfänge des Schichtungsgedankens in der alten Philosophie" in *Kleinere Schriften* II Berlin 1957, 164-191 not only gives a perceptive account of the relation of Plato and Aristotle to the idea of four members of the human being but also explains why modern philosophy (*sc.* also psychology and anthropology) is largely unaware of these members *as a system* (that is, an explanation of human reality):

> "This situatiion has, of course, arisen from the following circumstance. The historian of philosophy can recognize in his array of materials from texts *only* those insights that he has himself already worked out in the sense of a systematic philosophy. The nineteenth century interpreters and compilers who created the modern view of Aristotle lacked the sustained ability to do this—and most particularly in regard to the question of ontology, which plays a fundamental role in any evaluation of ancient thought."
>
> (Translated by J. L. Benson.)

That statement, written in 1943, was followed by an expression of hope that improvement in this critical matter was on the way. Certainly, in Hartmann's case, there is no doubt that the power of the four-member system was felt. Hartmann does not give a detailed history of the concept but does treat that aspect casually.

18. Besides Steiner's books and voluminous published lectures, an enormous and ever-growing secondary literature exists dealing with, among other things, research on the various physical and life sciences. His work is often tangential to the traditional "Panpsychic" stream (see M. Tuchman *The Spiritual in Art: Abstract Painting 1896-1985* Abbeville 1986, p. 187ff.) but eludes exact classification. It is of some interest that the concept of the etheric body, which in Steiner's view regulates the rhythmic processes of an organism, has been paralleled non-conceptually in recent years in medical parlance by the "biological clock."

19. The general framework of the macrocosmic-microcosmic view of Hellenism historically has to be based on Plato and Aristotle, that is, at the most developed stage of the Four Elements philosophy. Whether or not one takes a teleological view of the development itself does not in any way exclude the importance of unstable and even contentious attitudes towards aspects of it at various times, any more than it excludes powerful background guidance on the part of the Pythagoreans. I do not consider it my task here to trace the history of the concept of soul both because this has been done by others and because it is in effect not essential to the large picture I am trying to sketch out in this study.

20. A measure of the difficulty is the temptation felt by some commentators to treat ancient philosophical-scientific matters in a somewhat mechanical way. An example of this is the claim made by B. Farrington 1961, 143 that existence of the economic class structure in Athens that Plato wanted to improve by organizing society into rulers, police and workers gave him the idea of dividing the soul into reason, spirit and appetites. Further: "As with Plato, the master-and-slave relation provides the basic pattern for his (Aristotle's) thought in *every* sphere (italics mine): *ibid,* 145. Again he ascribes the specific originality of the Ionian thinkers to the fact that they applied "to all major phenomena of nature modes of thought derived from their control of technique": *ibid,* 135. A one-sided viewpoint thus obscures what might otherwise be useful observations.

21. See, e.g., Arthur Zajonc *Catching the Light* New York 1993, 301-302.

22. The precise nature and urgency of this crisis have been recently defined by Brian Appleyard *Understanding the Present: Science and the Soul of Man* Doubleday 1993, *passim.*

2.

Making a Picture of
the Four Elements Theory

Although the canonical four color grouping of black, white, red, and yellow is not documented in ancient literature before the first half of the fifth century, it can easily be noticed that these same four colors, separately, together, or in mixtures giving the so-called earth colors, predominate not merely in Greece but all through early cultures.[1] The Greeks, specifically the Attic ceramic crafts-men, had a special relationship to this "canon" in that they refined their color choice, presumably out of a passionate attachment to it, to a glossy black and orange-red as an aesthetic norm.[2] Beings and objects in the pictorial frieze (see Plate 1) are shown in black, suggesting the obvious conclusion that this color represents the corporeality, the density, of earth substance. And the frieze itself, be it noted, is reserved in the black density of the pot, also fired earth-substance.

The orange frieze used in black figure work (Plate III) misses maximum contrast value with the black, so why was it chosen? Perhaps a kind of instinctive insight has always led people to refer to red, or reddish hues, as the color of life. For our purposes that is far too general a statement. In the circumstances we are considering—at least if the artists were not irrational—the reddish hue can really only represent air (atmosphere), in which all beings and things are bathed. For example, if we consider animals or men, they unremittingly draw in life force for the blood through breathing air, whereupon the blood maintains both physical and emotional existence. Red, therefore, represents the air on the macrocosmic plane and in the extended microcosmic sense it represents soul life.

We can now take stock. The two opposite fix-points, earth-air, provide a contrast that is more spatial than dynamic, for earth and air are fundamentally contiguous, and in an undisturbed state do not act on one another but simply preside over, as it were, the spheres of below and above, respectively. (Fire and water, on the other hand, are by nature hostile to one another, eliminate themselves when, forced together, they must attack each other.) Just as in the relationship of earth and air, the colors black and red have a complementary, not an adversarial, relationship, and it cannot be accidental that as prismatic colors of the Dark spectrum (fig. 16), black and red are precisely contiguous. Nevertheless, the juxtaposition is decisive: black is heavy, immobile, hence can function as support; red as a chromatic color has also a certain density but, as Goethe already noted, it is the least mobile color, so that without forcing a point we could say that it hovers over black. In this way one can feel why the Archaic painters remained so long satisfied with this combination: it gave superb expression to their passionate pursuit of physical reality in a way that no other color as background, e.g., white, could have.

During the Archaic and Protoclassical periods the Ionian philosophers consistently pondered the nature of the elements on the basis of the polarity principle. Similarly, the colors black and white were certainly seen as polar opposites, like cold and warm; but these colors could not be connected with the actual pair of polar opposites in the elements (fire and water) in view of the factors discussed above. Indeed, apart from black-earth, we shall find that a little leeway must be allowed in assigning colors to elements (even red-air). In any case, at this point fire and water are open to apportionment to white and yellow. According to the criterion of density already established, yellow, visually the stronger of the two colors, will go to water, the denser element, leaving white for fire (warmth) as the most rarefied substance of all (just as Empedokles took for granted).

Yellow accordingly is the expression of the principle of fluidity, the functional principle (circulatory system) of the earth planet and all its creatures. Yellow therefore can be called the active color *par excellence*. At a later point it will be seen how closely this purely logically derived conclusion approaches the thinking of the ancient physiologists. White, on the other hand, characterizes the element which is the least physical—which in fact can almost not be conceived of except as an invisible connective (warmth) of the other elements. And indeed on the visual plane white is passive, lacking specific expressionality. It does not in any sense importune us but kindly provides without preconditions an empty space for inner freedom. This makes it highly suitable to represent, at the macrocosmic level, the sphere of pure thought, the goal of *nous*; the relative loftiness of this sphere may suggest, but does not compel, a connection to the Godhead. I say not compel because the Godhead is logically prior to and beyond all color. Moreover, white can be sullied by the admixture of impure elements, as can pure reason.

* * * * *

My suggestions for equating elements and colors so far have already uncovered one basic reason why the ancient philosophers did not try to think this problem out fully—at least on the macrocosmic level: whereas the four elements can easily be thought of as two pairs of opposites (earth and air as under and above; fire versus water), this is not the case with the canonical four colors (the origins of which will be considered later). There is only one absolutely unequivocal pair (black and white) and that pair does not correspond in a fully logical way with either of the two pairs of elements. Without modern knowledge of the spectrum (inclusive especially of

Goethe's), dialectical thinking cannot take this problem much further. Thus the lack of a systematic assignment of the four colors to the four elements in theoretical philosophy as handed down can hardly be accidental. There is moreover the circumstance that Pseudo-Aristoteles (*De Coloribus*), so close in time to the great theoretical physicists, deals with this matter in a naïve-realistic way, devoid of historical polemicizing.[3] Therefore, what these Greek thinkers—and artists—knew or at least instinctively guessed concerning a correlation of elements and colors can only be put in perspective if we ourselves attempt to think it through to the end with all the arsenal both of dialectical reasoning and modern color knowledge.

The Four Elements and the Four Colors in their Macrocosmic and Microcosmic Relationship

Til God, or kindlier Nature,
Settled all argument, and separated
Heaven from earth, water from land, our air
From the high stratosphere, a liberation
So things evolved, and out of blind confusion
Found each its place, bound in eternal order.
The force of fire, that weightless element,
Leaped up and claimed the highest place in heaven;
Below it, air; and under them the earth
Sank with its grosser portions; and the water,
Lowest of all, held up, held in, the land.

—Ovid, *Metamorphoses*, 1, 1.21-31.
Translated by Rolfe Humphries

As a point of departure for attempting a coherent presentation of the vast problem set out in the title of this section I offer in tabular form a summary of the results so far obtained:

ELEMENT	PROCESSUAL DESIGNATION	COLOR
Fire	Combustion	White
Air	Rarefaction	Red
Water	Liquefaction	Yellow
Earth	Condensation (Compression)	Black

It will be seen at once from the processual column that the order of listing is not accidental but from least dense to most dense (following Aristotle, as does Ovid in the passage cited); yet this table presents only one possible condition out of many. For it is a fundamental experience in the study of color that every color is subject to movement through the dynamic processes in the earth's atmosphere. Even the pigment colors are subject to this to some degree, with the possible exception of black. To grasp this I found it necessary to ask, how are the remaining elements affected when, for example, combustion is the dominant process—and then when rarefaction is, etc. One could try to use tables like the one above but in fact, if a pictorialization of the processes should be possible, that would be even better. But pictures, even diagrammatic ones, are subject to the laws of picture-making, and these are seldom articulated. Here it is all the more necessary to do this because we are considering the very basis of human existence and human experience. In view of the importance of this matter I have chosen to present a formal investigation of the theme.

Prolegomena to a Study of the Four Elements Theory and Its Relation to the Canonical Four Colors

No comprehensive history of the actual origin, emergence and effectuality of either of these theories, let alone both in combination, in ancient and later times, has ever, to my knowledge, been attempted. The question as to whether specific colors were in antiquity attached to specific elements (*in the macrocosmic sense*) has been variously evaluated. Although a very few authors have proposed or assumed such actual correspondences, no comprehensive reasoning about the fundamental interrelationships of elements and colors has appeared.

Without prejudice to the possibility that such correspondences really were accepted in antiquity without being recorded or that such really do exist whether contemplated in antiquity or not, our first step must be to establish a coherent, logical *visual* means of conceptualizing the relationship of at least the four elements among themselves. There is no inherited scheme for this from antiquity, even though, again, one could have existed. Indeed, the possibility of some kind of overall geometric scheme may be suggested by the fact that Plato did visualize each individual element as a geometric figure:

FIRE :   TETRAHEDRON

EARTH :   HEXAHEDRON

AIR :   OCTAHEDRON

WATER :   IKOSAHEDRON

To these Heaven was added as a fifth—let it be noted—extraterritorial element; its figure was a pentagon dodekahedron.[4] To suggest how to combine all these is beyond my competence. Furthermore, for the purpose of this study, it is essential to invent a "picture" that can also suggest in spatial terms the concept of the miscibility (*krasis*) of the elements, since these were understood by the ancients to be processes[5] whereby a constant metamorphosis of the visual configuration of the world at any moment is actually taking place. The descriptive determination of such momentary states lies within two pairs of opposing conditions: hot-cold and wet-dry. These qualities in effect give the parameters of two of the elements, fire and water, whereby it can be concluded that fire and water have a particular axial quality, a central governing position in the total concept of four.

The most obvious and striking aspect of this relationship is, as already suggested, the uncontested polarity of fire and water. The archenemy of fire is water; equally, fire opposes water but with much less immediate impact and finality. Fire is quenched by water; water is evaporated (goes into air) by fire. This stronger quality of water allows it to determine how to pictorialize the relationship. Since the inalienable tendency of water is to seek the horizontal, we may use a horizontal line, whereby the placement of fire and water to left or right is still to be discussed: liquefaction opposes combustion.

ILLUSTRATION 1

With this given, a second less dramatic but equally inescapable polarity remains: earth and air. Their normal relationship is to be contiguous, with the earth below and the air above. Their difference in density results in the phenomenon of gravity, which would not be observable without a contrasting medium through which things can fall and, for that matter, rise. If gravity is a force—as science proposes—beyond earth itself, then dialectically an opposing force, levity, must also be postulated.[6] This relationship is logically to be illustrated by a vertical line: condensation opposes rarefaction.

A

E

ILLUSTRATION 2

Given the interaction of the four elements observable by the senses, we can now cross the two lines.

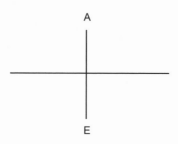

ILLUSTRATION 3

Whereas the positioning of A and E is given by physical characteristics of the two elements, the placement of fire and water involves the relationship of left and right. Therefore the concepts of science and the laws of picture-making, if there be such, must meet and interact. There is no left and right bias in fire and water as such, but there is a fundamental difference between left and right visually. While this is generally recognized as vital by artists and critics alike, it is generally discussed, if at all, using psychological considerations, which plainly are irrelevant here. It was the merit of Vassily Kandinsky,[7] acting on a suggestion of Goethe, to have conceptualized the picture plane as an area—blank or not—that is alive with tensions of weight. Indeed, that plane is an excerpt of each observer's bodily relationship to the horizontal-vertical conditions of earthly existence. Thus, the horizontal and vertical represent, respectively, earth's plane from L to R and space from up to down. The visual resistance experienced in a defined rectangular pictorial space is naturally strongest below and weakest above. The next strongest resistance (tension) is offered by the right side; this is reduced on the left side but not so much as up and down. Thus, there are four degrees of density (sc. visual density) as represented by the following scheme:

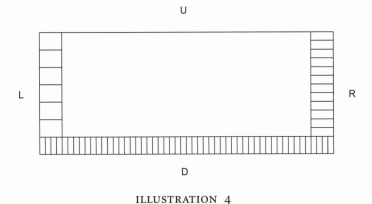

ILLUSTRATION 4

The applicability of Kandinsky's reasoning to the problem at hand, if any, must be axiomatic, as indeed all geometrical reasoning lies inextricably rooted in the human body/mind condition. We may therefore criticize the suggested scheme with fire and water inserted.

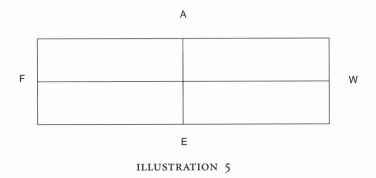

ILLUSTRATION 5

No conflict exists in the vertical plane. The potential conflict is in the horizontal. Although W is correctly placed on the right in relation to A and E, fire cannot easily be related to density in the sense of the other three. That is because, in contrast to ancient (and some current esoteric) thought that warmth is a (primeval) substance, present scientific theory sees fire (warmth) as a condition of other substances. In terms of our picture, a resolution of this dilemma may be sought in regarding the elements not as substances but as processes, where there can be no conflict. In this sense we then have the completed diagram as follows:

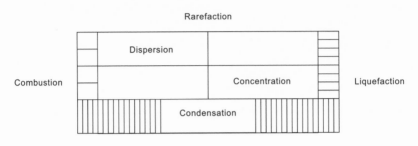

ILLUSTRATION 6

Taking into account again Kandinsky's criteria and visualizing the *results* of the four processes in terms of changes of density in weighable and measurable materials of earth existence, combustion is clearly in the right position. Combustion can lighten matter, leaving ashes which are lighter than water or earth but still ultimately heavier than air; and on the other hand it may intensify the process of rarefaction and thus contribute to lightness.

The next problem is to show the opposing pairs of elements in the descriptive sense-analytical terms of early thought. These are described by Empedokles (under A in *GCTFE*, Testimonia) as hot/cold and wet/dry. The existence of four quadrants allows us to arrange these terms in the sense of equally balancing contrasts;

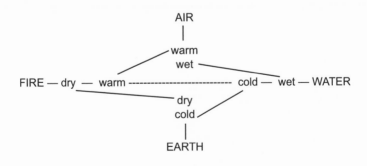

ILLUSTRATION 7

In this way we have accounted for the nature of the four elements but what of the fifth element? In order to include that in this picture we must find a way of showing that, besides the planet earth and its atmosphere with which we have so far been dealing, there are outside of these the heavens (universe). We can accomplish this by enclosing the above cross in a circle, representing first of all the shape of the planet—if not the arch of the horizon—thus giving an inside and outside, so to speak, and also functioning as a symbol for relationships among equal elements.[8] Furthermore, Kandinsky showed how the four arms of the cross function as axes being displaced to the left and right but maintaining the center connection and, in effect, becoming radii of a circular form. Such movement of the arms is particularly meaningful in the circumstances because it literally shows the process of *krasis,* whereby the four elements constantly intermingle as they create and define the quality and quantity of all physicality.

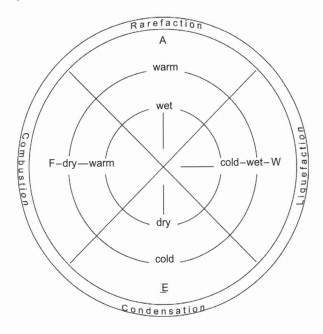

ILLUSTRATION 8

If we now reinstate the picture plane containing (or contained by) the circle, we can see that Kandinsky's characterization of the four quadrants of this plane actually corresponds, to a remarkable degree, to the process of miscibility (cf. e.g., ills. 9 and 6).

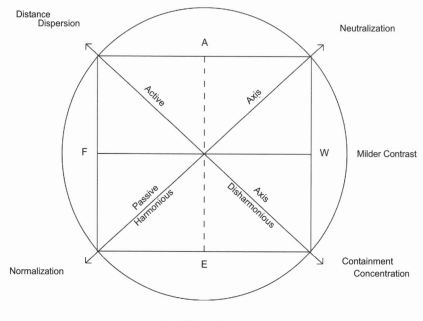

ILLUSTRATION 9

While Kandinsky did not propose that the pictorial framework gives more than symbolical meaning to the qualities of the various quadrants, his considerations nevertheless demonstrate a new degree of sensitivity to the problem of pictorial thinking, without which complicated relationships cannot be prepared for discussion and evaluation in any sphere of knowledge. His apprehension of the pictorial plane as a living entity was deduced exactly from the fact that left and right relationships are not mirrored passively from the observer's point of view. This should be taken into account in all diagrams, for these should correspond to the laws of visual perception. This will become increasingly clear when colors are added to the characterization of the four elements.

N.B. the data about the elements contained in Ill. 8 can also be rendered, and more conveniently, by attaching the information about hot/cold and wet/dry to the vectors, as in the diagram below (which has been preferred in the text).

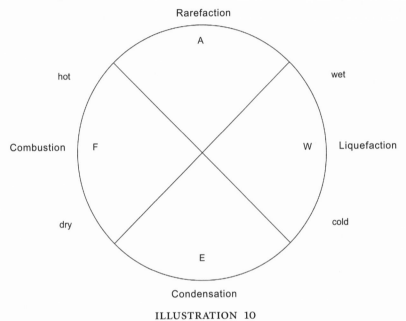

ILLUSTRATION 10

The persistent implication in the method of constructing the picture of the Four Elements theory arrived at in Ill. 8 and 10 above, namely, that this is an irreducible explanation of earthly realities valid for all of humanity, requires a further comment. The elements qua substance require to be thought of as occupying real space: they are in a sense the planet we live on, they are our own body/mind entity. As such they are Being. But they are also synonymous with processes, so that one could just as well speak of the four processes theory—and as such they belong to the realm of time: they are Becoming. There is evidence that the Greeks themselves conceived of this latter idea without, however, living so much in consciousness of the *technical* potentialities of the processes which dominate *our* minds, but rather in the blessedness of feeling the processes as earthly projections of realities inherent in higher worlds. Nowhere is this so explicitly put as in a dialogue of Plutarch (*De Defectu Oraculorum*, 10):

> Others (other authors) say, there is a transmutation of bodies as well as of souls; and that, just as we see of the earth is engendered water, of the water air, and of the air fire, the nature of substance still ascending higher, so good spirits always change for the best, being transformed from men into heroes, and from heroes into Daemons; and from Daemons, by degrees and in a long space of time, a few souls being refined and purified come to partake of the nature of the Divinity.[9]

If we consider this passage in microcosmic terms, the reference to men, whose highest earthly member is *nous* (fire), translates into an overlapping of the circle of the four elements by a higher circle of which *nous* is the lowest member with three stages above it, each of a finer and more (spiritually) rarefied nature: heroes, Daemons and the Divine itself. The result of this merger of Heaven as the fifth element and fourfold man is therefore a sevenfold picture in all.

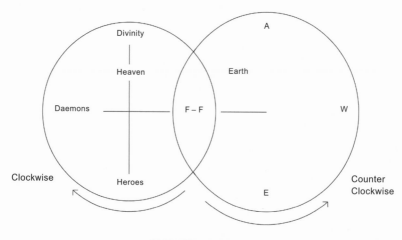

ILLUSTRATION 11

NOTES

1. One need only examine the artifacts in any ethnographical museum to establish this visually. As an example for many, I cite here a tradition related by a Maya descendant, Giacondi Belli (Belize) in an article entitled "Journey to the Lost City of the Jaguar" published in *Nature Conservancy 44* (1994) 14: "I look up and see the ceiba tree. A sacred tree for the Mayas. In their cosmogony, the world was thought to be a square, flat surface, suspended between 13 successive heavens and nine underworlds, each of them ruled by a god. On the geographic center of the Earth, a great ceiba tree grew, while four smaller trees stood on its four corners. Each corner had a separate color: white for the North, yellow for the South, red for the East, black for the West."

2. The hue of Attic soil is sometimes supposed to be the reason (i.e., sheer convenience), but nothing compels artisans to accept unchanged what is at hand, and concealing ground color—as Attic potters long did—is a common phenomenon in ceramics: cf, for example, the blue ceramics of the New Kingdom in Egypt.

3. *Aristotle Minor Works* (Loeb Classical Library) Cambridge, Massachusetts 1955 Vol. I Translated by W. S. Hett: *Aristotelous peri Xhromon* (from the Peripatetic School, of unknown authorship: Theophrastus? Strato?) *passim.*

4. Plato, *Timaeus,* 55A. A detailed discussion of the relationships among all these shapes is to be found in Plutarch's "Why the Oracles Cease to Give Answers" (De defectu oraculorum) 32-34 in *Plutarch's Essays and Miscellanies* edited by W.W. Grodam (Boston 1906) Vol. IV.

5. This conclusion arises inevitably from a fragment of Empedokles himself: see under his Testimonia A (*GCTFE,* ch. II) and, of course, the elegant disquisition on qualities by Plato *(Timaeus,* 49).

6. Ernst Lehrs, *Mensch und Materie* (Frankfurt-a-M 1966) Goetheanismus Ch. VII.

7. *Punkt und Linie zu Flache,* 1926 (*Point and Line to Plane,* Dover, 115 f.)

8. J. Pawlick, *Praxis der Farbe* (Cologne 1981) 214.

9. See translation reference in n. 4.

3.

The Colors of the Four Elements
and Their Relation to the
Remaining Colors

Having established a structured visual paradigm for the relationship of the four elements among themselves, we can now consider the associated *colors* when the paradigms are repeated to show the effects of the respective dominant process. Although the impulse to ask how this works arose for me out of the original paradigm itself, the procedure was later found to be quite in the sense of what Empedokles himself envisaged: "Those elements and forces are to be understood as equally strong and coeval, yet each of them has a different function, each has its own characteristic and *in the rounds of time they take their turn being dominant*[1] (my translation)."

It must be emphasized that the progressions in Ill. 12 relate to the macrocosmos, that is, more precisely, the universal, external and objective—as it were—basis of physical/physiological processes. Whatever echoes or premonitions of such progressions may be discernible in the ancient literary tradition (probably even including the medical writings) seem to be related to the macrocosmic sphere. However, Goethe's great pioneering work on the psychological and mental/moral aspects of color implicates another dimension to this problem, namely, the microcosmic or individuated realm. Therefore, it would be unconscionable for the modern investigator not to attempt to understand the implications of elements and colors on the specific level of the human being, whose form and functions—physical, physiological, psychological and mental/moral—constantly interact with the macrocosmos. This is shown in Ill. 13.

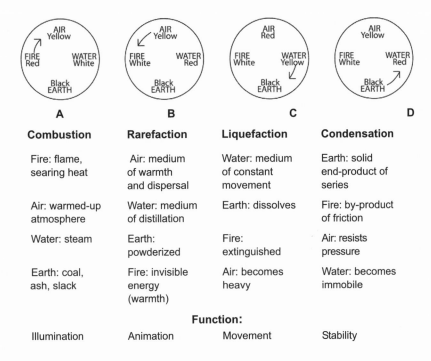

A	**B**	**C**	**D**
Combustion	**Rarefaction**	**Liquefaction**	**Condensation**
Fire: flame, searing heat	Air: medium of warmth and dispersal	Water: medium of constant movement	Earth: solid end-product of series
Air: warmed-up atmosphere	Water: medium of distillation	Earth: dissolves	Fire: by-product of friction
Water: steam	Earth: powderized	Fire: extinguished	Air: resists pressure
Earth: coal, ash, slack	Fire: invisible energy (warmth)	Air: becomes heavy	Water: becomes immobile

Function:

Illumination	Animation	Movement	Stability

Fire is the creative principle in (B), (C), (D), hence white; it materializes only in A, hence red (physical).

Air expands in (A), (B), hence yellow and increases its efforts to do so in (D) hence really a deeper yellow; it loses this quality by taking on weight in (C), hence red (immobility).

Water is the least stable in color. In (A) it is white (diminishingly physical). In (B) water signifies (retains) liquidity even in distillation (oxygen) hence red, yet it also becomes gaseous (hydrogen) thus tending toward yellow; in (C) it achieves maximum movement (yellow) and in (D) it tends toward immobility (red).

Earth is always stable to the extent that it remains the darker part in any condition. In principle, yellow is the color of dispersal, black of concentration, red of intensity or arrested movement and white of non-physicality or minimal physicality.

In all cases the colors share the tendency of the elements to mix themselves constantly and must therefore be taken as in constant gradation from one to the other.

ILLUSTRATION 12

E	F	G	H
AIR Yellow FIRE White WATER Red Black EARTH	AIR Red FIRE White WATER Yellow Black EARTH	AIR Red FIRE White WATER Yellow Black EARTH	AIR Yellow FIRE White WATER Red Black EARTH
Condensation/ compression	**Liquefaction**	**Rarefaction**	**Combustion**
Earth: ground of physicality	Water: agent of assimilation	Air: agent of psychic event	Fire: solid end-product of series
Air: warmed-up atmosphere	Water: medium of distillation	Earth: dissolves	Fire: by-product of friction
Water: steam	Earth: powderized	Fire: extinguished	Air: resists pressure
Earth: coal, ash, slack	Fire: invisible energy (warmth)	Air: becomes heavy	Water: *becomes immobile

Function:

Incarnation	Digestion	Animation	Reflection

Earth is implicit in life processes* at all stages providing physicality or its shadow, hence always black.

Water is more subject to movement in (F)-(G), hence yellow but more balanced and stable in (E) and (H), hence red.

Air is more subject to movement in (E) and (H), hence yellow but more stable and dense in (F) and (G), hence red.

Fire is the invisible presupposition of all processes, hence white throughout.

* in the sense of physiological processes.

ILLUSTRATION 13

∗ ∗ ∗ ∗ ∗

It may be useful to repeat that the progressions of Ill. 12 relate to the macrocosmos, that is, more precisely, the universal, external and objective—as it were—basis of physical/physiological processes (such as meteorological). Whatever echoes or premonitions of such progressions may be discernible in the ancient literary tradition (probably even including the medical writings) also seem to be related to the macrocosmic sphere. Extending this, Goethe's great pioneering work on the psychological and mental/moral aspects of color implicates another dimension to this problem, namely, the microcosmic or individuated realm. Therefore, I have made an attempt in Ill. 13 also to understand the implications of elements and colors on the level of the human being, whose form and functions—physical, physiological, psychological and mental/moral—constantly interact, as noted, with the macrocosmos.

In structuring the macrocosmic pictures (Ill. 12), I employed, as explained above, the hierarchical evolutionary principle of organization: fire, air, water and earth (as solid matter, the finished product of evolution). By contrast, since the psychological and mental/moral effects of interaction can be realized only by an individual consciousness, the microcosmic series (Ill.13) is therefore organized according to the biographical principle. The order is exactly reversed since the human being begins with earth (physicality) at birth and rises in the end (ideally) to mental/moral ripeness.

* * * * *

A comparison of the two sets of figures shows that only the color of earth (matter) remains constant in all cases. Further, only the picture for the dominance of water accords both macrocosmically and microcosmically with the original table that served as the point of departure (p. 33) for the study of variations. That original table was obtained from an analysis of the characteristic colors of Archaic ceramics. Yet, quite apart from color altogether, it had appeared from the analysis of sculptural form that Greeks of the Archaic period were at a stage of development that took for its concern the aqueous constitution of man (water-man).

Correspondence of the color series occurs at the earth stage as well as at the water stage of the two systems. Logically this is to be expected, since an individual human being is, as far as physical and physiological aspects are concerned, identical materially and constitutionally with the surrounding macrocosmic environment. As far as the air stage is concerned, the air-being (soul) corresponds to the color arrangement of the macrocosmic water stage, whereas the

individual fire-being (mind) is in accord with the colors of the macrocosmic air stage. This amounts to a chiastic relationship. Tentatively
one might argue that individual souls are necessarily limited by a
common parameter emotionally, that is, by a certain given range of
possible human emotions, whereas individual minds (I-beings)
have—theoretically—unlimited freedom to transcend cultural
parameters into the sphere of uniquely original creativity. If there is an
intelligible pattern in this, it must be stressed that the working out of
the tables took place at a comparatively early stage of this study with
sole concentration on the separate processual conditions; patterns
and implications like those just discussed were not noticed until later.

The various paradigms of Ills. 12-13 show the planet in terms of
color, that is, the planet as a four-membered unity with its manifold
subordinate, organically living, feeling and even thinking beings, in
elemental colors. These tables also go together in the sense of a
higher and a lower—though not necessarily oppositional—order.
Not as yet taken into account are the functional equalities and oppo-
sitions of the separate living beings (microcosms). The very intention to do this brings one to the particular way that philosophy and
the rational healing arts of the Greeks were interfaced; for the
founders of the latter were, according to the sensitive and sympathetic account of the medical historian, Henry Sigerist,[2] the
Pythagoreans, including Empedokles himself—the famous Hippokrates being by this account his successor. In any case, the paucity
of the record obscures what contribution these thinkers actually
made to the physiological model of the Hippokratean school. On
general grounds I am inclined to assume that the contrapposto-like
structure of this scheme as conceived by others from the purely medical standpoint (cf. Ill. 15 with basic macrocosmic figures Ill. 14)
makes it indeed a genuine product of the contrapposto principle,
and thus an achievement of the High Classical period—that is, a
mental model whether visualized as it is here or not. Still, the design
quality of the resulting inversions (presented in Ill. 14) is so striking
and artistic that it could possibly have been symbolized visually in

some way. Again, I must stress that the model I justified on pp. 37-43 was worked out before I became aware of its virtual existence, together with the same color scheme, in the writings of the Hippokratean corpus and Galen—but there *only* for a microcosmic purpose and apparently without conscious macrocosmic implication.

By the same token, the method of putting the basic macrocosmic model through four variations was anticipated in theory not only by Empedokles (p. 47) but also by Hippokrates in that he reckoned with a rotating ascendancy of each of his basic substances according to the progression of the four seasons, four ages of man, etc.,[3] as visualized by H. Schlepperges in a scheme exactly like mine (Ill. 15). I must leave it to the medically cognizant to ring the changes on that theme in a fully dynamic macrocosmic/microcosmic way. Although I do not feel qualified to attempt anything so ambitious, I believe that nothing else could give so vivid a conception of the mixture of the elements and the colors going on all the time as Empedokles proclaimed.

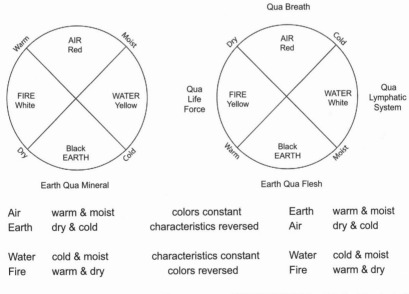

Air	warm & moist	colors constant	Earth	warm & moist
Earth	dry & cold	characteristics reversed	Air	dry & cold
Water	cold & moist	characteristics constant	Water	cold & moist
Fire	warm & dry	colors reversed	Fire	warm & dry

MACROCOSMIC (*postulated model*)   MICROCOSMIC (*model after Hippokrates*)

ILLUSTRATION 14

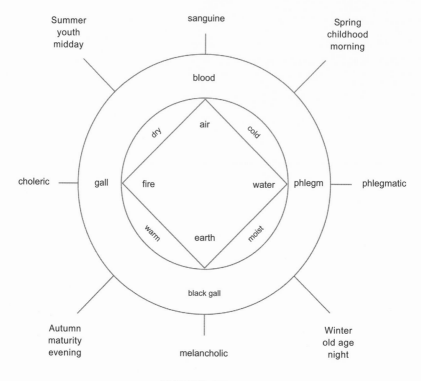

ILLUSTRATION 15

The diagrams I have used so far as an implementation of a Four Elements/Four Colors theory based on written sources and vase painting (by implication also major painting, as I tried to show in *GCTFE*) have served relatively well up to this point. But it is impossible to go further without being able to see the four color system itself in a larger framework that can elucidate the nature of that system relative to the other colors. For one is virtually forced to conclude that there was no scientific interest among the Greeks in any but the four colors before the fourth century, and even then—and thereafter—not much. On the other hand artists had been dealing with an extended range of colors, particularly with blue, in a pragmatic way from at least the seventh century. A reason for this situation will be suggested.

Attempts on the part of present day art historians to explain Greek color on the basis of the so-called Newtonian spectrum are subject to the severe limitation of Newtonian thought in general: it is confined to treating color as a purely physical phenomenon. Yet everyone knows that color exists not only in that sphere, but has psychological and even moral dimensions as well.

Having found no help from that quarter, I turned to Goethe's work on color. In the end this proved to be not only suggestive of an explanation for the Greek preoccupation with the four colors, but also richly evocative in realms he opened up but did not go into. Thus, my results seem to have application not only to the Greek situation but beyond it.

The Other Colors

Our point of departure for expanding the four color system is the fact that Goethe rejected Newton's conception of color out of hand and through his own experiments with the prism acquired a quite differently structured understanding of the phenomena of color. The defenders of Newton's conception (which has since become largely a matter of mathematical calculations) against Goethe habitually point to pragmatic achievements in color science—really staggering technical innovations. Thus, in order to master the basics of materialistic color science today one must virtually study mathematics and physics. By the same token, in order to grasp the basics of Goethe's color theory and—with appropriate adjustments, as we shall see—of the ancient Greek color system, one has to get some direct or indirect experience of the prism (this may require some guidance) and think *logically* about the phenomena it shows.

Then, just as Goethe intended, one *experiences,* one *sees* the actual coming into being of colors, their *phainetai eon,* instead of contemplating thought-pictures of wave lengths. A reverse paradox in this situation is that one can also experience the prismatic phenomena— at one remove—through such technical inventions as color slides and photographs—which would probably not have come into existence without the Newtonian mind-set. I take advantage of this by presenting in the Appendix guidance from Hans-Georg Hetzel who has spent many years developing just such visual aids and explaining authoritatively what they show. This allows me to proceed in the knowledge that any reader wishing to understand my discussion of the larger aspects of Greek color has the information necessary to do so within the covers of this book.

The Greek use of color suggests a limited but coherent theory of color which apparently was never thought out systematically, judging from ancient references to four basic colors: black, white, red, yellow in connection with Greek ceramic tradition and with available testimonia. Obviously, all this heavily involves the so-called subtractive (fixed) colors, that is, pigments. At this point it is worth emphasizing that the Greeks were necessarily more restricted to those in their color experience than we are. For modern technology has more than accustomed us to the additive color mixtures (called by Goethe *werdend,* incipient), such as are found in films and television. The Greeks, however, could experience such mixtures virtually only through natural occurrences, particularly the rainbow. E. Keuls[4] calls attention to the fact that Aristotle designated the three "frequencies": green *(prasinon)*, red *(phoinikoun)* and violet *(alourgon)* as the main colors of the rainbow, quite in accordance with the three additive colors of modern color science. Yet I cannot find the slightest indication that the Greeks at any time were familiar with the use of the prism or any other means of studying or even registering spectral phenomena.[5]

Despite this, since it was maintained as a truism that the chromatic colors arose through *krasis* (mixture) of black and white, one can suppose that either through some mystery tradition[6]—or else quite spontaneously—the Greeks recognized what Goethe established through countless prismatic experiments, namely, that the atmospheric colors arise through the interweaving of light and darkness in certain well-defined circumstances under appropriate conditions. About the same time as the Four Color theory was being given expression more or less consciously (as in the Hippokratean school)—a theory that in the light of prismatic phenomena is quite intelligible and defensible—the formula black + white = color became so deep-rooted in Greek thought that the interchangeability of white with light and black with dark probably seemed obvious (but was not used as a point of departure for reasoning about color problems).[7]

If, therefore, all that concerned the four color system simply remained below the threshold of conscious theoretical interest, there are even fewer indications that the other side of the prismatic spectrum (of Goethe) embracing black, white, blue, violet was part of any systematic thought procedure, even though again the *implications* of this other side were understood in the practice of painting. We are confronted here with a mystery of the first order; insistent questions arise. How could the Greeks—and for that matter peoples who preceded them—have such a sure understanding of the nature of colors when this is intellectually possible only through knowledge of the prism? And how, in these circumstances, are the origins of the pigment colors, as belonging more specifically to earth substance, to be related to the atmospheric colors as manifestations in the sphere of air?

An answer to the first question is perhaps to some extent inherent in the Greek conception of the Four Ages as this is given in the *Erga* of Hesiod (who, however, distorts this somewhat by inserting an Age of Heroes as a separate entity; that he did so may suggest that he was embroidering in an eighth-century manner on an older tradition). The general meaning of the myth seems clear; humanity lived at one time quite intimately with the gods (in a divine order) and was directly guided by them. Gradually, however, the gods gave up this supervision and thus forced humanity to stand on its own feet, regardless of what bitter consequences might ensue for it. Thus, much that had previously been simply handed over by the gods was no longer offered and had to be consciously and laboriously reacquired. A feeling for the attraction of this view of things can still be found in the Age of Reason; J.G. Herder writes in his *Ideen zur Philosophie der Geschichte* (V. Buch I. Teil, VI.Kap.):

A divine management was certainly operative for the race of men from the time of their first appearance, which was thus launched on its way with the least trouble. But the more human faculties came to be exercised, the less they needed to be subject to this assistance.

An important part of the Hesiodic myth is the connection of the Four Ages with four appropriate metals in the following order: gold, silver, bronze, iron. Obviously each metal has a hue. Gold could be described as yellow, perhaps more accurately described with Plato's *lambron* (bright, shining). Silver is naturally connected with white,[8] bronze is certainly in the red/brown frequency and iron is black in the *Erga* of Hesiod, whose tale is beyond any doubt a moral one, an earnest conversation with his countrymen. Thus, it serves incidentally as a prime example of the way the macrocosmic metals with their colors are interwoven or interfused with microcosmic (psychological and mental/moral) associations. My intention here is to point to an existential quality in the Four Elements/Four Colors theory, not to extract any specific historical content from the myth.

The second question articulated above is on all counts too difficult to discuss in a general way. I have worked out a hypothesis by extending the logic of the laws of optics as I understand them. Since this hypothesis does take account of modern viewpoints as well as of what seems to be inherent in using the Four Elements/Four Color theory as a model, it is unavoidably technical and seems best relegated to the Appendix for readers interested in the scientific implications of the subject.

The Two Spectra of Goethe's Color Theory

It is at this point incumbent on me to explain in my own words (that is, in addition to those of H.G. Hetzel in the Appendix) how I conceive of the interconnection of the two spectra derivable from Goethe's work, because that interconnection has led me to establish particular values for the various colors according to their connotation as macrocosmic or microcosmic. These values are presented in chart form in Ill. 16.

First of all, strict logic indicates that no prismatic scale, including Newton's, can appear without the cooperation of both light and shadow. In the case of Newton's experiment the wall of the dark chamber around the hole through which he admitted a light ray furnished the darkness necessary to allow the "refracted" colors to appear on the opposite wall. Nevertheless, he deduced from this experiment that colors existed purely in the form of bundles of rays constituting the light. Goethe's first contact with color theory did not happen to take place in a *camera oscura*. In his haste to use a borrowed prism he simply put light rays through the prism onto the white walls of the room he was in. To his surprise—for Newton had said that colors were contained in the light—nothing happened.[9] No color appeared on the wall. Only where he encountered a shadow on the white did it appear. In systematic experiments he then examined how colors appeared when there was more white than black on the surface and vice versa. In this way he discovered a polar reversal in the order of the *same set* of colors that appeared in these two circumstances. Furthermore, he found that by manipulating the prism he could either keep these colors intact or—by approaching the two innermost colors in the series—mix them and create a third, new color: green where dark predominated and magenta where light predominated. These relationships can be visualized in the following way:[10]

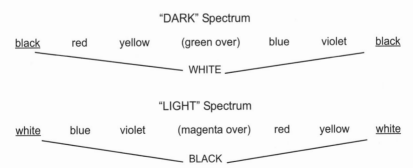

"DARK" Spectrum

| black | red | yellow | (green over) | blue | violet | black |

WHITE

"LIGHT" Spectrum

| white | blue | violet | (magenta over) | red | yellow | white |

BLACK

This polarity corresponds quite exactly with the world view of the Greeks, who preferred to deal with polarities in all phenomena. The relation of dark and light as well as the relation of specific colors to each other was on their minds from their first "Protogeometric" pots to Aristotle's speculations (note 5). And it was exactly that portion of Goethe's spectrum corresponding to the popular concept of "earth colors" that most concerned them, particularly so in the earlier periods; whereas the other part of the spectrum with the blue and violet corresponding to the popular concept of "heavenly colors"; increasingly attracted their interest in the later periods.

To repeat, for absolute clarity: the famous four colors of the Greeks are in effect one half of the Dark spectrum of Goethe:

BLACK   RED   YELLOW   WHITE

The white in this case is the "trench" between the two pairs of colors of the whole spectrum and as such plays an important role. For, although the Greeks at all times freely used yellow and also, when appropriate, the blue poised across from it, they seem seldom to have bridged the white gap between them to mix up a green; in fact, they may have been more interested in mixing black and yellow to produce a dull olive, as in certain ceramic fabrics, and this would have a different expressivity than true green. This downplaying of a radiant green helps to define their relationship to nature. Their subject was first and foremost that part of nature which is the human body and which in its nurture subsumes the green of plants and the oxygen produced by trees; it must not then have seemed necessary constantly to refer to all aspects of the environment literally, as in various other (later) cultures. Nevertheless, since green *is* a mixed color, not a primary, traces of blue left on stone, particularly on statues, might in some cases be the blue component of an original green (see below), although the blue might simply represent a local color.

The nature of black and white *as colors* in the four color system remains elusive. There is no other way the spectrum as a whole can be called up by the prism except that dark (sc. black) and light (sc. white) are played off against one another.[11] Modern color science, ignoring this, applies the adjective "achromatic" (colorless), which has a proper use in optics, illogically to black and white. Artists of virtually all periods have wholeheartedly used black and white as colors of the utmost expressivity and, as we have seen, some Greek thinkers regarded them as the only true colors or, more precisely, the original colors (*Urfarben*). The use of black and white as stand-ins for dark and light must lie behind this. By that token Ill. 16 can be read as the relationships of pigmentary colors reflecting, reduced from, the atmospheric colors.

An Attempt at a Holistic Interpretation of Color Meaning

My experiences over a number of years in studying the prismatic laws and applying them to the interpretation of works of art of all periods have led me to make a visualization of the relationships I found; this is in the form of the schema given in Ill. 16. My debt to Goethe as a point of departure is fundamental. Yet I have proceeded to derive the fullest consequences of his rather generalized, really incipient, thoughts from the spirit of his work, that is, the insight into polarities, applied here in the most radical fashion. The more uncompromisingly one applies the concept of polarities to colors, the more generously they yield up the nuances of their expressivity, which nevertheless remains inexhaustible. The nature of the case then admits of, even requires, characterizations of color quality by single keywords or phrases. This makes it apparent that Ill. 16 cannot be justified by a long verbal disquisition (although a few features of it will be explained in due course) but rather by use of it in understanding the prismatic experience and by applying it to the (largely nonverbal) appreciation of the choices of artists in the coloration of their works. This in turn implies that artists have always intuitively understood the lawful potencies of macrocosmic/ microcosmic color handed down from earliest times. This occurred normally in terms of conventions individually administered but agglomerated into larger units recognizable as workshops and schools. In effect, many of the concepts offered in Ill. 16 have long been intuitively understood by critics as well as artists; hence a more precise delineation of the concepts suggested here could be an incentive to further methodical refinements.

At this point at least a few explanatory comments to Ill. 16 are in order. Atmospheric green, induced by manipulation of the prism to combine yellow and blue over white ground is similarly produced in painting by mixing blue and yellow pigments on a white support, as in watercolors. From this fact it can be seen that the invention of oil paints was a distinct step toward materiality, since the white support is not necessary, even though white as a surrounding color has much of the same effect. The preparation of green pigment directly from natural substances, such as minerals (whose color implies an earlier evolutionary process, as discussed in *GCTFE* Ch.11) is a further step in this direction. The corresponding color in the Light spectrum is the delicate hue magenta, induced by mixing violet and red over a black ground. If one imagines black paper used as the support for mixing violet and red water colors, the delicacy of magenta can be easily comprehended. Add to this the indication that in their normal state all the colors of the Light spectrum are especially delicate in that they embody non-material qualities.[12]

This can perhaps be grasped in the case of the blue and violet of the Light spectrum which I have designated as transcendental colors in contrast to blue and violet of the Dark spectrum which are called transatmospheric; these latter (as atmospheric colors) actually owe their darkness (shadedness) to the backdrop of cosmic darkness against which they are apprehended by our eyes. To put it another way, they conduct the vision from the lightfilled earth atmosphere toward the darkness of the surrounding universe. The blue and violet arising in this way are not so much in the earth's atmosphere as at its very edge, its boundary; it is as if blue were the inner skin and violet the outer skin of that boundary. For this reason they have always been felt as drawing our sight outward and away into the distance. Thus the expression "transatmospheric" is an attempt to do justice in a completely neutral way, with no overtones, to the physical/ physiological phenomenon just described. By the same token the diagonally positioned blue and violet of the Light spectrum are actually backlighted. Hence they refer in this context exclusively to the sphere of Being (the moral sphere) and do most decidedly have overtones. Put in another way, they are transcendental in that they transcend the physical realm which is the everyday setting for human existence. Therefore, at one time blue is purely physical (sensory), at another time it is supersensory, the criterion being how it is positioned (understood) in relation to light and dark.

Therefore I emphasize again that *all* the colors of the Dark spectrum are to be understood on the purely physical/physiological level and are therefore highly suited to be grasped in exactly the way that modern color science does grasp them. It is historically inevitable that the Dark spectrum would be discovered through a materialistically oriented scientific problem and then used as a basis not only for defining the sensory nature of color but even of refining that definition in the direction of a sub-sensory (purely mathematical) system of color science. So congenial is the Dark spectrum to this point of view that it has been hailed as the *only* existing spectrum (to which, of course, Goethe reacted violently) and no lengths have been too laborious to go to in order to defend this assumption.[13] This is obviously controversial ground and the challengers of the assumption also have exerted—and do exert—themselves to a corresponding degree. It is also somewhat ironic that Greek thinkers—even Plato—immersed themselves in exactly the earthiest part: the "earth colors" of the physical spectrum, as something they wanted to know more about, at the same time unwittingly supplying a basis for a coming western science of the material.

Dark Spectrum (Sensory)   Light Spectrum (Supersensory)

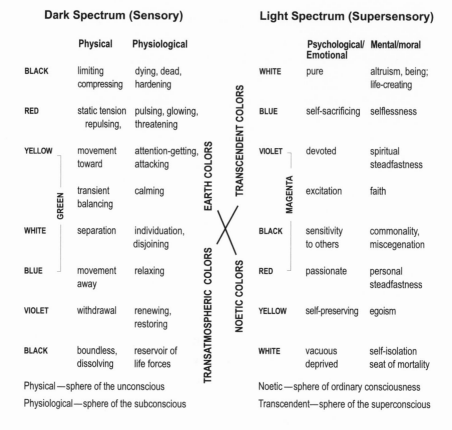

	Physical	Physiological					Psychological/ Emotional	Mental/moral
BLACK	limiting compressing	dying, dead, hardening				WHITE	pure	altruism, being; life-creating
RED	static tension repulsing,	pulsing, glowing, threatening				BLUE	self-sacrificing	selflessness
YELLOW	movement toward	attention-getting, attacking				VIOLET	devoted	spiritual steadfastness
	transient balancing	calming				MAGENTA — excitation		faith
WHITE	separation	individuation, disjoining				BLACK	sensitivity to others	commonality, miscegenation
BLUE	movement away	relaxing				RED	passionate	personal steadfastness
VIOLET	withdrawal	renewing, restoring				YELLOW	self-preserving	egoism
BLACK	boundless, dissolving	reservoir of life forces				WHITE	vacuous deprived	self-isolation seat of mortality

GREEN · EARTH COLORS · TRANSCENDENT COLORS · MAGENTA · TRANSATMOSPHERIC COLORS · NOETIC COLORS

Physical—sphere of the unconscious   Noetic—sphere of ordinary consciousness

Physiological—sphere of the subconscious   Transcendent—sphere of the superconscious

HOW TO READ THE CHART

The characteristics of physical colors are adapted from the concepts of statics and dynamics inherent in the four elements. The characteristics of physiological colors transfer the physical characterizations to the basic organic (vegetative) realm. On the psychological plane reactions are subconscious but can instantaneously release motor activity as in the case of red and yellow traffic signals (emotions are not necessarily involved). On the supersensory level the order of colors is reversed and their effect—as given by nature or acculturation—arises in the noetic sphere. On the mental/moral level one encounters a fluctuating relationship of the emotional factor and the social (ego) factor. The latter includes the highest moral concepts traditionally associated with religion and philosophy, hence transcendental.

The color values proposed here, based on the principle of polarity, are representative central concepts. Nuances arise from mixed hues and from (situational) interaction of hues.

ILLUSTRATION 16

Yet those very same Greeks almost certainly could not have experienced difficulty in conceiving that the colors of the Dark spectrum can become totally (and chiastically) inverted and back-lighted and thereby more delicate. Such colors, in any case, can dialectically have a connection only with mental values (yellow and red as the truest colors of the innermost *nous* and with spiritual values (blue and violet as belonging to the sphere of the divine). By this reckoning green refers principally to the transience of the physiological sphere, just as it is in fact the color of every blooming landscape. If used metaphorically, it could then refer to transient beauty or to the peacefulness of organic well-being. The opposite, special prismatic color, magenta, has logically to be the link between the noetic and the spiritual spheres, just as green is the link between the materials of earth and the animating forces, for example rays of the sun, that descend to nature through the transatmospheric boundary.

On this basis it is not surprising that Goethe considered magenta, which is used here to translate his term *Purpur,* to be the ultimate intensification—*Steigerung*—of red (vermilion); the combination of the highest noetic color, red, with violet, which in low saturation offers a delicate atmosphere of spirituality, creates a bridge from the mental to the divine sphere. But at a price, for this color alone in the light spectrum is not backlighted by white but hovers over black, which holds it down to mortality.

Finally, in order to make the concept of the transcendental quadrant of the spectra comprehensible to the maximum degree, I refer again to the idea that the Greeks probably could have accepted the concept of the colors of their four elements as capable of being chiastically inverted and backlighted, because in fact they *used* colors in the noetic and also the transcendental sense effectively, when that was appropriate, but without speculation. Their more conscious concern was plainly to grasp intellectually the earth quadrant of the Dark spectrum.

What they achieved in that respect became part of the heritage of a firm, balanced conception of human life valued by the Roman intelligentsia, such as Cicero and the Plinys, to mention a few, and which was passed along to become, with or without the blessing of the Church, a powerful factor in the civilizing of northern Europe. It seems possible to associate the earth-bound solidity of Romanesque architecture with this. Yet, when an unprecedented surge of faith swept over Europe in the so-called Gothic period, it fell to architects and painters to overcome that earth-bound practical solidity which is so rightly preserved in the very name (Romanesque); they did so by inventing soaring, seemingly weightless architectural forms and, to go with them, stained glass windows. Anyone who has stood in a great Gothic cathedral like Chartres has felt the unique refulgence of its lofty windows (generally dominated by blue, red and violet—on the religious significance of these colors see my discussion in *GCTFE* Ch.V—and white). One is seeing pigmentary colors liter-ally backlighted by natural light. But is that all there is to it? The total effect is often described as a supreme spiritual experience, even in our jaded times; and the reason is that transatmospheric color is transformed into noetic (red) and transcendental (blue, violet) col-ors by atmospheric light, which becomes at the same time meta-static divine light. With the chiastic spectra of Goethe this event can be explicitly described and understood, insofar as human under-standing reaches. Without those spectra the experience can easily become lost in an amorphous mysticism.

Expanding the Basic Four Color Paradigm

In order to offer the reader the ultimate intellectual consistency I can muster, I offer below an expanded version of the basic Four Color paradigm to suggest how green, blue and violet could be related to the basic earth colors. In Ill. 12C or the identical 13C, which may be used as the most familiar operative form of the para-digm, the circumferential line marks the separation of all terrestrial phenomena, macrocosmic or microcosmic, from outer space. Obviously this paradigm is a drastic simplification owing to Greek concentration on only the earth color quadrant of the Dark spectrum (Ill. 16). That is, the Greek philosophers were, accurately enough, analyzing the functional (dynamic) processes that take place in the earth's atmosphere but ignoring the visual phenomena that actually result from those processes. This is another way of saying that they ignored the transatmospheric quadrant of the Dark spectrum (Aristotle makes a slight exception to this statement).

In order for these facts to be apparent in an expanded version of the paradigm, it must be understood that the circumferential line of the basic paradigm (Ill. 12C) separates the earth *plus* its atmosphere from the outer cosmos; in the new version (Ill. 17) this same line actually separates the purely mineral earth *from* its atmosphere. The latter now contains the separate realms of the colors green, blue and violet which are visible to us—in what way I will mention shortly. Meanwhile, the *original* four colors are to be thought of as dynamically active under, on and above the earth's ground line and visible where appropriate. The outer circumferential line of Ill. 17 separates the earth *plus* atmosphere from the outer cosmos.

In the new version (1ll. 17) green hugs the surface of the earth, just as does the green mantle of vegetation in reality. The transitory, shifting nature of the latter can be understood through its being a combination of finely moisturized earth represented here by yellow and the cosmic light of the sun (white) penetrating through the blue sky. This circumstance is exactly reflected, as, of course, it would have to be, in the Dark spectrum. The outermost color, violet, is principally visible in the rainbow, since otherwise it is above the blue.

While this final schema goes beyond Greek theoretical values, it was nevertheless explored and understood to a considerable extent by Greek artists, who at first in advance of the philosophers and by mid-fifth century in tandem with them—and then leaving them behind—worked pragmatically on into the Hellenistic period (and what I designate as Graeco-Roman painting). By that time they had discovered and used freely many, if not most, of the technical properties of color—apparently at a completely informal level—which are now discussed routinely in art training and in textbooks on art history. But while such technicalities would apply only to the Dark spectrum (to which Ill. 17 is limited), the insights of the Greek painters reached into the Light spectrum, since only that could serve them as a bridge to the divine world and the world of deepest human meaning. That spectrum, being a total inversion of the Dark spectrum, eludes the kind of abstraction which can try to pictorialize it (the Light spectrum) in a paradigm—however useful that may be (see Ill. 17). In short (to use familiar terms), one must exercise the soul as well as the mind.

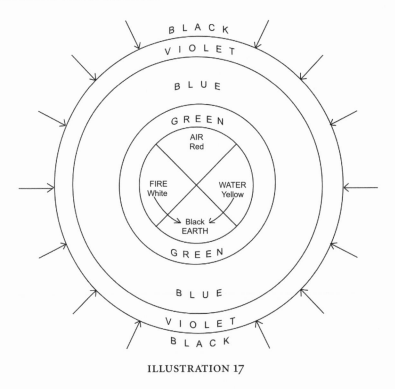

ILLUSTRATION 17

The Epicurean View of Color

In this somewhat curtailed treatment of Greek Four Color theory as far as it can be reconstructed, it was not feasible to include any detailed consideration of the insights obtained in *GCTFE* through a close consideration of actual ancient references to color. However, I append here, as a supplement to what was presented there, a review of references to color in the poem of Lucretius which, being a veritable encyclopedia of the world-view of the Epicurean school, of course includes color. (By the same token, the relation of that world-view to evolution will be discussed in Part II in connection with Darwinism).

My discussion here has the aim of establishing whether, being beholden to a kind of imaginary physics, the Epicurean view produces a rival color theory to that of the mainstream Empedoklean-Hippokratic School. The ideas about color derived from Epicurus go back to the atomism of Leukippos/Demokritos of probably the second half of the fifth century B.C. Relatively little is known about either man except that they launched an abstract view of nature, or of the work of Epicurus as their chief convert except what Lucretius tells us.

In Book II, beginning at line 730, Lucretius discusses at great length the shapes and movements of atoms with a vividness that guarantees us that he is seeing a mind-tableau in which—despite its totally imaginary character—he has the utmost faith. His exposition includes the atomic understanding of colors about which otherwise there are only a few—though very important—scraps of information attributed to Demokritos. These have been discussed in detail in *GCTFE* and cannot be repeated here. They are, on the whole, inconclusive, owing to the difficulties of the subject and the illogic inherent in the atomic position, but it is worth seeing what Lucretius, who was much closer in time than we are to the original source, made of them.

The first principle he propounds contradicts the physiological conviction of Empedokles (that colored rays: black and white, emanate from the eye—Aristotle reversed this) by claiming that the primary particles of matter have no color at all. The proof for this is (for him) that the unsighted can touch colored objects and thus get an impression of them which obviously cannot include color. In this way colorless bodies are quite thinkable and atoms must be such bodies since, if a substance—for example, sea water—changes color, something must be left behind to prevent that substance from disintegrating. That "something" would by this reasoning be the atoms. Ergo, if the basic atoms *have* to be colorless, the *effect* of coloration must be given by the shapes and combinations of shapes of the atoms. What must have taken place is a churning up and re-shuffling of the atoms with some additions and subtractions. [The Empedoklean principle of *krasis* (mixture) is borrowed here with the substitution of atoms for elements.] This train of thought is to demonstrate that the sea is not composed of blue atoms, since otherwise the effect of white wave crests would not be possible. He uses this to suggest that white and black objects are not created from white or black materials respectively, but rather that the colors of both the objects and the materials are the result of the mixing of various colors, But no proof of this is given.

No colors are visible without illumination, but in light itself (*lumen*) no atoms can be seen. Therefore, when colors are observed to change, this must be owing to the angle at which the beam of light (*lux*) strikes the atomic shapes (l.800). The eye's perception of white, etc. is thus the result of a particular type of impact. On the analogy of touch already used, this must be owing to the differing shapes of the atoms involved because, on this premise, otherwise specific shapes would have specific colors. Further, that conclusion seems to rest on the grounds that, if the atoms were *not* colorless, their compounds might be tinted in any unpredictable way regardless of the shapes of the atoms. This seems to me to be a circular argument, and the examples given do not help much. In fact, the whole section concludes rather lamely and one wonders whether the author would have tried to revise it had he lived longer.

Such is the extent of a color theory that could be put together on the basis of atomism by a highly intelligent Roman poet. It clearly remains on the level of a very limited, abstract "proto-physics" and has only the most limited application to actual hues in nature, as when the poet comments on the phenomenon of the rainbow in his treatment of meteorology (VI, 524-26). The fixation on basically indefinable atoms blocks access to the universality of color phenomena implicit and explicit in the Four Colors/Four Elements framework described in this study.

NOTES

1. Diels B17, 27-29: B26, 1-2. Historians of ancient philosophy traditionally interpret the cyclic aspect of Empedokles' philosophy as an alternating dominance of love and strife, i.e., of "forces." Undoubtedly that had high priority in the thought of the ancients. Yet this approach neglects a possible similar significance in the other term of the Empedoklean statement quoted here: dominance of the (four) elements in rotation. Coming to this problem from the direction of color, I found it necessary to conceive a way of doing justice to the processual quality of the elements (a Greek concept though not usually mentioned) and to the differentiation between macrocosm and microcosm (also implicit in ancient thought). Obviously, I do not claim that Empedokles or anyone else actually systematized his philosophy in my conceptual terms; yet certain conclusions from them concerning colors and Hippokratic medicine, if not more, are implicit in fifth century culture and all the more in the pragmatic achievements of Hellenistic engineering and chemistry.

Thus there are now two parallel interpretive streams: that of the traditional scholarly analysis of cycles, e.g., D. O'Brien's *Empedokles' Cosmic Cycle* or in B. Inwood, *The Poem of Empedocles* (Toronto 1982)46-52—in which there is no mention of any of the factors I have just brought up; and the one I am developing here out of analysis of art and from diverse clues in previous scholarship. In stressing processual quality I do not exclude the operation of love and strife— indeed that has to be the essential mover of the rotation of the elements to dominance. That is not, however, to say that I can offer any definitive suggestions about the technique of its operation—any more than can O'Brien and those he reports on, who do not agree on how or even whether love and strife operate in turn. In any case, the two interpretive streams under discussion seem to me to express complementation rather than contradiction and to demonstrate again the richness of fabric of any creative moment in world history, going beyond the ability of human consciousness to exhaust.

In the foregoing sense, it can be pointed out that my demonstration of triadic stages in the rotation of the elements in Greek sculpture *(GSFE)* opens the way to a new hypothesis. Empedokles' mention of a "double tale" *(dipl'ereo)*: the coming together and growing apart of roots, can hardly exclude a middle phase in which the process starts to reverse itself, comes to a balance and then starts on the opposite course. Logically this is more plausible than the assumption of a single abrupt and dramatic turning point whereby things are completely turned around. It could therefore be supposed that the thinking stage is dominated by the creativity of strife (in reaction against an old order) and that in the feeling stage the new creation is then gradually harmonized by the increased activity of love so that in the final (willing) stage, all things desire each other in the now refined conditions of the cycle in progress. In due course the cycle begins over again. In this way, the *simultaneous* rotation of the elements *and* love and strife can be accounted for.

N.B. I follow Diels and K. Freeman *Ancilla to the Pre-Socratic Philosophers* Cambridge, Mass. 1962 in the interpretation and translation of the passage under discussion. However, if one is going to doubt that Empedokles was referring to elements as well as forces—as does H. Lainbrides, *Empedocles A Philosophical Investigation* (University, Alabama 1976) 67-69—then it must be counterclaimed that the whole thrust of the section (fr. 17) in which it occurs would leave no sense in these lines without elements but could if necessary be understood without forces.

2. Sigerist 1961, 101-106.

3. According to the astute arguments of W. Muri in "Melancholische und schwarze Galle": *Antike Medizin* (ed. N. Flashar, Darmstadt 1971, 165-191: excerpted from *Museum Helveticum* 10, 1953 21-38) the systematic differentiation between black and yellow gall first turns up in "On the Nature of the Human Being", which he dates to about 400 (cf. W.H. Jones in the Loeb edition of this with the date of 440-400). Muri rightly calls attention to the mental agility of the Greeks in recognizing such subtle distinctions as four instead of three seasons and keeping "psychological" apart from "mental". Yet it is surely a modern preconception to propose some systematic compulsion toward fourfold division. Who was forcing whom to do this? I prefer to assume that Hippokrates—if not Empedokles himself—had absorbed the artistic model of contrapposto, perhaps in stages as it was being worked out, and simply applied that to his own concerns. Just when the results were written down cannot, of course, be known but the detailed structure of the scheme rather suggests the spirit of the High Classical Reaction (430-400 B.C.). Another problem is whether the statement in the Hippokratic work *On Diet* which A. Krug *(Heilkunst und Heilkult:* Medizin der Antike, Munich 1985, 21-38, 49) takes to be evidence of an alternative system, represents the refusal of the author of that work to relinquish the old macrocosmic system in favor of new ideas, given that the definitions of the elements fire and water in *On Diet* remain unchanged.

4. Keuls 1978, 69-70 ad Aristotle, *Meteorologika,* 374b, 31-34.

5. The word *prisma* is used by Euklid (II Deff. 13) in connection with its geo-metric shape: cf. Pauly-Wissova *s.v.* Euklides, 1018. Hellenistic Greeks were at least interested in the refraction of light as it affected katoptrics (*Hdbh d. Altertumwiss.* V,1,21:L. Herberg, Geschichte der Mathematik und Naturwis-senschaften im Alterthum: IV Optik, 73-79). It is my understanding that there is at least one natural means of access to the spectral phenomenon, *viz.,* quartz crystals. However these are said to produce *double* bands of each color at the border of the light ray—a perhaps confusing impression (cf. Rudolf Rykart, *Quartz-Monographie,* OH-Verlag Thun 1989: I have not personally been able to consult this publication).

6. I am thinking of temple geometry as this is recovered by Tons Brunés, *The Secrets of Ancient Geometry and Its Use* (Copenhagen 1967).

7. Goethe concerned himself with this problem in *Beiträge zur Chromatik,* Par. 29: "…thus pure white is a representative of light, pure black a representative of darkness." Rudolf Steiner, in editing this (Kurschner edition, Weimar) commented: "white then in Goethe's view is only the representative of light, whereas Newtonian optics claims it as light itself. But at most one could say that white is a condition of matter under the influence of unadulterated light, or that white appears as matter that resists light by its opacity." This is obviously a, if not the, central problem in color studies and has been thought about extensively by philosophers such as Wittgenstein as well. It therefore seems pertinent to quote a rather long passage from an exceedingly astute commentator whose work is hardly known in the English speaking world, and perhaps only marginally to German art historians: E. Strauss, *Koloritgeschichtliche Untersuchungen zur Malerei seit Giotto* (Deutscher Kunstverlag 1972) 125 (my translation):

> Through this process there is a firming up of those elements of color which are supported by a system of linear structuring, foremost among them being those that most purely represent the phenomena light and shade, colorless as these are. That only black and white are capable of doing this has, of course, always been understood and accepted, and yet the whole long route to complete autonomy of picture colors had to be traversed before this article of knowledge could finally be accepted in the practice of artists. Not even Otto Philipp Runge—who in his color theory gave more room than any other artist-theoretician before him to reflections on the manifestations of light and dark and the problems these present to the painter—succeeded in consistently incorporating

into his own painting his own pregnant observations about the two "polar colors". Nevertheless, he came to the remarkable realization that white and black are to be considered "figures" of light and dark. Through this important insight color acquires a form-quality: the "etheric essence" of light and darkness first of all takes on a definite reproducible shape. On this point Runge's ideas come very close to Klee's evaluation of white and black as the primary components of chiaroscuro in painting. For to Klee's way of thinking what consists of white is simply the light itself, whether this is applied pigment or simply part of the surface color of the picture support itself. By the same token pure black stands for pure darkness.

This materialization of darkness through the deepest, most absolutely scaled color quality signifies at the same time a decidedly upward valuation of darkness as a picture element. It also contains a basic innovation. By identifying darkness with pure black, Klee gives the former the same color status as that which light gets through being represented by white—and makes it, through this opposition, for the first time tangible to the senses. He creates a balance between these two potencies which could not exist so long as the conception of the natural primacy of light as the only animating force had uncontested validity also in regard to pictorial light. But "what may be true in Nature, the dominant activity of the white pole, must not seduce the painter to a one-sided view." In fact, Klee goes so far in this relativizing of light and pure white as its equivalent as to deny it even in its isolated state any automatic power of its own. It can perhaps acquire this in its "interaction with opposites." Painting thereby does not reckon only with a light-energy set against a specified darkness, but just as much with a black energy set against a specified light, and so with two forces that work in opposite directions.

8. Cf. the title of J. Boardman's article, "Silver is White" *Revue d'Archeologie* 1987, 279-295.

9. However much Goethe's expectation in this case was an—understandable—misunderstanding of Newton's *cruces experimentum,* it also harbored intuitively an inevitable criticism of Newton's legacy in its capacity as an absolute model for the world view that swept all before it. That legacy starts from the premise that the phenomena of nature can be understood as mathematical abstractions which in turn can be used to manipulate said phenomena quite arbitrarily to serve human convenience. Curiously, this premise is not inapplicable to the way that Newton himself silenced his contemporary

critics: Hook, Huygen, Marcotte, etc., more through his great authority and clever politicking than through honest consideration of their doubts. The problematical nature of this whole side of modern science troubled Goethe more than any other factor of the culture of his time. Despite the fact that he hardly made a breach in the impregnable fortress that was Newtonian science at that time, the problems he aired have never ceased to exercise theoreticians of science (e.g., Helmholtz and Heisenberg). A number of studies have appeared recently in the Anglo-Saxon world which attempt in an unprejudiced way to do justice to Goethe's concerns: J.P.S. Uberoi, *The Other Mind of Europe: Goethe as a Scientist* (Delhi 1984); Frederick Amrine, ed. *Goethe and the Sciences: A Reappraisal* Boston Studies in the Philosophy of Science, no. 97 (1987); and D.L. Sepper, *Goethe Contra Newton Polemics and the Project for a New Science of Color* (Cambridge University Press 1988). Particularly the last mentioned sets out trenchantly the ramifications of the controversy not only for the science of Goethe's time but also of our own age. He concludes that Goethe's conception of the scientific method represents an ideal which—despite his inability to gain a hearing for it—has in many ways been validated in the twentieth century through sheer necessity. Thus "we have seen that rejecting Goethe's science as the imaginings of a poet is false; perhaps it is not fanciful to suggest that as poet Goethe recognized with unmatched clarity the role of language in science, its symbolic and inalienably metaphoric character" (p.192).

10. This scheme is based on that in Ott & Proskauer I 1980, 327.

11. The rainbow is a special problem. Individual atmospheric colors arise according to the polaric rule: dark before light makes red, while light before dark makes blue, interfacing with such physical factors as rain drops and dust. But the position of white at the center of the Dark spectrum seems to me not to be taken sufficiently into account in explanations of various phenomena.

12. One could try to formulate it in this way: although the prism can make these colors physically visible, they are by virtue of their inverse relationship to light-dark more hovering over than entering into physicality.

13. In the experience of H.G. Hetzel (see p. 54) many scientists condemn the physical theories of Goethe without having investigated them, that is, on hearsay. More fair-minded scientists, such as R.M. Boynton *(Human Color Vision*, Rineholt, 1979, 22) and P.J. Bouma (1947, 204), recognize that a holistic interpretation of reality such as that of Goethe would naturally produce a quite different understanding of color than Newton's.

4.

The Supersensory Colors
of the Four Ethers

In the preceding study the colors assigned to the four elements were worked out by combining analysis of written historical materials and actual objects preserved from past times with an intuitive mode of thinking which approaches what can be called the outermost reaches of academic method—that is, what can be grasped by logical considerations available to everyday consciousness. Yet, (as already noted in the Preface) I could hardly have achieved a workable epistemological relationship to those historical materials and objects, had I not simultaneously and on an ongoing parallel track been studying the thought-world of Rudolf Steiner. That, however, constituted an enabling factor only and did not in any way dictate the course of my work on the ancient materials.

Despite the foregoing disclaimer—or perhaps in view of its efficacy—it was clear to me that my results could at best not be anything more than a reorientation to, or a plausible imagination of, an historical tradition, which might be of some value in understanding how Western intellectual theory has become so indifferent, or even hostile, to a spiritual explanation of the world.

Furthermore, it was clear to me from the beginning that Steiner had already gone far past the stage I was concerned with, and had, with his world view, pushed far ahead in his mission of laying out new paradigms for a future benign development of humanity. These are paradigms that build upon, as he himself stated, and transform the heritage of the ancient world, particularly that of the Classical Greeks. On that basis I had promised myself to "look into" his discovery of the four ethers *when* the right moment came. I had more or less purposely avoided doing this because I realized that I must first really understand as well as possible the modern philosophical implications of the Greek Four Elements theory—and on its own terms; for this was a task ignored by the typical academic consciousness because of the frozen condition of current epistemology.

Upon completion of that task, therefore, I felt as well prepared for the four ethers as I could be: prepared in fact to follow with rising gratitude the patient guidance in, and sorting out of, the theme by Ernst Marti, who in effect summarized and modified the by now almost unknown foundation-work of Guenther Wachsmuth. Marti's vantage point as a medical doctor, furthermore, made him precisely a successor of the Pythagorean-oriented medical school of Hippokrates which, as is well known, worked creatively with the physiological aspect of the Four Elements theory. Marti's work offers the life sciences a way out of the *cul de sac* into which their cognitional rigidity has brought them, and one may say the same of the physical sciences in relation to the work of such scientists as Bodo Hamprecht. With guides such as these, even my incomplete knowledge of their fields could not prevent me from realizing that Steiner's discovery of the four ethers (actually discovery of the inner structure of Aristotle's *aither*) is as brilliant and promising for the creation of a new epoch as were those of Kepler and Galileo in their time. Deepening the knowledge of extra-terrestrial factors discovered by them, Steiner's ethers present also sub-terrestrial transmutations in the realms of the "adversary powers"—those unthinkably destructive forces hidden in substances like uranium. Thereby he gave a tool for a truly "spiritual-scientific" understanding of planetary reality—with full emphasis on both of those terms, as is appropriate for the consciousness soul stage (Steiner's term for what lies above pure intellectuality) of humanity.

The tool just spoken of obviously implies a possibility of conscious-ness-widening; but this cannot, of course, be achieved by the mere transmission of "information" from author to reader, however useful that may be. The opening and widening of consciousness must be indi-vidually worked for, so that what follows can be no more than a chal-lenge to be taken up or left aside. What I can offer is an attempt, inspired by, but necessarily going beyond Marti, to separate the con-cepts: elements, ethers, colors and world origins. I do this in the full knowledge that such a process is only an intellectual convenience which may, nevertheless, prove to have been a necessary step toward experiencing the divine and dynamic unity of these concepts, as the Greeks did on a purely intuitive level. For it would seem that the god they felt behind each physical element is none other than the cosmi-cally active ether which Steiner discovered in the same position. To underscore the seriousness of my intentions in regard to researching the concepts listed above, I refer the reader not only to what immedi-ately follows but also to my essay on the philosophy of color (chapter 5), which presents an example of my personal experience in striving for something of the consciousness-widening I referred to above. More-over, this should be taken in conjunction with the section of the Appendix, "The Four Elements and the Origins of Fixed Colors."

* * * * *

The core of my attempt to separate the elements and the ethers is a set of defining characteristics of each in axiomatic form. These will be followed by a brief discussion of the problem of assigning colors and—in fig.18—an extended version of fig.17—to suggest how etheric and formative forces interact. A second diagram (fig. 19) concentrates more specifically on the functions of the ethers. Finally, a large chart (fig. 20) summarizes and widens the characteristics of the elements and ethers and includes a new factor: the differentia-tion of celestial and subterrestrial ethers. There is no separate dis-cussion of the world's origin, since that subject is implicit in various aspects of my treatment of elements, ethers and colors.

The Cosmically Real Nature of Etheric Colors

Ernst Marti (p. 37) writes: "Like the elements, the ethers are ideas. In which phenomena does their collaboration appear perceptible to our senses? Since the Greeks knew only one undifferentiated ether, they could neither ask nor answer this question. We have to look for the answer by way of thought and have to find the phenomena in the realm of the organic." From this point Marti explores the interaction of pairs of etheric forces and its results in terms of the maintenance of the natural world. As a convenience I have incorporated these in chart form in Ill. 20 along with color indications. For the Marti quotation is equally a point of departure for the question of the inner nature of color. To begin this I have expanded Ill. 17 in the sense of the Dark Spectrum alone (see Ill.16), wherein transatmospheric black, characterized as the sphere of boundless creativity, can now be understood as in reality the sphere of the ethers (Ill.18). Finally, *after* the following discussion, the reader can find in Ill. 19 a similar schema wherein the colors of the various elements and ethers are specifically differentiated.

Undoubtedly "idea" in the context of Marti's statement is to be interpreted as Schiller interpreted Goethe's idea of an *Urpflanze*: principle. Principles are leading thoughts that reveal themselves to exact observation and contemplation of a given phenomenon. Almost without doubt the Greeks, at least by the time of Aristotle, were capable of realizing that the principle of the four elements which had gradually come to expression could not explain all known phenomena in a truly scientific manner, and even that the fifth element, the ether—out of which the other elements had perhaps precipitated—might be amenable to being subdivided so as to correspond to the inner driving force of each of the elements. Indeed, in their experience, the four elements were already an intellectual reduction of four separate divine beings who must have existed in the ether. However, the Greeks were going in precisely the opposite direction; they were increasingly engrossed in experiencing

the more tangible physical, particularly the physiological, manifestations of the four elements themselves. That was quite enough to do.
Rather it is *our* task to work *backward* toward the supersensory
aspect of what now we experience as a densely material and, because
of that, an often stifling world.*

The association of colors with the four elements was a Greek
inspiration, and this was one of the factors in their culture which literally opened their eyes to the physical world in a degree unique
among ancient peoples. Their intuition of the actual origin of colors
in the omnipresent experience of light and darkness, which were
also associated with deities, attests to that balance between the physical and the non-physical worlds which is the key signature of the
Greek experience at its apogee.

* * * * *

It may be recalled at this point that I had already been obliged, out
of practical considerations, to make a distinction between colors
which arise *as a physical phenomenon* at the border between the outermost limits of the earth's atmosphere and cosmic darkness and, on the
other hand, colors that exist virtually only in the astral (pyschological)
and noetic realms (and beyond), which I called transcendental or
supersensory. This is the distinction, as Goethe had to discover bit-
terly, over which "rational," that is, sense-based, thinking stumbles
and then, to be rid of the problem, denies that the spectrum in question, with its magenta, really exists. Yet the phenomenon of transcendental colors at every stage of human culture is totally real and
undeniable, unless one wants to deny and condemn along with the
Goethean Light spectrum all religion, all philosophy and all art that
exist only in that sphere. Thus, "rational" thinking, which generally
assumes that those finer things of life *do* exist (to the point of investing
heavily in Old Masters), harbors a cancerous contradiction, for the
prism itself, manipulated as Goethe demonstrated, gives visual, factual

---

* I believe this to be the real explanation for numerous teenage suicides.

proof of the reversed position of the supersensory colors—which now reveal themselves, in the lower right-hand quadrant of Ill. 16, as the colors of the four ethers; these are the colors or, more accurately, the "idea" of colors which exist in the outer astral darkness surrounding our living atmosphere. All the supersensory colors, as can be felt most strongly in the case of those of the upper right-hand quadrant, are implanted in human consciousness as the higher meaning of visual experience. However degraded this consciousness may have become through materialistic thinking and the reckless exploitation of color psychology in modern advertising, it undoubtedly still remains as a potentiality and certainly as a challenge—at least for a while!

Defining the Four Elements

1. No "pure" element exists in nature. There is always a specific natural manifestation as, for example, different varieties of water at spas, in blood, tree sap, etc.

2. Each of the four elements represents an undifferentiated (physical) potentiality, with which spiritual forces from stars and planets create specific substances through *krasis* with other element-potentialities. Such substances are qualitatively infinite in number. The process of substance-creation takes place in the etheric realm but results in a physical substance. This sequence can be reversed: for example, an inorganic substance like gold, being a condensation of stellar forces, can rise again from the physical state toward the creative forces.

3. No specific substance created by cosmic *krasis* (mixing) has shape or form by definition but may acquire this through the action of natural or human forces.

4. Each of the so-called inorganic "elements" recognized by modern chemistry is, in the sense of Four Elements theory, a subdivision of earth, air or water and has a characteristic structure which can be combined with or assimilated by, other substances or combinations of them. Thus, the Greek concept of *krasis* is retained but

reduced to a mere facilitator of combinations from a "menu" of given (materialistically conceived) elements. This view necessarily reduces Fire to a functional facilitator of such combinations. (See further treatment of this theme in Part II, Afterword). The gain in exactitude is offset by total loss of philosophical overview and imprisonment in a sclerotic world view which degrades nature.

Defining the Four Ethers

1. No "pure" ethers exist; all are "clothed" by formative forces which can be understood as the gestures of the consonants (zodiacal) and of the vowels (planetary). With this insight into the phenomenon of continuous creativity we are reminded of the Logos as proclaimed in the Gospel of St. John.
2. Astral forces (beings) from stellar regions stream down to the transatmospheric boundary, thus stimulating the various ethers.
3. These astral forces create for the stimulated ethers the formative forces which are thereafter available for use by the etheric body of the planet and also by the etheric bodies of individual organisms on the planet. The formative forces thus have their origin in the astral realm, then descend into the etheric realm, and terminate in specific (living) forms in the physical realm. This progression, however, is not reversible in the same sense as substances, for a living form is a unique, one-time phenomenon—as Schiller knew— and can dissolve into its constituent elements only upon its death.
4. Any etheric body constructs, like a master architect, and then maintains, a corresponding physical body by deploying—via the formative forces—inorganic and organic substances from the realm of the four elements as required.

Summary

Substances are physical manifestations of the work of cosmic forces on the elements (planetary influences on metals were established by years of research on the part of L. Kolisko, *Sternwirken in*

Erdenstoffen Stroud, England: Kolisko Archives, 1952). Nature's beings consist of substances unified into working forms by etheric bodies (*cf.* Aristotle's vegetative souls) using etheric forces existing in the etheric world. That is, nature's beings are dynamic force and movement localized within individual members of a species. This conclusion is as far as the reasoning in this chapter can take us. The all-important problem of the definition of "species," which Darwin approached but did not solve, is the subject of Part II of this volume.

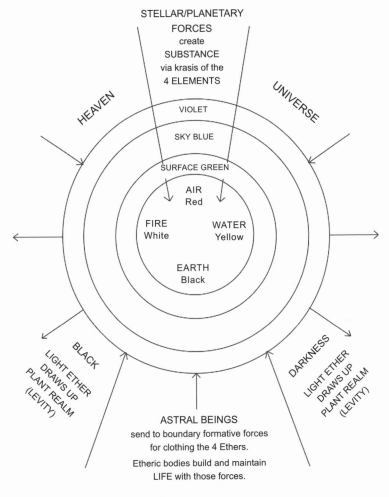

ILLUSTRATION 18

MANIFESTATIONS OF THE SPIRIT

TERRESTRIAL ELEMENTS
(RECIPIENT POTENTIALITIES)

	QUALITIES	ORIGIN
FIRE	WHITE combustibility	SATURN warmth & fire not separated
AIR	RED rarefactive tensile (elastic) pressure- producing (downward)	OLD SUN primaeval substance (gas) hence beginning of time Proto Plants
WATER	YELLOW liquefactive planar, merging homogenizing	OLD MOON Proto Animals
EARTH	BLACK solidifying 6 spatial directions tricomer symmetry	EARTH STAGE full distinction between "lifeless" minerals and organic individuals "bestowed energy" (human thought)

The elements separate and contract toward a center.

CELESTIAL ETHERS
(ACTIVATING AGENTS OF COSMIC FORCES)
CONSONANTS = ZODIAC   VOWELS = PLANETS

WARMTH	BLACK "Intensive movement" (zero dimensional) "Proto-Time" "uncreated energy" (divine thought)	
LIGHT	YELLOW "Extensive Movement" (one dimensional;) purely directional (linear, radial) drawing (upward)	Electricity
TONE (Chemicals)	RED planar (two dimensional) dividing, separating by nodes, symmetricizing	Magnetism
LIFE "Third Force"	WHITE cubic (three dimensional) differentiating into life-driven, separate organisms building life from matter	Radioactivity

SUB-TERRESTRIAL ETHERS

		As the primal, fundamental, all pervading and indispensable gesture of uncreated divine being toward a world of substance, warmth has no reductive manifestation: yet its presence or absence is vital to all levels of being.
ELECTRICITY	(light)	APUD the subphysical astral reality of Lucifer: contributes to consciousness of space (light bulb) emancipates physical process from space (telephone) heat and light-creating (radiant fire)
MAGNETISM	(tone)	APUD the Lower Devachan realm of Ahriman: combines with electricity (electromagnetic waves) prefers cold produces mechanical force
RADIOACTIVITY	(life)	APUD subphysical Higher Devachan (realm of the Asuras): creates enormous heat deconstructs substance (even natural radioactivity) has a time-release relationship to terrestrial processes

The ethers expand confluently to the periphery.

ILLUSTRATION 19

5.

TOWARD A PHILOSOPHY OF COLOR*

Part I: Where is Color?

The problems that attend the philosophical critic of ancient or later color theory are prefigured in the way that Greek philosophers dealt with, or did not deal with, the relation of color to the physical and mental world on the level that could then be experienced.

As a group, the early Ionian school and the Pythagoreans, culminating in Empedokles, worked with percepts (sense impressions) as the basic stuff in weaving their concepts back and forth among themselves, creating a rich fabric of thought that was taken up and organized more systematically by Plato and Aristotle. In a seemingly sudden way, in perhaps the third quarter of the fifth century, Demokritos[1] burst onto this scene with a totally different approach, one that tried to go directly to concepts and from these explain and define percepts. In that incipient abstract atomism the "western" world experienced its first "alternative" view and the accompanying freedom of choice at a deep level. Demokritos' attempt to institute a color science on the atomic basis failed, but Aristotle could not create one on a perceptual basis either, in the absence of the prism.

This task was not taken up again until Newton, in an age which did have the prism, found himself seeking an explanation for the spectrum in the course of following his many interests. While it is true that the inception of his optics was perceptual, he turned at an

*The author wrote this article in clarification of problems arising out of his long-term study of the four elements in relation to form and color in Greek art.

early stage of it to thoroughly abstract concepts deriving from Hellenistic and Arabic science, such as light consisting of "rays", and proceeded to lay the foundation for a mathematicized color science perfectly adapted to absorb the increasingly subatomic inclinations of the modern era. For example, John Dalton[2] quite specifically associated himself with a revival of the ideas of Demokritos.

It is, in fact, worth noting that apparently neither Demokritos nor Newton drew on the work of predecessors in their own time (but see p. 186 for a possible influence on Demokritos). P. J. Bouma, (his p. 204), writing about the history of color science, fails to note the parallel and begins immediately after mentioning Newton's discovery of the "center of gravity" rule on an algebraic basis as follows:

> In the few pages Newton devotes to the arrangement of color sensations he sketches, as it were, the plan to be used in later ages for the construction of the whole edifice of the science of color. If we then remember that *Newton did not have a single predecessor on whose discoveries he could build further,* we may draw the certain conclusion that even on this subject the master had no equal. (Italics mine).

Further, in commenting on Goethe's opinion that light does not "contain" colors because it is an indivisible entity, Bouma (p. 206) says:

> The last opinion is quite understandable coming from such a man as Goethe. Many people have wondered how it is possible for colorless daylight, which psychologically makes an impression of simplicity, to contain all these bright colors. Which of the two opponents is right depends mostly on individual philosophic taste. Most people, however, will prefer Newton's opinion, as it enables us to give a much simpler physical description of the phenomenon.

It should be noted, moreover, that Bouma (p. 205) also points out that Goethe's theory can be dealt with via mathematics (color equations), albeit more cumbersomely. It is almost certain that Goethe—like Plato—would not have encouraged doing this. How very different the course of modern world history would have been if its scientific mentors—like Bouma himself—had not swept aside Goethe's viewpoint as irrelevant and a hindrance to industrial progress (e.g., Philips Research Laboratories, Eindhoven, where Bouma was employed) and had tried to understand to what Goethe was really objecting.

In any case, Goethe's criticism of Newton seems to have been historically inevitable. To make color totally a child of particles (or waves) in rays of light, while ignoring darkness completely, is so arbitrary that it could only belong to a world age of extremely dogmatic one-sidedness and was bound sooner or later to provoke a protesting reaction. The conviction of Aristotle that the interpenetration of light and dark (he said white and black) accounts for colors is so much more balanced, so much more logical, that someone, someday, would surely have revived or reexperienced it.

And yet, did Newton sense a deeper level of explanation, but owing to his preoccupations and personality simply turn the concept upside down? In the deeply occult landscape of his mind, was he searching almost unknown to himself for a spiritual explanation of color? If light is spiritual, could it not contain spiritual beings, those lovely Beings of color? Enticing as this vision may be, it does not accord with the fundamental visual experience of the prism that there is no color without shadow and turbulence, nor with the fundamental mental consideration already mentioned by Bouma (above). If not in light, then, where are the Beings of color who reveal themselves to those seriously questing after spirituality, such as Kandinsky? The very consistency of colors and color experience through time seems to militate against a notion that they are momentary *ad hoc* "reactions" called up by a virtually accidental clash of two quite opposed entities (light and dark)—but only under certain conditions—and then dissolved again into nothingness when those conditions disappear. Surely that is unworthy, and the higher *persona* of Newton must have felt that he had satisfyingly, if illogically, located colors in light—after all, a noble entity—even though his lower *persona* began reducing them to patterns of "particles" (but note, they are *patterns* to him).

In fact, Newton virtually had no other choice than to locate color in light, heir as he was to a long tradition not least at home in various aspects of early and medieval Christian theology, of treating the concept of polarities with blissful inconsequentiality: for example, postulating vividly heaven and hell but admitting no such polarity for good and evil, that is, holding only the former to exist, the latter to be merely the absence of good.[3] Already an ancient tract on color, *Peri Chromaton* assigned to Pseudo-Aristotle, a name used to designate an unknown successor of the great master, wondered whether darkness was not merely the absence of light.[4] But if it is logically impossible for color *qua* darkening to be part of ineffable, indivisible light, then in a truly polar world it should be possible for darkenings of the most varied gradations to rest within darkness and wait to be "revealed," "illuminated," by the action of light when it encounters darkness. When the encounter is over, the so-activated colors would de-activate themselves by slipping back into their nurturing element of darkness, as do brilliant sunsets into twilight. Obviously, when I speak of "colors resting in the darkness" I am thinking of them as invisible signatures, patterns, if one must use that word, in the same sense that Newtonian physics sees constancy of hues in their makeup of long and short waves. And nothing is changed in regard to the conditions that bring forth colors. It is only our understanding that makes a shift to a new spot from which the admitted darkness of all colors can be *logically* understood as part of their very substance and essence. And from the same vantage point we could suppose, on the spiritual level, (a) that color beings are awakened—and then held in place—by light, or (b) that color beings could be thought of as something more active, striving toward the light for self-realization in the physical world to be at the service of human creativity. This is obviously a very large issue and I will return to it in due course.

Thoughts in this direction had already occurred to me as a possible route to understanding the tremendous power of Newton's reversed explanation when I came across André Bjerke's somewhat similar suggestion,[5] that Newton could be turned against himself. Bjerke actually presents the experiments by which the same postulates that Newton obtained on the basis of light can be obtained by substituting darkness. Then, however, he turns this demonstration into no more than a vehicle for satirizing the Royal Academy for its role in the all-too-uncritical acceptance of Newton's thesis by his contemporaries. What is gained for Goethe's insistence on the principle of polarity in the genesis of color by simply changing the location of color from light to darkness? That would be to believe that Newton was totally wrong, pig-headedly wrong, in every respect, and I hope to have shown that this is not fair to that powerful thinker. In other words, he may have been wrong as to *where* he located colors, but not wrong in his instinct that they must be located somewhere. And the fact is that—while his choice of color-space in light may seem illogical from the commonsense visual considerations I have brought forward—it could only have recommended itself the more strongly to Newton as the inventor of calculus. To him, color/light was, as Arthur Zajonc pointed out to me, a new field to deconstruct and then resynthesize.

Indeed, abstract mathematics did lead to control and manipulation of colors in the laboratory environment that is stunning, even if it also brutalizes the color beings I have just proposed as a hypothesis. (Such beings are not to be taken too seriously by the reader at this stage but there is something of note in the idea). Indeed, the methods developed, one-sided and even dangerously so, have been so successful that few *scientists* have been willing to consider any criticism of them. This is the first lesson for those dissatisfied with Newton's solution to take seriously: to criticize it for being illogical and one-sided is to criticize the *entire* frame of mind in which many if not most scientists have worked and continue to work since Newton's time. That is, it is to be exclusively concerned with what Goethe called *das Was* (the what), eventually to a totally irrational degree, careless of—perhaps even unaware of—logic (i.e. philosophy) as the highest and most valuable human capacity.

Johann Wolfgang von Goethe, by instinct, nature and tradition, valued *das Wie* (the how) more highly than *das Was* (the what).[6] Being concerned with *how* one approaches reality more than how to control at any price what it is, he found himself counterattacking the long-since departed Newton. He brought together an enormously impressive logical armament in the entirely erroneous belief that he could demolish a structure which was impervious to logic. He thereby wasted much time and energy, for which he has been roundly criticized even by people sympathetic to him. In fact, by failing to evaluate what was positive in Newtonian color science, he virtually guaranteed that his hostility would be ignored. Furthermore, it left somehow incomplete his own enormously creative approach to color, which was to show *how* color arises and *how* it affects body and soul, all questions to which a one-sided Newtonianism could and can give no sensible answers. Incomplete, in my view, because Goethe never really came to grips with the problem of the *Was* in color—and a *Was* has to be somewhere in our four-dimensional world, as Newton grasped immediately. So Goethe never decided where color, as a spiritual reality, is. But that it *is* a spiritual reality he understood better than anyone else (*Farbenlehre* B919-920). Yet he withdrew diffidently from the problem. In the circumstances he was probably wise to do so, both because of the drift already in his time toward a self-contained materialism and because the time was not yet ripe (see below). It is therefore most unfortunate when any of his followers insist on maintaining his total early nineteenth century hostility toward Newtonian color science, rather than seeking to transcend it with new and adequate concepts that were not available to Goethe.

Basically these concepts seem to exist only in the world view, or one could better say, the multifarious life work of Rudolf Steiner. If this sounds like an inflated claim to those still unconsciously—or it may be even willfully—frozen into the icy impersonality of modern science, that is not surprising. Neither would it carry any urgency if the purely physically oriented methods and explanations of reality of that science were not dangerously far along in making the continuance of rational life on our planet extremely doubtful. Because of that dangerous situation, one feels a great pressure to find a way to work with Steiner's methods in order to found (among other things) a color science that is fully logical in that it does not stop with sense phenomena and their mathematical manipulation, but also consciously includes the spiritual dimension of color. To this end no *one* discipline has any longer a privileged position. Physicians, priests, farmers, artists, art critics and many others have as much to contribute as physicists. A diversity of viewpoints is thereby guaranteed and should prevent dogmatism. Nevertheless, there must be an agreement on *principles* however arrived at; that is, there must emerge a *philosophy* of color. This portends a new stage in human consciousness, for it has never before been even feasible for there to be a true philosophy of color, even though conscious ideas about color first emerged among Greek philosophers.

What are these principles, these *principia* of a new color science? In a general way they have been beautifully prepared for by Michael Wilson of the Goethean Science Foundation in Sturbridge, Clent, England, in a short but pregnant discussion[7] called "The Evolution of Light, Darkness and Colour." Insofar as this is a summary of Rudolf Steiner's *Outline of Esoteric Science* as that work pertains to the origins of color, I shall extract what suits the purpose of the present investigation.

Obviously, however, the following reasoning, both of Wilson and myself, presupposes that Steiner's *Outline of Esoteric Science*[8] as a view of evolution from the clairvoyant perspective in no way discounts real physical facts of the evolutionary record; rather, it provides these, if anything, with a setting that makes them comprehensible on more than a merely physical level. Steiner was a keen student of Darwin and particularly of that researcher's German counterpart, Ernst Haeckel. Yet Steiner understood that the physical record of evolution, to which the eyes of humanity were rather suddenly opened within one generation, could never be adequately related to the total physical, physiological, psychological and mental-moral reality in which we live, on the basis of physical laws alone. For "laws" have to be made by some agency, and no science, however much oriented to sense observation, exists without axioms, which ultimately represent a *communis opinio*. Thus, he contributed a plausible departure point, by no means new for it has a long creative history, that the very existence of the planet earth and its cosmic environment is based on a very long but entirely rhythmical process—a process initiated and guided by the intentions of supersensory beings acting out of a cognitive faculty and on a moral level of which any human intimations of these qualities are merely pale reflections. With the utmost courage and candor he described the origins of the universe in this sense as a four-step process (Saturn, Sun, Old Moon, Earth) and did so with a degree of compression and forward movement that gives his account an epic quality.

With all this in mind, we can make use of the summary provided by Wilson as follows:

(1) After the preconditions of physical warmth and light had been fulfilled in the Saturn and Old Sun stages (these, and Old Moon are meant here as conventional designations), there came to these factors, in the Old Moon stage, a polarity in the form of "new forces of Cooling, Darkening and Condensing". These forces give the original substance for Goethe's idea of "active darkness."

(2) The real activity in darkness was provided by retarded Archai (members of the Hierarchy at the rank above Archangels) who

had stayed at the level of Saturn warmth, never acquiring light. As Beings of Darkness, they stood opposite the advanced Beings of Light and Warmth. In the second half of the Old Moon period there was "a very real active darkness... responsible for the further organic development" through the fact that light, coming at this stage entirely from the outside, was absorbed and transformed into organic life (cf. chlorophyll). In effect, the active dark forces came to long for the light-warmth sphere (now manifesting as an outer "sun"). "The forces of attraction and repulsion, which were a gift of the Spirits of Movement, now began to be woven into the evolving 'bodies' or vehicles of consciousness, with which the Old Moon-body was now populated" (basis of present astral bodies: see p. 26).

(3) From this point onward one can speak of a polarity of Light and Darkness. Color can now be defined as a "dimension of tension and movement... between the poles of light and darkness". It is a "sea of astral tensions...a sea of astral colour will" which worked on the plastic, pliant bodies of the moon denizens as a formative force.

(4) In the recapitulation of the Old Moon stage in the present incarnation of the earth, this sea of astral "colour will" actually became embodied as permanent color tendencies within the astral bodies of physical, pre-human organisms as well as in substances. At the same time, organs to apprehend these, until now invisible, colors as outer reality were activated. In this way we can understand that color existed first as inner soul sensations (of which remnants still remain) and secondly as objective qualities outwardly apprehended and at the same time inwardly felt and understood as to their nature. Wilson makes it clear that in studying color one is confronted with a phenomenon that has cosmic-history roots in the four different planetary stages and that research into it must be adjusted to take into account which level in the evolution of color we

are concerned with. This enables a new degree of subtlety of thinking about color relationships that can only be hinted at by the above statement.

* * * * *

To return at this point to the main problem with which this investigation has been concerned, we can first recall that the inner-most nature of light is to be sought in the second half of the Saturn stage. It emerges out of the warmth of love of the various Hierarchi-cal Beings who made the Saturn stage possible. It then takes over the basic *generative* role throughout the rest of creation right to the present day, as opposed to the non-generative but active role of Darkness, which I have already characterized in one of its aspects as a reservoir of life forces (fig. 16). The first principle, then, that was instinctively grasped by Goethe, is that light does not *contain* color; on the contrary, it is uniquely indivisible and primal. But it created the *basis* of color through its irresistible attraction for the Beings of Darkness in the second half of the Old Moon stage. Thus it could mold them, interact with them.

The second principle, virtually a corollary of the first, is that as a facet of warmth light is invisible in itself, but by virtue of its sacrifi-cial nature has the power to illumine darkness—literally so when darkness becomes physical matter and there are physical eyes to per-ceive the process. Normally matter is not luminous, but it *can* con-tain light which can be released in certain circumstances and thus continue the process of illumination. How can these principles be applied to the Newton-Goethe conflict?

It appears that the inner patterns of coloration, the "signatures" of specific colors in Beings (and subsequently in the least conscious form, the elements), evolved from the interaction of light and dark-ness on the Old Moon and beyond. The lawful relationships which Newtonians describe as particles or short and long wave combina-tions are thus the apprehensible expressions of this coloration goaded to self-revelation by the action of light ("deed of light") in certain circumstances (concentration through the prism—itself a particular form of matter—presence of atmosphere, itself also a particular form of matter).

In this appraisal the distinct quality of hue inheres in its material matrix, hence in darkness. Moreover, by this account of the location of color the often-used term, "colored light," is a figure of speech. What is actually being referred to is some form of matter with its color shading revealing itself through the activity of light.

The foregoing relationships can be expressed in the form of a rule: Light can be in color (as a transmuted constituent of matter) but color cannot be in light (it can only be revealed by light). This gives a rational explanation for the Northern Lights as pure color appearing out of total darkness (see below). Goethe approached this complex of problems without being impressed by, or interested in, the subsensory patterns which can be conceived of intellectually, since he was concerned only with the lawful relationships perceptible to normal human sight, particularly the physical and physiological aspects, with a side-glance at the psychological and noetic aspects.

It can be seen at once why Newtonian color science is one-sided. It is a particular—and by far not the only—dimension of the purely physical side of color. Yet, in the sense of cosmic evolution, this particular dimension is of crucial importance for the human apprehension of the *moral* quality of the universe. By ignoring, if not actually denying, that quality, Newtonian science has discovered secrets that force humanity to confront its own limitations. Thus, that science belongs inevitably and inalienably to the stage of the Consciousness Soul (on this see p. 100). Goethe himself as a dramatist showed how this world view was taken up triumphantly, but without the necessary critical acumen, by a high culture releasing itself from the shackles of an outmoded theology.

It was Goethe's apprehension as an artist of the dire consequences of that one-sidedness that pushed him into an exposé of its lack of acumen. And since Goethe's time that one-sidedness has led to inconsistency even on its own premises. It was Goethe's tragedy to reject the entirety of this theoretical direction along with its short-comings, even as he himself blazed a trail in the opposite direction.

At this point, on the strength of my conviction that the world entered upon a new subphase of the Consciousness Soul Period around 1980—based on analysis of Western artistic and scientific creativity in the sense of periodicity—I offer a stern, though not intentionally moralizing, balance-sheet to locate the state of color understanding at this new juncture of opportunity.

Newtonian color science, seen in the light of the philosophical position worked out above, bases itself on indefensible tenets. Even in the realm of mathematical explanations—its greatest boast—*total* exactitude eludes it.[9] Certain technological processes, such as Land polaroid photography (Retinex Theory of Color Vision), require other assumptions. Above all, its tenets cannot be honestly reconciled with the phenomenon of the Northern Lights—*aurora borealis*—the colors of which arise in darkness, that is, in the total absence of "light rays." While the electrical nature of these colored light displays could not, of course, have been known to Newton, or his successors until fairly recently, this phenomenon of (rarified) substances revealing their identity (signature) in terms of spectral colors in total darkness suggests that cosmic reality has depths and complications to which Newtonian thinking cannot give full access.[10] Yet it has become an historical pattern (as Goethe learned) that practitioners of this type of thinking (in whatever scientific field) in all situations of embar-rassing shortcomings do not examine their ultimate premise philosophically. Instead, they have become marvelously adept at forming ludicrous explanations and justifications such as imagin-ing a physiology of the eye that allows them to avoid admitting that Goethe's Light Spectrum exists.

This way of reacting to challenges, understandable as a collective defense mechanism, is unfortunately in keeping with the amoral foundations of materialistic science. One of its greatest historical sins has been the attempt, out of lassitude and *Besserwisserei* as well as self-preservation, to dismiss Goethe's scientific impulses—particularly in their Anthroposophical form—as largely "unscientific" and dilettantish. Blind self-approval stands in the way of any genuine revisionism. Yet—through the wisdom of world guidance—this very persistence in pursuing a one-sided viewpoint has led to uniquely valuable discoveries which at any time could be *used* to see the value of taking a modified approach, that is, one less neutral toward the human and social consequences of scientific discoveries. The greatest positive contribution of Newtonian optics is undoubtedly the discovery of spectral analysis which, as applied to astronomy (among other facts of color research), has literally forced all of mankind "over the threshold" into a new (and bewildering) level of consciousness of the universe.

Goethean color science is philosophically on better ground. Its successes on the physiological and psychological levels are tangible and enjoy general acceptance, although this is very little in the public consciousness owing to Newtonian hostility to Goethe's ideas in general. On the noetic level, which Goethe left unexplored, artists, mostly of Anthroposophical persuasion, have begun to experiment (beyond, though not unavailable to, the public eye). Unfortunately, these efforts are disturbed by factionalism which may point to a lack of concern with philosophical principles. Dogmatic sclerosis in Goethean color studies has been a danger from the very beginning, starting with Goethe himself in regard to physical problems. It is difficult to see how spectral analysis would have been arrived at by his route, for example. A built-in historical problem is the relationship of Steiner to Goethe. Given Goethe's largely cognitive and seminal role, only Steiner's reconstitution of his ideas on a totally new level can make them really viable and fruitful for a world which has succumbed, as if under a spell, to total (because often not easily detectable) materialism. Yet the very polarity of Steiner's Anthroposophy to that materialistic world view offers a stumbling block to many people when they first hear of it.[11]

Part II: What is Color?

This is the message we have heard from him and proclaim to you,
that God is light and in him is no darkness at all. — I JOHN 1, 5

Previously I have mentioned color beings only in a somewhat poetic sense. At this point, however, it is desirable to look further into this concept. To do so, it is necessary to expatiate on the final statement of Part I (p. 95). That profound polar difference between Steiner's account of the origin of the universe and the materialistic account—which has saturated modern consciousness—is that he seeks the origin of matter in the sacrifice, in the transmutation, of extremely high spiritual beings, so that in effect everything in the universe originates from life and then devolves, quite purposely, into apparently inert material substance as its last stage (it is, of course, not inert but highly charged). The materialistic view, on the other hand, begins with this inert material substance, which it has ultimately found to be dynamically charged, and proposes an evolution by purely physical laws—the origin of which it obviously cannot account for—with no discernible goal or ascertainable meaning. The final intellectual consequence of this is existentialism *qua* philosophy of the absurd, whereby giving "absurd" a meaning contradicts the intention of the concept and thus invalidates the whole stream of "materialistic thought" as a gigantic non-sequitur.

Opposite to this latter is then a devolution of certain spiritual beings, obviously guided by spiritual consciousness all the way, via staged processes, ultimately contraction (condensation) to the present ground of the physical universe. Thus, the whole of reality, even this final stage of it, consists of thought—a conclusion that has emerged recently from an unexpected, since non-philosophical, source.* To make this utterly concrete one must say thought-beings, which is not necessarily comparable with what is meant in ordinary language by intellectual beings. There is no other reality, by this

* See entry for Vartosick in Bibliography.

reckoning, than a mental/spiritual one, from which all came and to which all will return. The final intellectual manifestation of this view is not scholasticism or Berkeleyism, but the dynamic, multi-facetted modern structure of Anthroposophy, which builds not only on its own insights, but on the spiritual heritage of earlier ages and on the later materialistic heritage in those cases where its concepts are justified, that is, in the realm of the purely physical (but not, obviously, accepting the materialistic definition of physicality).

Even for those thoroughly familiar with this explanation, it is necessary constantly to review and repeat it in new contexts, as Steiner's own writings demonstrate, in order *consciously* to counteract the insidiously deadening effects of the materialistic malaise. So pervasive are those effects as not even to be identifiable in all departments of life by the beleaguered human beings of the present, many of whom, however, are quite aware that all is not well in a society in which senseless, rampant violence—with or without war—is rapidly becoming a shoulder-shrugging norm. In the 1920s, Steiner predicted this state of affairs if another generation or two of the university elite upheld the materialistic dogma (for even then "scientific authority" had become the only accepted norm in all matters).

All this is necessary to say in order to make it at all intelligible to speak of Beings of Light (and of Warmth) as absolutely self-contained entities. For only on this basis does it become fully evident that they cannot, in their pure state, best represented by our physical sun, contain color, for color by any rational definition is to some degree a darkening of light. Even white is, as is universally agreed, not *in* light but is only its purest reflection in matter. As opposed to Beings of Light, the term Beings of Darkness covers a much broader spectrum, for in the devolution spoken of above, darkness/matter became subject to an exceedingly complicated, multifarious process, guided in the first place by all ranks of the hierarchies. This guidance resulted in all manner of sentience through the various combinations and permutations that took place during the Old-Moon phase on the basis of attraction and repulsion of sentient organisms (Empedokles' Love and Hate). It cannot be stressed enough that most of these sentient forms were durable enough to survive into the Earth stage, as witness the thousands and thousands of species we see around us, and that the ultimate slack in this process, our minerals (the element earth), was the final stage of that process. Even this has at least potential sentience in the sense of being restorable to a non-physical state in the future. Irresponsibly and perversely restored, however, as in nuclear reactors, it releases blindly destructive power.

To state what has been said in another way: within every physical manifestation there is pure life, present in every stage of evolution and, whether treated with respect or misused, awesome beyond rational understanding. It is this concept, which can perhaps be equated with the German word *Geist* in its deepest sense, that modern positivism cannot even remotely grasp. Thus, the art historian, Sixten Ringbom, assumes that Rudolf Steiner (who, incidentally, was trained at the Vienna Institute of Technology), was *naively* implying by a certain passage that "a stone (could) melt down in the air and become invisible".[12] Ringbom is certainly dishonest—since his intention is to jeer—in not pointing out that just such "magic" does take place in a nuclear explosion. That, however, is not what Steiner had in mind with *his* statement, nor the geological erosion of stone either, but something more like the conversion of minerals, as in food, to human energy (life). To a careful student of Steiner's life-work, the claim of Ringbom[13] that Steiner "re-worked" a simile of Lord Balfour into a "spiritualist model of the universe" is too absurd to refute, since the implication is that Steiner garnered half-baked ideas from proper scientists. It is fortunate that Vassily Kandinsky, of whose inner development Ringbom is so remarkably solicitous, did not let the richness of that inner life, which Steiner's ideas stimulated, ever be disturbed by the smugness of contemporary positivism, as Ringbom has to confirm again and again, to his own mystification.

Devolution thus explains how every facet of earth reality has its own relation to light and color, either having specific colors or reflecting color. In this way, any sentient being with fixed color can be called a "being of color." In the sense of the possessive adjective construction this could have an invidious ring, as when human beings with light skin call human beings with brown or black skin "persons of color" or colored persons —that is, having a particular pigmentation as one distinguishing characteristic. To preclude all misconceptions: the term "color being," in which color is *not* a descriptive term but the qualitative modifier, is a totally different concept. If "color being" were meant as mere description, any particular hue would be an intact entity—so, for example, atmospheric green or greenness would be a separate, permanent spiritual entity. Given the transitory way in which any atmospheric hue comes together out of light and darkness and then vanishes, such an assumption is a logical absurdity. Moreover, if this were the case, there would have existed in the occult tradition a Hierarchy of Colors, which, of course, there is not. Yet it is not unimportant to dwell on this point, because any attempt to rescue a spiritual quality for light in the *Newtonian* universe would almost inevitably call up a vision of angelic color beings ascending and descending in shafts of divine light, for example, a spirit of red with a particular constitution. Kandinsky may have come to or close to this view, subconsciously at least, since it is not clear that he took Goethe's color theory seriously.

＊ ＊ ＊ ＊ ＊

Out of the considerations brought forward in this discussion of a philosophy of color, we can now attempt a summary of the problems that arise for western thinking from Newton's starting point. Whereas he located colors in light, we have argued that they belong in principle to the sphere of darkness, into which, however, some light has been woven in varying degrees. But this solution to the where? seemed insufficiently supported until we came to grips with the what? of color, about which Newton also had definite ideas. For his school, colors are purely abstracted, sub-physical patterns that are conveyed to the eye and there *subjectively* turned into color sensations. Philosophically vacuous though this may be, it does convey a half-truth. During the Old-Moon phase, colors *were* sub-physical, or at least invisible, patterns *outside* the nascent organisms, but also were being woven into these by the beings whose interactions had created the colors in the first place. Because of that implantation, present sentient beings have an *inner* feeling-relationship to the qualities of the various colors. Thus, color *is* in one sense "subjective". Nevertheless, when organisms became physical during the Earth stage, their inwoven color patterns were incarnated into matter, the color of which had also become precipitated into visibility. In the case of the resulting "chemical" colors (Goethe's expression) or "fixed colors" (current expression), either in the mineral world or taken up and further transformed by living organisms according to their color tendencies, the physical eye does see the actual physical colors (not abstract patterns) as an objective part of objective nature in *addition* to being able to feel them inwardly.

It would be possible, then, to say that in the physical colors which the eye was created to see, it has an image of the relationships[14] that once prevailed among non-physical beings. On the other hand, the prismatic (spectral, that is, atmospheric) colors, in the sense of Goethe, do not image or represent any past relationships; rather, they are, existentially, those relationships actually being entered into, carried on, by non-physical beings right before our eyes. Mankind had always had a glimpse of them in rainbows, the spiritual nature of which was recognized. But it took the development of the prism, as a key tool of the era of the Consciousness Soul (beginning, according to Steiner, in 1413 A.D.) to make it possible for human beings to see and study *physically* the order on which these relationships are based. When beings more given to darkness are in the ascendancy, through the preponderant presence of dark colored surfaces, the Dark spectrum and *its* line-up of colors results. When beings of light exert the more powerful influence through the reflection of light offered by white surfaces, the Light spectrum with *its* line-up results. One could equally say, the Dark spectrum shows the beings of darkness yearning for the light, while the Light spectrum shows the requiting gesture of love by the beings of light.

NOTES

1. The two names: Leukippos and Demokritos are traditionally coupled as the first proponents of a theory of atoms. Leukippos was apparently the older, while Demokritos systematized the theory (for which no predecessors are known). It is Demokritos who appears in the extant fragments drawing the consequences of the atomic theory in relation to the nature of color.

2. *Encyclopaedia Britannica* 11th ed. 1910, p.778 s.v. John Dalton.

3. On this originally Neoplatonic view and Augustine's process of absorbing and adapting it see, e.g., V.J. Bourke, *Augustine's Quest of Wisdom* (Milwaukee 1945) 58, 237-38; E. Zum Brunn, *St. Augustine Being and Nothingness* (New York, 1988) 107.

4. See Aristotle Minor Works (Loeb Classical Library) Cambridge, Mass. 1955 Vol. I Aristotelous Pen Chromaton, 1.

5. *Neue Beitrage zu Goethes Farbenlehre* (Stuttgart 1961) 86-88.

6. *Faust* II Act 2, 6992.

7. *The Golden Blade* 1982, 53-66.

8. *Die Geheimwissenschaft im Umriss*: first published in Berlin in 1908, with many following editions; translated as *Outline of Occult Science*; *Occult Science An Outline*; and most recently, *An Outline of Esoteric Science*.

9. In a course dealing with optics at the Rudolf Steiner Institute in 1982 Hans Gebert referred to a statement by a scientist named Wood of the U.S. Bureau of Standards in the 1940's to the effect that Newton's theory is wrong, but in such a way that if it were right it would be so neat that the world goes on using it as far as possible (he admitted that light waves are produced by *interaction* of light with the material of the prism). This may be Lawrence Wood, whose reports appear in various publications of the Bureau of Standards in that period, but I cannot find such a reference and it may have been an oral communication to Gebert.

10. This phenomenon may also require a *philosophical* rethinking of Goethe's rules of color. When the aurora borealis manifests, the spectral colors appear out of complete darkness. There is no contact with the light of the sun, there are no rays or beams of cosmic light involved. Harald Falck-Ytter in *Aurora* (Floris Books 1992) 99 writes: "Planetary space remains dark, for the (solar)

plasma is not light and not even, like the corona, light-related. On the contrary, this stream of ions and protons (the solar wind) is related to matter.... the direction of the plasmic stream is diverted from the magnetic fields of other planets. As plasma in the earth's magnetic sphere, it produces light and color in the terrestrial darkness in the form of the aurora, by colliding with highly refined terrestrial matter."

Obviously the color produced in this phenomenon is not connected with light as we know it. What is involved seems rather to be a kind of primordial "cold light," which Falck-Ytter (his p. 100) describes as a remnant of, or better yet an imaging of, the first flickering light of Old Saturn associated with the first emergence of matter: "the streaming solar wind conceals embryonically within it—combined with and tied to material occurrences—primordial light substance." Thus, under certain conditions (as described in the foregoing quotation), the color potentialities in matter (darkness), which, in the evolutionary sense, have to be younger than cold light, are somehow activated by or with that light. Thus, the awe-inspiring spectacle of the northern lights is, as it were, a glimpse into the evolutionary history of our solar universe.

11. It is apparent from the collected observations of Rudolf Steiner on color (*Gesamtausgabe* no. 291a, Dornach, 1991) that he realized this while working on his commentary to Goethe's color theory in the *Deutsche National* literature series in the 1880's and repeated it from time to time thereafter; but even shortly before his death in 1925 he was obliged to admit that the time was not yet ripe for gaining a hearing for alternative approaches to science.

12. S. Ringbom, *The Sounding Cosmos* A Study in the Spiritualism of Kandinsky and the Genesis of Abstract Painting (Abo 1970) Acta Academiae Aboensis, Sr.A Humaniora Vol. 38 nr. 2 37-38.

13. *Ibid.*, Ch. VI; idem, *Kandinsky und Munchen* Begegnungen und Wandlungen (1896-1914) ed. A. Zweik (Munich 1982) 90.

14. The basis of these relationships can be thought of as provided by the lawful, ordered, inviolable patterns which cause each specific color always to be recognizable. These patterns are by nature invisible (supersensory) qualities of the physical substances that formed when the Earth planet incarnated in matter. These substances, insofar as they remain visible or form anew, are at the same time the expression of the dynamic processes understood by the Greeks as the Four Elements. Supersensory beings of any kind, degree or rank who clothe themselves in these substances to achieve their purposes constitute themselves thereby as beings of darkness and interact unremittingly with beings of light.

6.

Rudolf Steiner's Color Qualities:
Image and Luster

"When yellow plays from one side and blue from the other to a quiescent white, green arises." *Colour*, p. 32. This statement is entirely in accord with Goethe's first spectrum (which I designate as the Dark spectrum) because all the colors except the central one, white, appear on a dark ground.

"When this evenly shining colour (red) illumines white and black which are in movement, peach blossom arises." *Colour*, p. 32. This statement may be surprising since it does not conform to the strict polarity inherent in Goethe's Light spectrum (in which all the colors except the central one, black, appear on a white ground). Nevertheless, in another context Steiner reproduced the relevant parts of the two spectra side by side (GA 291A, p. 54), exactly as Goethe had discovered them. It may be noted that the term "peach blossom" (*Pfirsichblüte*) is one of the two words for the color at this position of the spectrum used by Goethe. Peach blossom, despite its somewhat poetic implications, is actually used in the more technical contexts (as in *Optics* par. 59), while *Purpur*, a straightforward color term, connotes mental/moral qualities for Goethe.

Thus we are confronted by the fact that Steiner changed the constituents of a specifically defined Light spectrum color: red + violet over black, to red behind black and white. He seems to refer to this directly when he wrote: "We cannot look for the nature of peach

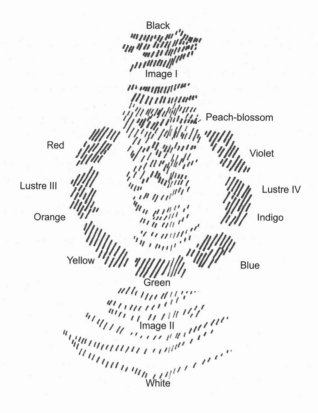

ILLUSTRATION 20

blossom as we looked for green. We must try to find it in quite another way." *Colour,* p. 25. If one asks why it is necessary to look "in quite another way," no direct explanation is given. However, in the course of the second lecture in *Colour,* as Steiner develops his idea of the three colors red, yellow and blue as being lustrous, it becomes amply apparent that he is working not only with Goethe's spectra but also with Goethe's idea of a color circle.

Goethe's color circle has six colors. How did he move from the pattern of four basic spectral colors (red-yellow-blue-violet) to six colors? He did so when he began considering the two spectra he had discovered in the light of a single continuum — which would thus incorporate the two colors created by mixture, that is, green and magenta (*Purpur*), as integral parts of one color circle: In plate IV b, the final version of Goethe's color circle, one may imagine how it precipitated from the gradual blending of colors into one another.

It is worthwhile to pursue this further. John Salter (as editor) made the observation (*Colour*, p. 77): "From his study of prismatic and atmospheric colours (amongst many other aspects of colour) Goethe concluded that the colour circle was a qualitative organism. The primal phenomena (Ur-Phänomen) of yellow and blue were his starting point." Obviously, what is meant here is that yellow and blue represent two totally different spheres of the planet: the solid ground and the sky—a fundamental insight of Goethe. In their union green is created, a color which clothes the earth when ground and sky cooperate under suitable conditions. Yet this is not really a color polarity. While it has often been assumed that Goethe discovered true color polarities by means of physiological experiments with after-images, this has been disproved by Rupprecht Matthei (his p. 41), and Ott and Proskauer suggest more plausibly (I, p. 327) that a meditative contemplation of the scheme worked out in Ill. 16 here would yield the concept of three vertical pairs of precisely polar colors (red-blue, yellow-violet, green-magenta).

This hypothesis is supported by certain other considerations. Goethe himself stated in *The Color Theory* of 1810 (Matthei, p. 190) that the first impetus in his resolve to write a treatise was: "The requirement of the painter, who till now has not received any assistance from the existing theory." He further stated that the painter's feeling and taste had been totally dependent on the "uncertain transference [meaning tradition: *Überlieferung*] in regard to color, without any kind of physical fundamental to base his expression on." It is worth examining the situation referred to. The only theory at that time which dealt with the physical basis of color was, of course, that of Newton, which has no direct—or even indirect—relation to the aesthetics of color. It is admitted time after time in the literature of art criticism that there are two lines or facets of color: wavelengths and then visual perception, which is regarded as completely subjective.

What is therefore original in Goethe's work is his demonstration that such a division is not only arbitrary and upheld only by the most rigid partisanship but that, by putting color outside the sphere of objective artistic laws, one unnecessarily and unjustly deprives the artist of the consciousness needed to face the new situation that scientific progress was creating. Goethe was not alone in feeling that artists needed help. Since he had always been in close contact with leading artists of all kinds, he quite naturally cooperated with Otto Phillip Runge, who at that very time was probing deeply into the living experience of color. As a practicing painter, Runge could provide the professional expertise to stimulate Goethe, particularly in regard to the physiological effects of certain color combinations. It is significant that Runge's great work, *Farben-Kugel*, which Goethe had seen in manuscript form, appeared in 1810, the same year as Goethe's *Farbenlehre*. Leaving aside the greater profundity of Goethe's orientation, one may be grateful for this dispensation of destiny, since Runge could exert a more direct influence on other artists, particularly in Germany, right into the twentieth century.

To a considerable extent, however, the work of Goethe and Runge was — and still is — overshadowed by the efforts of Michel Eugène Chevreul, not himself an artist but the chemist in charge of colors at the Gobelin factory, to find a means of standardizing the dyes used in making tapestries. It is worth commenting that the desire to do this is in itself characteristic of the dawning industrial age. Chevreul accomplished his purpose with pragmatic thoroughness and, in the French spirit, formalized the results as a series of laws. The most significant of these is the Law of Simultaneous Contrast, announced in a book of that title published in 1839. Although his theory was, in the end, not very fruitful for artists, it was taken up, tested and given considerable publicity by the Neo-lmpressionists and several later French artists. Perhaps because of the extraordinary popularity of late nineteenth-century French art, Chevreul is sometimes given credit for being the first to present general rules on the psychological effect of colors (*Grove Dictionary of Art*). In fact, however, his laws seem more directly concerned with physio-logical effects, while the work of Goethe and Runge on both the physiology and psychology of color is far more profound as well as considerably earlier.

The foregoing excursus was necessary in order to put Goethe's color circle—our original point of departure for understanding Steiner's color reasoning—in perspective. If the *Farbenlehre* was Goethe's general gift to the world, his color circle was a kind of spe-cial summary of it for artists' use, particularly adapted to the tradi-tion through which European artists understood their relation to color. That this tradition took the form of a circle is purely a practi-cal matter. Faber Birren has researched this problem extensively in various articles and particularly in his *History of Color Painting*, which I have used in the following summary. For centuries artists had arranged their (oil) paints around the edges of the palette they held with one hand in an order corresponding, in the words of Goethe, to "their feelings and tastes". The first formal attempt to sys-tematize this in writing had been made only a generation before Goethe by Moses Harris (1766). Indeed, Newton himself may well be reflecting this tradition in his use of a circular diagram to show mathematical relationships of colors, even though this was not intended for artists and failed to accomplish the purpose he had in mind (*Optics*, Proposition VI, Problem II). This was picked up again in the mid-nineteenth century by H. G. Grassmann, who proposed a more organized circle of colors, still based on mathematics but in an order strangely like that of Goethe and Runge. In any case, a quite different Newtonian diagram was proposed by J.C. Maxwell a few years later. None of this was intended for, or of much interest to, practicing painters, who—if they took any notice of theory at all—went more into color perception.

At this point I must recur to the problem with which the discus-sion began: the three-color versus the four-color system. In my Ill. 16 the latter is presented—for the first time to my knowledge—as a complete conceptual system of polarities involving four levels of reality (consciousness) together with the color modalities corresponding to each of them. Although all of this is implicit in the work of Goethe, he had other things to do than work it out; moreover, even for him to have tried to do so would have been premature because, as the present study has demonstrated, two hundred years of archaeological and art historical studies beyond Goethe's time have been necessary to gain the historical perspective needed to throw light on the full significance of Greek color theory. Furthermore, it can be readily admitted that the presentation in III. 16 is a rather abstract construction which—compared to the living colors with which Goethe concerned himself—can appeal only to an intellectual understanding. In order to appeal to the creativity of artists, Goethe turned to actual colors that could be presented in relation to each other in a circle (Pl. IVb and Matthei, p. 51, Ill. 48). Nevertheless, I must point out that the four-color system on which Ill. 16 is based can also be presented visually, as shown in the excellent photographs created by H. G. Hetzel (Pl. IVa). The visual demonstration that there are *four* primary colors: red-yellow-blue-violet, might work like an electric prod on some artists.

Goethe had felt a powerful impulse to foster color sensitivity in artists and thus instinctively—perhaps even unawares—turned to an already existing device, the color circle. His contribution was to organize it so as to reveal a certain spiritual content (mental-moral qualities) inherent in colors that could stimulate a spiritual orientation, even a commitment. Yet, perhaps few artists (although among them some great ones like Turner and Kandinsky) could or would rise to this level. It seems safe to conclude that Goethe's color circle had minimal influence on artists in an increasingly materialistic age and, in effect, had to wait until Rudolf Steiner revived interest in it among his followers.

Since the foregoing statement implies that many artists now are taking an interest in color circles, it may be well to locate Goethe's version historically. What existed at his starting point was a system of three primary colors: red, yellow and blue. This system had begun to be customary in the earlier eighteenth century (for example, with J. C. Le Blon), bringing with it the idea of three secondary colors, thereby replacing a system of four colors: red, yellow, green and blue, going back to Leonardo da Vinci (about whom more must be said later). The three color system was canonized in 1831 by David Brewster (*A Treatise on Optics*) and still prevails.

In what ways, then, did Goethe in his color circle depart from (or perhaps unwittingly compromise) the ideal concept of the nature of color inherent in his own work—and what is the significance of these departures? First, he suppressed, that is, sacrificed, the fourth color which should be a primary, violet. Secondly, he did not include black and white as colors. In both cases this issue is highly complex and bears strongly on the color circle proposed by Rudolf Steiner.

In physical terms, that is, in the Dark spectrum, violet is a "sky" color, visible only with some difficulty if one is using the prism, and in actual observation of the sky virtually invisible in most atmospheric conditions. In fact, it might be characterized as only a prism color and, as such, could not have been noticed as a major color until Newton—and then only in a scientific context. Moreover, the delicate, almost wistful quality of violet as a pigmentary color in nature—as in certain flowers—would ordinarily deny it the commanding immediacy of red, yellow and blue in the context of art.

Thus, for artists and theorists of the rising Consciousness Soul era (from the fifteenth century), there have never been more than three primary colors. It is, however, an irony of history that Leonardo and his successors thought of green as a full-fledged color, thus anticipating Newton's claim that green is a spectral rather than a mixed color. Nevertheless, for artists the situation is somewhat different (for example, they were beginning to be concerned with realistic verdant landscapes) and they must have taken satisfaction in the control given by mixture to obtain the exact hues they wanted. In any case there were no tubes from which to take such hues until the later nineteenth century.

We have now defined an apparently insoluble contradiction between cosmic (spectral) and physical (color pigment) reality which invades even as high an achievement as Goethe's color circle in his omission of violet as a primary color. This is in itself a warning not to dogmatize that circle. Some relief from this impasse can be obtained by rising to a level beyond that of Goethe, to which we shall return shortly. First, however, it is necessary to introduce, or rather recall, one more equally intractable contradiction, that is, the absence of black and white as colors in Goethe's reasoning.

It may seem particularly ironic that Goethe—the very discoverer (or re-discoverer) of the crucial interaction of light and dark in the coming into existence of chromatic colors (which he demonstrated with strips of black and white paper)—should have then dismissed the latter as merely *representatives* of darkness and light rather than as colors in their own right. His predecessors in sound color theory, the ancient Greeks, did not make that mistake—nor have that great majority of painters done so who have always freely used black and white to depict objects of those colors in nature, as well as shadows. Leonardo da Vinci specifically stated that, "although philosophers want to raise black and white out of pure colors, painters cannot do without either, (therefore) we shall place them among the others" (quoted by Faber Birren, *History of Color Painting* p. 18). Rudolf Steiner (*Colour* p. 25) states: "We have found four colours (black and white must be counted as colours), four colours with an image character: black, green, peach blossom and white." Can it be that Goethe did not realize in this matter that he could be giving comfort, at least indirectly, to Newtonians, who deny reality to darkness and hence, if this proposition is thought through logically, to black as well, color or no color. Moreover, virtually the only artists, to my knowledge, who seriously degraded black (but not white!) in their interpretation of visual reality were the Impressionists. The resulting rather ethereal effect, especially noticeable in many works of Whistler and Monet, is perhaps a considerable factor in their lasting popularity, but subsequent painters have mostly ignored the aberration.

It cannot be doubted that this is at least one of the factors Rudolf Steiner had in mind when, despite his respect for the depth and significance of the *Farbenlehre,* he wrote as the last words of his lectures on color: "In Goetheanism we find a way of knowledge which embraces the realm of soul and spirit, but which needs to be developed further. Goethe, for example, was not able to reach the distinction between image and lustre colors. We must follow Goethe's approach in a living way in our thinking, so that we can continuously go further. This can only be done through spiritual science."

On the Structure of Rudolf Steiner's Color Circle

Steiner, like Goethe, undertook to raise color to "the next highest [*sic*] world," that is, from the physical colors of Newton to the etheric level (*Colour,* p. 33), but in a somewhat different way. He bent the linear spectrum of Newton completely back on itself, retaining the indigo for which Goethe had not found a place, so that peach-blossom came out at the top and green at the bottom (Ill. 18). Thus the main contribution of Goethe's color circle is retained, although now in a somewhat asymmetrical form. Yet Steiner still needed to include black and white which he said "remain hidden". How is this to be understood?

It can be understood quite easily by recurring to our Ill. 16 and reading across the line beginning with green. In the creation of green and of magenta by bringing together the two (vertical) halves of the spectrum, white and black respectively become reabsorbed and thus "hidden" but there is no doubt of their participation in the resulting color entities. Steiner therefore deconstructed this mixture and restored white and black to their proper place *while at the same time retaining the green and the magenta.* He shows this by placing the white lower and the black higher in the diagram than the other colors of the circle. Understood in this way, there is nothing mystical about the procedure he describes as bringing the white over (that is, upward or around) to ripple into the black during the creation of magenta.

We must now examine his color circle more closely to elucidate the all-important nature of magenta, usually called peach blossom by Steiner. Although green at the bottom is placed exactly over white, black reigns at the top with no color directly under it; instead, red occupies the upper left quadrant, while peach blossom and— slightly below it—violet occupy the corresponding upper right quadrant. This would seem to mean that red and violet constantly react on one another in the sense that red is defined as the luster of the living (*Colour*, p. 33) and violet as soul being (*Colour*, p. 59). Moreover, the dynamic quality does not end with this because, as we have seen, white and black play into red and violet to create the peach blossom. Thus, we are confronted with a concept so dynamic that it melts down the contour of the traditional two-dimensional color circle, with its fixed pigmentary relationships, and requires us to imagine a circle on a three-dimensional level: not merely with gradated colors shading into one another but with colors pulsing and combining with, and also against, a background of white and black. In an undeniable sense this constitutes an approximate way of visualizing our Ill. 16 and thus closes the circle back to Goethe's original discovery.

That a color circle in this sense was still evolving in Steiner's mind is evident from the fluidity of his diagram, from his color notes (as presented by John Salter) and by the numerous remarks and provisional diagrams in *Farbenerkenntnis* (GA 291a. 1990): for example, the possibility of a twelve-part color circle mentioned to Dr. Van Zeylmans in 1920.

Since the particular purpose of the foregoing investigation was to determine how Rudolf Steiner dealt with the shortcomings in Goethe's color circle, it is appropriate to summarize the conclusions reached.

First, he in effect concentrated on what is the horizontal axis of the diagram in Ill. 16. By giving every part of this equal weight he fully recognized the quintessential relationship of white and black to green and magenta. Indeed, this procedure is required in order to understand the concept of image colors which binds these four colors together.

Secondly, he concentrated on what is the vertical axis of that diagram to recognize the luster character of red, yellow and blue, which he discussed at some length in the text of *Colour.* Curiously, he did not include violet in this context, much less indigo and orange, although all of these are clearly indicated as luster colors on his color circle. The fact that indigo is included on the circle is explained by the requirement of polarity, that is, if orange is shown as an intermediate stage between red and yellow, then indigo must stand between blue and violet. In my opinion, the inclusion of indigo and orange has more to do with the practical aspects of color usage in painting than with the more theoretical aspects of the spectrum, since there can be an infinite number of gradated hues and Steiner did not attach specific characteristics to any but the four basic ones: red-yellow-blue-violet (the last named as "soul being"). John Salter, in his note 14 (*Colour,* p. 87) did not hesitate to reproduce the diagram shown below which was worked out as a process (for use as a painting exercise) by Hilde Boos-Hamburger in *The Creative Power of Colour.*

Red   orange   yellow   green   blue   indigo   violet

Lustre III   Lustre IV

radiating   encrusting

Connective Tissue

In the remaining essays I take leave of my role as scholar of ancient Greek color and its significance for the modern world and undertake to be a critic of color theory in the thought and artistic initiatives of Rudolf Steiner himself, and of several distinguished painters who were contemporary with him and influenced by him. In doing this I have always the expanded picture of Goethe's color theory as presented in Ill.16 as a touchstone. While this picture certainly corresponds faithfully with Goethe's *Idee* of color, it is also an ideal and, in measuring other things against it, I am fully aware that real life has its own imperatives. In this sense the role of critic is not to condemn deviations from that ideal but to try to understand why they exist and what consequences they had. However, I draw the line at considering what consequences artistic events in the first couple of decades of the twentieth century still have. To attempt this in the case both of the non-Anthroposophical artists and particularly of those artists who, in an ever-widening stream, draw inspiration from Steiner (sometimes very loosely, just as in other movements which originate in his thought-world), would be a vast undertaking more appropriate for younger art historians.

7.

Light and Color in Painting
at the Turn of the Century

This discussion begins with thoughts on Cézanne from an article by Stefan Weishaupt.* Cézanne gave supreme expression to a tendency that had already been announced in the most various ways by Impressionists. That tendency can be summed up in the question: "What is the role of light in the world of appearances?" Painters were no longer so much interested in objects themselves as in the way light makes them visible in particular circumstances. This led to a virtual dethronement of the object *per se* as the subject of painting in favor of the way color makes the object what it is. This prepared the ground for a further step: turning away from the object as a two-dimensional representation in simulated space in order to treat it as a composition of colors on a flat (two-dimensional) surface. Given that the space surrounding the object(s) is treated in the same way, a radically new effect is created. This was the contribution of Cézanne, and his posthumous retrospective in 1906 had a tremendous impact on the artistic world. The next step was Cubism, which totally dissolved whatever might have been left of the traditional conception of rational space on the canvas. Cézanne can be called the Father of Modern Painting in the sense that he introduced a new concept of color relationships which is an appropriate starting point

*"Film. Bild und Filmbildbewagung: Zum Illusionscharacter eines Mediums" (*Das Goetheanum* 66, 1987, 285-288).

for painters of the post-Kali Yuga Consciousness Soul period to work on (Kali Yuga is a Hindu term used by Steiner to designate an age of materialistic darkness ending ca. 1900, to be succeeded by an age of spiritual seeking).

Continuing the train of thought introduced by Weishaupt, we naturally turn to Kandinsky as the most original color theorist of the early twentieth century. He may be called the Father of Abstract Painting in that he presided dynamically, as well as thoughtfully, over the tendency to allow colors to strive away from object-form altogether—rather than merely remove object-form from the rational tradition, as in Cubism. Thus, he created totally new color relationships out of the sheer interaction of the colors on his canvas. Inasmuch as these relationships were of a spiritual nature, for him at least, he made the first and most important contribution of pre-World War I artists to the task for painters mentioned above.

His biography shows that he could not have achieved this without contact with the work of Rudolf Steiner, who in his turn was grounded in the spiritual and artistic tradition of Goethe. It is certain that Kandinsky also had contact with that tradition, whether or not through Steiner, but remained independent of both (to his disadvantage) in his own theory of colors and their significance. He wrestled his whole life with the problem of how his new color approach related to form; to solve this scientifically (as he thought) he gradually banished earthly, physical objects from his painting, thereby creating the new category of abstract painting. This led him, perhaps contrary to his hopes, ever deeper into an intellectualistic posture, not much different from that of his less spiritually inclined colleagues. It is paradoxical, if not ironical, that it was probably his Russian Orthodox apocalyptic spirituality that led him to Goethe-Steiner in the first place, and that then he could not, or would not, grasp their directly Hellenic, Four Elements balance as the uniquely fruitful and historically crucial impulse of the twentieth century.

One can perhaps underscore Kandinsky's position by posing a rhetorical question. If his belief that colors are Beings stems from an actual spiritual (but confused) perception on the level of Imagination, does this become an intellectualized concept that forever holds him at a Platonic (or Neo-Platonic) level, or did he ever advance beyond that perception into the realm of Inspiration and Intuition (according to Steiner's use of those terms), where the heavy mists of Imagination are lifted, to a view of the totality of human and cosmic structure?

That question, anchored in the year 1911 and thus considerably before Steiner had articulated an actual color theory, can to some extent be understood by moving forward to 1921. In that year Kandinsky ended his attempt to work in Communist Russia and went to Germany, where in 1922 he took up his long-term teaching commitment at the Bauhaus. His major preoccupation after this was with the laws of composition of painting, resulting in 1926 in the publication of *Von Punkt und Linie zu Fläche,* which is still not sufficiently appreciated for its philosophical depth; yet this study is concerned with a two-dimensional structural level and does little to clarify color relationships. In 1921 Steiner, in midst of incredible pressures from all sides, including the final touches to the first Goetheanum, gave his three lectures on color which effectively constitute his own color theory. The latter, like everything he did, is fully Aristotelian in that he not only uses Goethe's color theory as a point of departure—and fully understands it, as Kandinsky did not, by keeping the two spectra—but goes on to grasp color as a fourfold dynamic process continuing directly from the Greek Four Elements world view. This can be seen from the following table:

Mineral	(lifeless)	=	Lustre
Plant	(living)	=	Lustre-image
Animal	(ensouled)	=	Image-lustre
Man	(spiritual)	=	Image

* * * * *

In concluding this discussion I return to the first word of the title: Light, and review very briefly what cultural attitudes toward that phenomenon led up to the innovations of Cézanne. At the beginning of the Consciousness Soul period, Flemish painting documents clearly the fading of a direct experience of spiritual light as this had existed in the Middle Ages, and the experiencing of physical light as it illuminates physical objects; these are depicted in pristine clarity. By the later nineteenth century a turning point in the conception of light had been reached. This event has three facets. The first is a tendency to emphasize the original concern with physical accuracy, as seen in the naive realism of such still-life painters as William Harnett; the photograph became an accepted influence in painting. The second facet is the attempt of the Impressionists to understand how the eye actually functions in seeing. This represents absorption of artists in their contemporary world of burgeoning influence of the "scientific attitude"—in this case applied to the physiology of color, the ultimate manifestation of which was pointillism. The third facet is the breakaway from materialistic dogmatism toward a future spirituality. The most obvious manifestation of this was the rise of the Theosophical Movement, which attracted widespread interest in the whole artistic community, where organicism became an important impulse. In terms of painting, emphasis had to be on light: not only on simply lightening up the dark traditional palette, which theImpressionists achieved, but on sensing the approach of Kali Yuga in its deeper implications. Perhaps the most telling of these for painters involves the very reverse of what had happened at the beginning of the Consciousness Soul period (see above): that is, what happens to the physical object when it is illumined not by physical light but by spiritual light—the light of human consciousness? The very first tentative answer to this question seems to have been made by Paul Cézanne.

8.

Thoughts Inspired by Hilda Raske's
*Das Farbenwort**

First of all, Steiner's visual works cannot be grasped by considering them a reaction to the contemporary world of painting, for he was not a professional artist, had no formal training and no intention of establishing a new "movement."

Nevertheless, he was fully in contact with the heritage of European art through reading and visits to museums, and very much in contact with the world of poets, dramatists and other creative people, including artists such as Otto Froelich. Furthermore, he was thoroughly versed in color theory through his intensive study of Goethe and, early in the century, took an aesthetic initiative by designing a small structure at Malsch (1907).

It should not, therefore, be surprising that he made the central character in his first mystery drama, *Die Pforte der Einweihung* (1910) — *The Portal of Initiation* — a painter struggling with the dubiety of the whole practice of painting at that time. But what is perhaps surprising emerges from a comparison of a pastel sketch that Steiner made — in half an hour — with a painting by Kandinsky: "*Lyrisches.*"* Both were created in 1911, the latter, of course, quite intentionally, the former purely at the request of an actor taking the role of Johannes in the mystery drama, who felt uneasy about speaking the following words without actually seeing what the character was supposed to be putting on the canvas:

* See p. 125.

Im zarten Aetherrot der Geisteswelt
Versucht' ich, Unsichtbares zu verdichten:
Empfindend, wie die Farben Sehnsucht hegen,
Sich geistverklärt in Seelen selbst zu schauen.
                              —Nachspiel, 3. Bild

(In the delicate ethereal red of the World of Spirit I tried to express
what cannot be seen: for I felt how colors—once they are clarified in
spirit form—harbor a longing to view themselves in actual souls.)

The formal resemblance of the technique: dynamic lines scattered
throughout the composition, the flow of forms, even the shapes of
some forms, and the closely held color consonances are astonishing.
And yet, when closely inspected, the seemingly abstract forms in
Steiner's composition turn out to be heads emerging, as it were,
from an etheric misty warmth, whereas the shapes in Kandinsky's
composition reveal themselves as, principally, the notation of a run-
ning horse in a landscape with trees. The consistency of the color
field onto which the horse has been superimposed gives us no
choice but to describe it as a phantom, or at least phantom-like.

Steiner's figures, on the other hand, have a mysterious reality, an
actual activity on some plane other than in the mind of the artist, as
one would have to say of Kandinsky's horse.

The background of this difference is complex. First, one must
note that Kandinsky had attended lectures by Steiner in 1908 at the
Architectenhaus in Berlin. He was particularly inspired by the lecture entitled "Sun, Moon and Stars" (26 February 1908) in which
Steiner spoke of the spiritual essence of colors and of the Ariel scene
in *Faust II*. On that basis Kandinsky created an Ariel illustration,
later given to his pupil, Marie Strakosch-Giesler (some color prints
were also probably inspired by Steiner). In a certain sense, then, we
see in the two works compared above, the occult master demonstrating his teachings and the pupil—or better crypto-pupil, since
there was no direct contact between them—carrying on in his own
way but in the same general direction.

Yet we established a profound difference in content, and the explanation for this is obviously that Kandinsky, though fired by Steiner's spirituality, kept his distance by not joining the Theosophical Society, and even failing to mention it after 1910-11. Nevertheless, to the very end of his life he held to the task he had found for himself under the influence of occult inspiration (which he, *espressis verbis*, did *not* renounce).

It has been proposed that the explanation for the post-1911 silence on Theosophy was the necessity to create works that would be acceptable to the general audience of cultivated art lovers and collectors of the time. These could hardly stomach abstraction, but particularly not abstraction tied to occultism in any form. This idea would make a craven success-seeker out of a man of independent means and already somewhat of an outsider in the art world. He could very well have joined Steiner in Munich and then followed him to Dornach, as did his countryman Andrei Belyi, had he felt that would advance his goals.

In fact, however, Kandinsky's professional experience obstructed such a course, as we have seen by contrasting the basic orientation toward figural representation in the two 1911 works. The Russian painter's attitude goes back to his experience with the late Impressionist works of Monet, in which the represented object, such as rose or haystack, is virtually dissolved by light and color (Raske, p. 9). This caused Kandinsky to doubt the importance of the object as such in relation to the overwhelming presence of color on the canvas. From this he became absorbed in the latter, particularly blue, which, as he noted in *The Spiritual in Art,* draws the viewer deeper into infinity and, finally, the supersensory. He regarded himself thus as the first painter to dispense with the object. It would be natural, then, that he would harken to Steiner's words about the spirituality of color and, later, to Goethe's words about the lack of a generally accepted basis, that is composition, for painting pictures. The 1911 painting shows Kandinsky well on the way to giving up objective representation, for the horse can be regarded as a mere collection of strokes. Moreover, the goal he had before him was to herald the approach of the spiritual realm in which not the Christ tangible, but His surrogate, the Holy Spirit (*n.b.* Joachimism) would be depicted as flowing light of Divinity (which is non-sensory by definition). Thus, there is a total and complete orientation to painting out of color (which is Steinerian) yet painting without objective form (which is not).

In contrast, Steiner's point of departure is given by thoughts arising from his long study of Goethe's works. These thoughts are expressed in his lecture to the Goethe Society in Vienna in 1888 entitled *Goethe as the Founder of a New Science of Aesthetics*. Decisive are the following sentences: "Das Schöne ist nicht das Sinnlich-Wirkliche in einem göttlichen Gewand; es ist das Göttliche in einem sinnlich-wirklichen Gewand", (Beauty is not sensory reality in a divine garment, but the Divine in sense-tangible form) and "Der Künstler bringt das Göttliche nicht dadurch auf die Erde, dass er es in die Welt einfliessen lässt, sondern dadurch, dass er die Welt in die Sphäre des Göttlichen erhebt" (The artist does not bring the Divine down to earth by letting it flow into the world, but by raising the world up to the sphere of the Divine.). Thus, Steiner had no reason to give up objective form *per se;* instead, he wanted to see that form metamorphosed into a higher reality.

This was therefore in direct opposition to the trend represented by Kandinsky and Mondrian programmatically to banish objective representation.

The task proposed by Steiner was actually much more difficult and demanding, that is, to paint out of color in such a way as to let the very colors chosen suggest a spiritualized objective form. Artists who have since struggled with this problem have hardly attained to the degree of spirituality of Steiner's Christ figures, for example, since one must already *possess* deep and true spirituality in order to envelope the visible in it. In this respect Steiner's painting gives a standard as new and difficult to reach as the standard of philosophical thinking in his *Philosophy of Freedom.* Just as the latter transcends classical philosophy by reaching a new dimension, so Steinerian painting transcends classical painting not by abolishing part of it—as did the abstractionists—but by pointing the way to a new dimension that can be added to it.

Thus, the triumph of non-objective painting did not in the end revolutionize classical painting because it was insufficiently grounded in a true understanding of the spirituality required by the new Michaelic age, especially after the end of Kali Yuga (1899). Instead, that movement ended in an arid formalism. Yet Kandinsky's version of it continues to have both a fascination of its own and some relevance, for he never lost sight of two important spiritual goals which have yet to be realized in the world at large: (a) the task suggested by Goethe of giving the composition of painting a solid theoretical foundation; and (b) heralding the approach of the Holy Spirit. The latter can really be identified, as far as effectiveness is concerned, only with the best of Kandinsky's pre-war paintings, which in that sense presage a major task of the Russian folk soul in the distant future. Had Kandinsky not abandoned Theosophy as it turned into Anthroposophy, he would have been able to see that in the present age the immediate task of artists is to find the Archangel Michael. However, as we have seen, to do so did not, and really could not, lie within the karmic parameters of Kandinsky's career.

Those parameters determined that Kandinsky's initial successes would be followed by at least relative obscurity, no matter what he did. The career he did choose led to the desiccation of his original impulses, so that his later work faded from the public consciousness and is now largely a matter of specialized scholarship. On the other hand, the task proposed by Steiner to artists has been difficult to the point of not even reaching the public consciousness, so that public success has been automatically denied to those of his followers who attempted it. This would almost certainly have been Kandinsky's fate as well. Moreover, the exception that proves this rule—and guarantees that Steiner's difficult message was valid—is Pablo Picasso. It was he who sensed that the classical object had to be transformed spiritually, not abolished. But whether by design or a Faustian bargain, he changed the qualifier from spiritual to demonic, and for this became the sensation of the art world and remained the wildly successful darling of the cultured public. Somewhere between the deliberately demonic and abstractionism are to be found the Expressionist interpretations of the human figure.

These developments raise the insistent question of how form is related to color. Is form simply synonymous with object (*Gegenstand*)? A naive answer might be yes, as long as object is loosely enough defined (shifting clouds, for example, or vapor mists). But there are complications. Lionel Venturi[1] noted that the Cubists denied the value of form as representation and shifted meaning to the creative act, an idea which emerged conceptually with the Abstract Expressionists. This would seem to beg the issue.

The problem, if soluble at all, must be considered on more than simply the physical plane. Kandinsky was prepared to think about this in terms of the etheric and astral planes, where the inner essence of color can be pursued. There Steiner experienced the most diverse Beings. Since these had *moral* qualities that gave the *effect* of particular colors, it would be inappropriate to deny similar effects to physical colors when they pertain to situations *above the physical plane.* Whether one is actually aware of such Beings depends on how far one has progressed in the exercise of imagination, inspiration and intuition (these were called by other names by Kandinsky, according to Ringbom[2]). Even lacking such dynamic experience in higher realities, which is both difficult to attain and retain, as the case of Kandinsky shows, one may still allow to colors symbolic values which then associate themselves inseparably with commonly experienced forms. An example of this is the blue cloak in which artists envelop the Virgin Mary.[3] This example demonstrates that at some time in the past artists experienced by some means the higher content referred to above, whereby the colors were selected and eventually became "symbolic," that is, after the original inspiration paled and was no longer directly experienced by artist and viewer.

NOTES

1. Venturi, Lionel *History of Art Criticism* New York 1962 p. 302.

2. Ringbom, Sixten "Die Steiner Anotationen Kandinskys" *in Kandinsky und München 1896-1914* ed. Armin Zweite Munich 1982 pp.102-05.

3. Further discussion of this factor in *GCTFE* Ch. IV (Archaic Panel Painting).

———————

* The purpose of Raske's book is to document, as far as they are preserved, the various colored motifs designed by Rudolf Steiner for the interior of the Goetheanum in Dornach, Switzerland. These were applied to the building in the course of its construction during World War I but then destroyed in the arson of the building in 1921. The sketch he made at the behest of the actor playing the role of the artist in *The Portal of Initiation*, having been created earlier, was not lost and is published by Raske, p. 13 with the title "*Lichtesweben.*"

The achievements of European painters in the early years of the 20th century as they bear on Steiner's motifs are briefly discussed by Raske in her introduction, and reviewed by me on pp. 119-121 above. This gave me the idea of comparing Steiner's *Lichtesweben* with Kandisky's *Lyrisches: Kandinsky in Munich 1896-1914* Solomon R Guggenheim Museum New York 1982 no. 267. This comparison then provided me with a framework for the development of my essay.

9.

THE SPIRITUAL QUEST OF PIET MONDRIAN

THE LONG CAREER of Piet Mondrian (1872–1944) falls into several phases that are fairly easy to discern. Its beginning was more or less conventional, but nevertheless included at one point strong influence from (contemporary) post-Impressionist French art which had hardly penetrated to Amsterdam (which thus appears to have been rather provincial). He also came early into contact with Theosophy and, shortly thereafter, with Cubism. The effect of concerning himself with occult spirituality seems evident in the color choice in paintings that show influence from Cubism: the strong reds of the earlier phase give way to a predominance of blue that is not transatmospheric but—consciously or not—supersensory blue. At the same time his tree studies become less naturalistic and more abstract. They soon fit into a mode that ideally illustrates the supersensory spectrum: black is prominent in the linear forms, while the background is blue with a modicum of violet (which is best used sparingly in this spectrum for the best effect). White as such is little seen, except that it is implied in the rather light, low-saturation hues. It is also implied in the grays which sometimes supplant the blue and violet, thus leaving a gray field articulated by black lines. In this case, he slips into the vagaries of earth colors and thus reveals an unsteadiness of (avowed) spiritual intent that was to plague him throughout his life.

It may be that such depictions of tree-scapes show preoccupation with the death-side of nature or are merely an expression of Dutch gloom. In any case the artist sensed that he was "on to something" with his linear abstractions and removed to Paris for better exposure to the art world. He continued with trees and then added facades as a motif. He showed a tendency to let violet drift back toward a light brick red. Especially when he painted an exposed inner wall of a ruinous building opposite his studio, he experimented with a fairly prominent patch of brick-red set off with pale yellow—thus anticipating a color combination that became increasingly important to him. Nevertheless, in my opinion, the years 1911 to 1914, when Mondrian left Paris, represent the high point of his contribution to a new spirituality in art, thus corresponding exactly to the case of Kandinsky (although there seems to have been no personal connection between them and their contributions were totally different).

Kandinsky specifically denied a presentiment of coming war in his paintings, and there is no reason to suppose that Mondrian had such foresight either. Their common goal of spiritualizing the painting of their time must surely have originated in the perception of the dawn glow of Kali-Yuga by their higher beings and the corresponding efforts of the counter-spirits to divert humanity from this with promises of material comfort and artistic refinement. To counter the falsely optimistic mood of the opening years of the twentieth century, these two painters sought inspiration in the Theosophical Movement, a rather recent phenomenon at that time. It is, however, perfectly clear from their biographies that, even though they retained an ideal commitment to theosophical values, in their artistic practice they strove to conjure spirit directly onto the canvas—which is not authorized by a true understanding of spiritual realities—and ended up by abstracting physical objects into, essentially, lines of color. At first this created a powerful and attractive effect.

Inherent in the logic of that situation is that what they achieved was too little, whether or not too late. For the materialistic insanity of "The Great War" swept art in general into a cynical mode, even as it pushed artists opposed to materialism deeper into abstraction for its own sake. Here one can speak of confusion and distraction from the real goal: in effect they simply externalized what should have been absorbed in a new way into a living entity and remained invisible—that is, the underlying linear structure (of the contents of the world). Kandinsky did this more with forms, and his colors became uninteresting; Mondrian did this more with colors, and his forms became boring. In the later career of both artists we seem to be confronting intellectualized skeletons of the world. The fact that these nevertheless exercised a powerful influence on various other artists who created "schools" of abstract art confirms their importance. Even more, it testifies to the continuing influence of the negative spiritual counter-power who inspired two inconceivably massive world wars and thereby blinded humanity to the phenomenon of the Kali Yuga and its cosmic-Christian implications.

To return to the career of Mondrian: inadvertently trapped in Holland for the entirety of World War I. Mondrian at first actually gave up chromatic colors in favor of black on white (this is not really comparable to Munch and other artists who from the beginning expressed themselves as much through graphics as in paint). Mondrian evidently was exploring the line quality of his customary themes. When he returned to color in "Composition, 1916" he let a strong red seek to dominate the blue, violet and gray background. After this the linear element moved steadily toward geometric form, including passages of checkerboard design. Reds and blacks tended to overshadow yellow. Blue merged into black and violet disappeared. From 1917 Mondrian came under the architectural influence of the De Stijl group. His canvasses emerged from the frame (for the first time in history) and thereby eliminated the Renaissance idea of the frame as a window. The surface itself became a distinct object intended to communicate with the viewer as directly as a piece of sculpture. By 1920 Mondrian was ready to launch Neo-Plasticism on the art world. Exciting as this progression may be, it reveals that the artist has almost exclusively embraced the earth colors of the Dark Spectrum (black, red, yellow, white) to express what he still considered to be his spiritual quest. He thus capitulated to the materialist color fashion of furniture and architecture (where it was appropriate). While these colors, confined and combined in an infinitude of geometrically designed rectangles, are stimulating, they also risk over-stimulating the viewer.

In short, after experiencing a few specimens, the viewer has got the message (on which see below). Does he/she need to experience it a hundred times in slight variations? As studio exercises, they may be justified, but if they comprise an artist's sole production, they will obviously characterize that artist as too narrowly focused. Perhaps the best that can be said of the doggedly uniform geometricized output of Mondrian from 1920 to the end of his life is that it insistently proclaims that reality has a structure and that (taking these colors both in their physical and noetic sense) the world is not so formless as one might well conclude from the public and private chaos that began gripping more and more aspects of civilization in those fateful years. The extreme difficulty of maintaining balance in a spiritual mission at that time is evident in the fate of the Anthroposophical Society itself. The total ascendancy of the "Beast"—as Hitler's inspirer in 1933 was spoken of in esoteric circles—in conjunction with the whirlwind expansion of technology in World War II and afterward, had an extremely dehumanizing effect on humanity in general and ushered in ruthless exploitation and destruction of nature. That Mondrian's message was still important to artists in these dire circumstances is demonstrated by his influence on mid-century abstract art. Yet by the 1980s at the latest, all that had played itself out, with still no resolution to the problems artists were struggling with. Even great figurative artists like Edward Hopper followed life rather than leading it into the future. Will the tender strivings of truly spiritualized art that began with Rudolf Steiner (apart from the efforts of Josef Beuys) ever break into public consciousness?

The foregoing thoughts arose in connection with an exhibition of Mondrian's work at the Museum of Modern Art, New York (October, 1985–January, 1986).

Appendix

Understanding Goethe's Color Theory

An Introduction for non-specialists as a conversation between the author and Hans-Georg Hetzel, formerly technical Research Photographer (Medical Division), University of Freiburg-i-B, Germany.

What are the so-called spectral colors in terms of Newton and in terms of Goethe?

For Newton the spectral colors are those that he produced in his first experiment in a camera obscura in the following way: he admitted a light ray through a small hole in the shutters allowing it to pass through a prism held in front of the hole, whereby he refracted ("broke") the colors on the white wall opposite the hole. These colors constituted his famous color spectrum. On the basis of his observations and reflections about this, Newton came to the conclusion that these colors must have been contained in the light and refracted into various lengths by the prism. On this basis a scientific theory came to be built up.

Goethe, however, came to a different conclusion. He discovered that he could produce colors by focusing the prism (in an open space) on black and white edges. Colors appeared along the edges in accordance with the deflection caused by the material of the prism: dark before the light always results in yellow-red color boundaries (Pl. IV) and light before the dark always results in the blue-violet color boundaries (Pl. IV). These effects, according to Goethe, are the fundamental principles governing the *genesis of* all color (including what Newton saw). Additionally when Goethe caused, in the first instance just mentioned, the opposing borders to be narrowed over the white space between them (by manipulating the prism), the yellow and the blue poles combined to produce green (Pl. IVa). In the second instance, he narrowed the red and the violet poles over the black space and produced what he referred to as pure red (or *Purpur*—not our ordinary purple): Pl. IVb. This is sometimes referred to as magenta.

Given results of Goethe's experiments involving the producing of colors, how did he react to Newton's assumption that all colors are contained in light?

In thinking over the phenomena, Goethe reached the conclusion that colors arise on the boundaries of light and dark (whenever and however these occur). The prism itself, through its distortion and deflection of the light ray, produces the necessary turbidity *(Trübe)*. Goethe's view thereby differed fundamentally from Newton's assumption that the colors which are supposed to exist in light are refracted into differing lengths. For Goethe considered all surfaces that he viewed through the prism as displaced and distorted; to put it another way, the dark-light and light-dark parts of the surface are shoved over and into one another through the levering action of the glass on the light. In the first case yellow/red arises, in the second blue/violet. It must be emphasized that in the experiment the prism furnished the turbidity through leverage and distortion. Without this turbidity on the borders between dark-light and light-dark, colors can never arise. Without turbidity there are no colors. This is a great, but not sufficiently regarded, insight of Goethe.

In scientific contexts we hear of spectral colors and pigmentary colors. How do the two differ in the Newtonian view and the Goethean view?

Spectral colors arise, according to Newton and Goethe, on the basis of refraction and displacement, respectively (see above). Pigments are called chemical colors by Goethe. Basically the two categories of color are the same in both systems.

How do the atmospheric colors arise according to Goethe, who does not work with refraction-of-light rays?

Goethe's color theory gives us to understand that at sunset the atmospheric mist, becoming denser near the earth's surface, is to be regarded as darkness before the setting sunlight. Accordingly, the colors red and yellow manifest—conforming to the general rule that dark before light produces red/yellow. Conversely, blue arises when the sun shines obliquely through the illuminated atmosphere before the darkness of the universe—again conforming to the rule that light before dark produces blue/violet.

Is there a concept of additive and subtractive color mixtures in Goethe's system?

Goethe did not know these concepts nor can they be used in his system. He speaks only of a luminous and a toned-down mixture of colors. In the so-called additive color mixtures, three (or two) colored lights are projected over one another. These combine to register a white color or neutralize one another partially or wholly. The massive luminosity on the point at which the two or three colors come together fades off to be seen as mere brightness (white).

In the case of the subtractive color mixture, only one light source is used. Each colored filter applied to it combines with the already existing color and is neutralized wholly or partially to gray by the next filter applied to it. Thus translucence is progressively reduced.

How do Newton and Goethe compare in regard to the conception of the color circle?

Newtonian physics works with a linear scheme, that is, with ends which do not meet. Yet it must not be overlooked that various modern technical processes, particularly photography and color printing, *must* use Goethe's color circle. Goethe stated that he did not develop his color circle on the basis of the opposing, complementary spectra (hence, theoretically) but rather on the basis of the physiological colors, the after-image phenomenon, i.e., successive contrasts (hence, entirely by direct human experience). The after-image is achieved by staring for 10–15 seconds at a particular color, for example magenta. When the gaze has then been turned to a neutral light spot, the after-image sets in as the impression of the complementary color, in this case, green. Putting together successively the various colors and their complements obtained in this way, Goethe obtained the well-known complete color wheel (Pl. III c). Goethe, however, *also* used light blue and light yellow as two basic polar colors which, mixed together, yield green. But if one exposes yellow successively to augmentation—that is, saturates it—orange and then red arise by degrees (Pl. III b). Polarically to these colors, the corresponding colors of the other half of the spectrum arise, that is, to light yellow the violet, to orange the blue and to red the blue-green. When, in the final phase, the colors violet and red are mixed, the highest of all colors, magenta, results. This color contains, according to Goethe (B793 in *Farbenlehre*), partly *actu* and partly *potentia* all the other colors* The validity of Goethe's color circle enjoys general acceptance.

Since Goethe could not accept Newton's view that colors are contained in light, but instead made their appearance dependent on certain conditions, where did he propose that colors are before they manifest?

Goethe referred to this matter in only one passage, but there at any rate rather forthrightly. In the section concerning the psychological and mental/moral effects of color he wrote (*Farbenlehre*, B919; B920 continues the sense of this):

> "When the distinction of yellow and blue is duly comprehended, and especially the augmentation into red, by means of which the opposite qualities tend towards each other and become united in a third; then, certainly, an especially mysterious interpretation will suggest itself, since a spiritual meaning

---

*I believe that this point can be understood only in terms of the Light, that is, Supersensory, spectrum. JLB

may be connected with these facts; and when we find the two separate principles producing green on the one hand and red in their intenser state, we can hardly refrain from thinking in the first case on the earthly, in the last on the heavenly, generation of the Elohim.

But we shall do better not to expose ourselves, in conclusion, to the suspicion of enthusiasm; since, if our doctrine of colors finds favour, applications and allusions, allegorical, symbolical, and mystical, will not fail to be made, in conformity with the spirit of the age." (Eastlake translation)

What is the relation of Newton and Goethe respectively to the interpretation of color?

Newton and his successors have investigated and researched light exclusively in order to make use of the energy contained in it. The so-called magenta spectrum (*Purpurspektrum:* in terms of this study Light spectrum)—as complementary pole to the well-known and much used green (Dark) spectrum—remains outside the consciousness of current science and technology, since it is inexplicable by their concepts. Although Newton and many of his adherents had (have) some religious sensibilities, they do not take these into account in their researches and are therefore unable to enter into the psychological and mental/moral aspects of the colors. Goethe investigated color from the standpoint not only of its physical and physiological but also of its psychological and mental/moral aspects, the latter—as we have just seen—only in an indicative way.

What is a colored shadow and what is its meaning?

The colored shadow results from a particular lighting arrangement of an object, whereby the shadow of a monocolored light remains without direct illumination but is brightened to the status of a half shadow indirectly through another neutral light source, or even from a clear neutral reflecting light-shield. Therewith the complementary color to the light source illuminating the object appears in the main shadow. This colored shadow is called in physiology a simultaneous contrast, that is, a color arising in the eye. When Goethe discovered the phenomenon (12. 12. 1777) he described it as an objective color (that is, arising outside the eye), but shortly thereafter changed his mind. However, three years before his death, in a conversation with Eckermann, he admitted that the color of this phenomenon must after all be objective.

The colors of the colored shadow represent invariably and with exactitude the complementary color of the color illuminating the shadowed object. In terms of the doctrine of macrocosm and microcosm recognized by the Greeks and by Goethe, the microcosm is involved in the after-image and the macrocosm is involved in the colored shadow. (See an article by Hetzel: "Der farbige Schatten" in *Optometrie* 4, 1987, 177-179).

THE FOUR ELEMENTS AND THE ORIGINS OF FIXED COLORS

An Attempt by the Author To Justify an Ancient Physics
of Light-darkin Relation to Color

Characterization of the most advanced state of *krasis* with the elements progressively dominant:

> In earth: fire, air and water *solidified*
> In water: earth, air and fire *liquefied*
> In air: water, earth and fire *rarefied*
> In fire: earth, water and air *burned*

AXIOM I

Light comes from an extraterrestrial source and illuminates each of the states of *krasis*.

Additional comment: this corresponds to normal human perception that light itself is invisible but *reveals* a colored world.

AXIOM II

In reaching any of these states the light itself becomes subject to the appropriate functionalities of the four elements involved, that is, to warming, aeration, liquefaction and condensation. This constitutes the fate of light in the terrestrial milieu.

AXIOM III

Light illuminates *inter alia* the pigmentary colors black and white. Both of these have full earth character: opaqueness. Yet the opacity of black is harmonious with the non-material darkness of outer space, while the intensification of light by white is harmonious with the dynamic activity of light itself (as an illuminant). Hence, pigmentary black and white in their color-referrant polarity (color sphere) symbolize the color-precipitating activity of light in contact with darkness as this can be experienced in boundary observation with a prism.

On the basis of the foregoing reasoning, it is possible to postulate that the color properties which were summed up by Newton as the definition of light belong instead to the elemental world. By this reversal of standpoint we leave light undefined as to its composition but clearly defined in a functional sense: it is purely and solely an illuminant of the utmost sensitivity as it absorbs and reflects the functionalities of the four elements.

Light could then be, as supposed by Goethe, indivisible. Since it has been found to have a speed of movement incommensurable with terrestrial circumstances and is therefore measurable only in a non-physical medium: (abstract) time, the historically consistent microcosmic perception of light as metaphysical is justified. By the same token, the persistent microcosmic reaction to (pigmentary) black and white as having religious-moral significance in a symbolic sense is justified. One may recall Aristotle's statement that "light is the entelechy of the Transparent" (*De Anima*, 418b, 419a).

The best possibility for a logical explanation of color in objects is given by this postulate. As an inevitable result of the conjunction of light and the four elements, the stability of color varies greatly. In the least physical of the elements (fire) color is the most volatile, apparently created and vanishing on the spot. In the most physical of the elements (earth) color is obviously a persistent quality (fixed color). While the impression of color may be continuously recreated for the viewer in varying nuances depending on changing circumstances, the rational mind knows that the basic (fixed) color remains, even in the absence of light, just as the basic shape of the object remains when it is not seen or touched (Lucretius garbled this point: p. 67). Just as the origin of other perceptible qualities has to be sought in the history of the earth and cosmos, so also that of fixed color: it is the agglutinative result of perhaps innumerable confrontations of light and *krasis*-states of the elements through which color has been woven into earthly phenomena in the same way as other perceptible qualities.

Additional comment: the usual explanation that the cause of color in objects is the absorption and reflectance of wave-lengths by the surface equally requires—*if thought through to the end*—the color determining property to reside in the object. For the selectivity of the surface in respect to these two processes is, in ordinary circumstances, constant. It would, therefore, be necessary to postulate that the particular selectivity of a particular surface is objectively fixed within the total nature of that surface (or its interior) and hence is a permanent quality as much as shape, weight or any other measurable feature. This would be a corollary of the isomeric phenomenon. It is, therefore, a non-sequitur to claim that color exists only in the perception in the sense that it is different from any other objective property of matter.

It is a short step from this to the concept that absorption and reflectance refer to (but do not necessarily exhaust) the lawful processual relationships of the earth (that is, the opaque) element to the other three elements at the second of their being illuminated (i.e., precipitated) by the light. Other processual relationships among the same elements are perhaps precipitated ("illuminated") by the darkness (i.e., infra-red and ultra-violet).

AXIOM IV

There is no white in the atmosphere corresponding to pigmentary white. But light reveals its illuminating power in the atmosphere and may therefore be called the prototype of white. Complete atmospheric darkness may in the same sense be called the prototype of pigmentary black.

> *Additional comment:* atmospheric black can be said to exist, as in an underground cavern or in a darkroom. To define this darkness as simply the absence of light is to ignore the difference between a blind and a sighted person, for the latter of whom this is a visual experience. Such a definition would be true but irrelevant, just as it would be true but irrelevant to define light as the absence of darkness. The opposite of true atmospheric black is not atmospheric white but full daylight, which is colorless (even snow requires light in order to be seen). Artificially produced atmospheric light—insofar as it approaches the quality of daylight— is also colorless. Light and Dark are therefore best described as simply the two polar conditions of our atmosphere, both of which exist.

AXIOM V

Given the principle of *krasis* the symptoms of any elemental process involved in a synthesis can be pried out of it by appropriate means.

> *Example:* if reduction to particles is typical of earth as element when it is subjected to drying, the action of particles (rays) should be detectable in pigmentary colors. By the same token, if wave action is typical of earth as an element when subjected to moisture, wave lengths should be detectable in pigmentary colors. Warmth should also be detectable in various syntheses, etc. Moreover, it is obvious that detectable functionalities of several syntheses which are considered together must impinge on one another, e.g., a fixed color object illuminated in atmospheric light.

PART TWO

Invocation to Venus

Faire Venus mother of Aeneas race
Delight of gods and men thou that doest grace
The starrie firmament, the sea, the earth
To whom all living creatures owe their birth
By thee conceivd, and brought forth to the day,
When thou (O Goddese) comest stormes flie away
And heaven is no more obscur'd with showres.
For thee the fragrant earth spreads various flowers
The calmed ocean smiles, and att thy sight
The serene skie shines with augmented light.
Then doth the spring her glorious days disclose
And the releast, life-giving westwind blowes.
The power possessing first birds of the ayre
They thy approach with amorous noates declare,
Next when desires the savage heard incite
They swim through strames, and their fat pastures slight
To follow thee, who sees in seas, rivers, hills
In the birds leavie bowers, and in greene fields
Instilling wanton love into each mind,
Mak'st creatures strive to propagate their kind.

Since all things thus are brought to light by thee,
By whom alone their natures governd bee,
From whom both lovlinesse and pleasure springs,
Assist me while the nature of these things
I sing to Memmius whom thou (Goddesse) hast
With all excelling guifts and vertues grac't;
Wherefore sweete language in my thoughts infuse
And lett not warrs harsh sounds disturbe my muse;
Make sea and land a quiet calme possesse
For only thou with peace canst mortalls blesse,
Since Mars, the mighty God that rules in armes,
Lies in thy lap, bound with loves powerfull charmes,
And resting there his head in full delight,
On thy rich beautie feeds his greedies sight;
Hanging with amorous kisses on thy face,
Whilst thou (O Goddesse) doest this God embrace,
While he doth in thy sacred lap remaine,
Sweete peace for Rome by gentle prayers obteine,
For neither can we with a quiet mind
In time of warre, persue the works design'd,
Nor can brave Memmius, full of pious cares
For publique good, neglect those greate affaires.

—FROM *De Rerum Natura* of Titus Lucretius Carus

Translated by Lucy Hutchinson

Introduction

PART II OF THIS VOLUME, written only recently and on an apparently different subject, complements in an unexpected way the impression of Apollonian order and clarity gained when, at our distance in time, we contemplate the *culture-building* artistic and intellectual achievements of the Greeks as I have presented them in my two on-line publications (*GCTFE* and *GSFE*). The present study providing this complementation was prompted by the dire straits in which humanity finds itself by the turn of events at the beginning of the twenty-first century. I believe that we are facing the culminating consequences of the gradual *deconstruction*, or at least distortion, of the Hellenic legacy that has served as the very basis of western civilization. This process seems to have begun slowly with the nominalist controversy around the turn to the second millennium, then to have proceeded to an andante tempo, increased to allegro and then risen to presto in the late nineteenth century, reaching finally the Dionysian frenzy of the late twentieth century.

That such a deconstruction was attempted (it never fully succeeded: see p. 25) is not, in an historical sense, surprising. Certain benefits accrued from it, at first on an intellectual, then a practical level. Yet it seems to be largely unrealized within the current materialistic world view that the attempt simultaneously released a potent virus into the very first stirrings of Western science when it departed from the Hellenic model described in Part One in order to pursue another method—one stemming from, or at least heavily influenced by, Arabic thought and given to unrestrained and unfiltered abstraction. Yet even within the Greek heritage itself there is a connective link, the atoms of Demokritos—at that time a deviation from an historical current flowing the other way. We have considerable information about this from the almost accidental preservation of the quasi-epic poem entitled *De Rerum Natura* of the Roman poet T. Lucretius Carus, which inadvertently testifies to the culture-creating power of the metaphysics he rejected. While this encyclopedic work adds a little to the scant references from Demokritos himself about color theory (p. 66), its importance to my theme has other dimensions.

Given the profound immersion of Greek artists and philosophers in the creativity of nature and my absorption in their works, it may not be surprising that it became clear to me, as I wrestled with the Dionysian chaos engulfing every facet of our age—recognized by more and more contemporaries—that the chaos cannot be adequately explained by any positivistic view of history. Rather this chaos was released by an unforeseen—and unforeseeable—concept of nature. That concept, constituting a new and virulent variant of earlier materialistic tendencies, was released into the cultural stream almost inadvertently and hesitantly by Charles Darwin at a crucial point in the nineteenth century, when a separate discipline of biology *had* to be born, that is, had to separate from the generality of natural philosophy as a separate discipline. Before Darwin there was no biology as we know it. Through Darwin's ideas the whole of biology with its sub-fields such as botany, medicine, psychology and anthropology sprang up like dragon's teeth and created what we call modernism around the apparently irresistibly infectious doctrine-dogma of Natural Selection. As an historian of culture, I have no obligation to evaluate this dogma in the usual reductionist terms *which have resulted from it* and generally praise it as a welcome release from a previous unscientific or even superstitious past. In reality, Natural Selection is conceptually so weak that its ability to launch precipitately an age of atheistic materialism capable of inundating the more thoughtful idealism and even non-programmatic materialism characterizing the Enlightenment as well as traditional spiritual currents of the earlier nineteenth century, is starting to be seen as a phenomenon with no logical (or even rational) explanation.

In this sense, color theory is not, as I attempted to show in Part One, an irrelevant part of the contemporary situation.

Darwinism from the Standpoint of a Humanist

My proposal as a humanist is to view Darwinism in its cultural context in more chronological depth than is usual (where the emphasis is on its relation to scientific theories of Darwin's contemporaries), and thereby to establish its effect on the intellectual *standards* of its own and ongoing times. I am acutely aware that the term humanist itself has virtually dropped out of popular usage and even in academe is a rather exotic concept, so that I feel obliged to explain how I am using the term.

"Humanism" was originally coined for such scholarly and literary eminences of the Italian Proto-Renaissance as Francesco Petrarch (1300–1374) of Florence. This city, under the patronage of the Medici banking family, became in the fifteenth century (Early Renaissance) the most renowned cultural center of Europe. Scholars, philosophers, and artists were attracted to its court, where a frenzy of enthusiasm for the civilization of ancient Rome and—as far as known—of Greece inspired the shaping of a new age that saw the concept of a re-born antiquity *(rinascimento)* as superior to what it regarded as the crudeness of the Medieval *("gotico")* past.

It is in the light of this broadened aspect that, as a practitioner of ancient studies and their later influence, I undertake this estimation of Darwinism. Nevertheless, the implications of the term Humanist are complicated and need to be discussed further, because the newly stimulated minds of the Florentines, desiring to enhance Christian values, were attracted not only by the wide range of philosophical speculation, but also to varying extent by the seemingly more ambiguous moral—that is to say worldly—quality of "pagan" lifestyle. It would, nevertheless, be disingenuous to suggest that either in the ancient or Renaissance milieu awareness of a spiritual world did not exist or in any case was lightly rejected. Antiquity was a "world full of gods" (Keith Hopkins' phrase) and this extended to philosophy as well, from the Pre-Socratics to the Neo-Platonists (the "man-measure" idea of the Sophists is of another order). The only quasi-exception is Epicureanism, knowledge of which is preserved mainly through Lucretius, whose work was hardly known until rather later (I will deal with this and his supposed materialism in due course). Accordingly, it is important to emphasize that the great cosmological and medical discoveries stemming from the Florentines, down to and including Kepler and Newton, took place in confidence in a divine universe.

The foregoing aperçu informs the present study and, at the same time, puts me in the midst of the controversy between Christian fundamentalist groups on the one hand and (Secular) Humanists[1] on the other—a controversy usually treated as a black and white issue, since efforts at accommodation seem futile. As a "Four Elements" humanist myself, I am in a position to see virtues and defects on both sides. Not being beholden to an anti-spiritual (anti-"supernatural") premise, I can sympathize with the fundamentalists who *feel* the presence of God and the power of the Bible so strongly that they cannot stand the world as it is; and yet I dread this when it leaves the sphere of the inner life and becomes translated into overt political action. On the other hand, as a classicist I am entirely sympathetic to the broadly liberal outlook of the Humanists who seek freedom for individual personal development. The great problem here for me is that, at the same time, the leaders of this movement, Corliss Lamont and Paul Kurtz, have accepted—uncritically in my view—the authority of a Darwin-based Science. By arrogantly rejecting all methodological criticism, that science has, along with all its benefits, put the very survival of culture in question. Yet free and searching criticism of *all premises*—however generally accepted—has to be the life blood of *forward* human evolution.

To return now to Florentine humanism: even in the more accurate historical sense I prefer, in the more than half a millennium which has elapsed since the apogee of the Medici family, the vibrant excitement of Renaissance artists and scholars for a multi-faceted exploration of human life qua the ancient spirit, perhaps culminating in the works of Winckelmann and Goethe, has been gradually replaced by what amounts to an exclusive respect for documented "facts"—in effect, information *about* ancient civilization. Valuable as these are, the process has largely forestalled perceiving that the *consciousness* of that earlier civilization was entirely different from, but not less astute than, our own.

* * * * *

In the last third of the nineteenth century the ideas and theories proposed by Charles Darwin proved to be a dynamic cultural catalyst. By implicating man himself in a direct linear descent (or ascent) from the higher primates, they touched—or rather attacked—every possible traditional aspect of human culture. In the earlier twentieth century, after some initial opposition, "Darwinism" settled down into a matter of elite university concern with the expanded disciplines of paleontology and paleethnology. Public interest subsided as these disciplines attempted to make sense of ever more fossil discoveries. My personal experience in the thirties and forties of the twentieth century was that ordinary people (in the mid-South at least) were vaguely aware that they were supposed to be "descended from monkeys" (and that one might be ridiculed for not believing this). But the implications of that theory were so far from according with the traditional values by which society lived that the whole subject was put out of mind as far as possible. A notorious exception existed (and exists) in the Biblical fundamentalist groups which denied evolution altogether and thereby became the butt of scorn by the entrenched Neo-Darwinists, who now ruled supreme in prestigious universities.

The general public, even the well educated, knew little or nothing of constant skirmishes that had gone on in the background about the position of man in the scheme of evolution. Nevertheless, the key doctrine of Darwin's explanation of evolution as it came to be interpreted is that nothing, nothing at all on the planet or, for that matter, in the universe, is exempt from the iron-clad rule of Natural Selection, that is, from a universal process of accidental linear accretion. But the often applied term "mechanistic" is out of place here because that implies an intelligent constructor (of the cosmic machine). Above all, to exempt mankind from the accidental dictum in any respect whatsoever would risk causing the whole theory to collapse as inconsistent. In other words that "elegant simplicity" so highly valued in modernist science would be forfeited.

In this respect it is important to note that Darwin himself in his most spectacular publication, *The Origin of Species* in 1859, hesitated to go so far as to include man in his hypothesis. The events following on this persuaded him to make this final step in 1871. Yet this delay proved beneficial to the popularity of his theory. The novelty of his approach, his exotic data, the vagueness of his criteria and above all his silence on the crucial question of man's place in his scheme made an intriguing first impression, even on such a confirmed Transcendentalist as Henry Thoreau,[2] who died in 1862 before the full implications of Darwin's ideas could be known.

Darwin's working years were embedded in the half century: 1830–1880 that in every respect produced the foundations of the modern(ist) period. It was in this span of years that "natural history," with its links to a philosophical-theological tradition, became "science," the purlieu of "scientists" who cling to their narrow specialties. Curiously, Darwin did not quite recognize himself as being of this new breed (and this may explain his many protestations of ignorance and uncertainty). Yet his work was catapulted by certain circumstances into the position of intellectual flagship of modern thinking. Perhaps the most important circumstance is that he came to be seen as the high priest of biology: life-science with its various ramifications. No other "specialty"—even geology or physics[3]—had the authority or a particular need to concern itself with evolution.

The Humanistic Vantage Point

Most studies of Darwinism concern themselves with its scientific merits, as shown in a recent review of literature about Neo-Darwinism by Frederic Crew.[4] The results of this approach are by now quite predictable, for the parameters in which it can move are narrow; in fact, it is exactly this restriction which makes the whole process unsatisfying to the humanist. In the background even of humanistic studies lurks the agreed-on (but never discussed) definition of science itself as the reduction of the entire universe—including the phenomenon of life—to some form of matter. Since, as I hope to show, this sense-robbing view is to a great extent derived from the assumptions of Darwin, argumentation about scientific merits is so self-determining that attempts to be really objective are doomed from the start. As soon as one grasps the humanistic imperative of excluding humanity from this paradigm, as Alfred Russell Wallace, co-inventor of the theory of evolution by natural selection, did late in his life, insuperable difficulties present themselves and frustration results. The classic example of this is Loren Eiseley, whose head and heart pulled him in opposite directions, as one can determine by consulting almost any of his writings.[5] The problem is, of course, that the "window of opportunity"—so far as there ever was one—to negotiate a "non-exclusive clause" in the definition of evolution existed only a very short time—perhaps 1860–1870—but Darwin and his closest advisers would not budge. In fact, they had no leeway to do so; it was already too late. The new definition of "Science" (if there had even been one before this) as impermeably materialistic had already congealed. The battle with the doubters had been won and only skirmishes remained. And won not only in connection with what we normally consider to be the legitimate purlieu of "science," but as providing the fundamental assumption in any field of human thinking—even theology—as well. All this should make clear why a humanistic appraisal, as defined above, is needed, however much it may be automatically written off in prejudicial terms in most quarters.

Darwinism as Cultural Artifact

The general situation sketched out above suggests that enough time has elapsed so that the phenomenon of Darwinism can be looked at in perspective with an unapologetic eye. In the intervening period the fledgling world view known as the scientific age reached an apogee of public credibility in the 1950's, only to be increasingly confronted thereafter in the public consciousness with the destructive effects of its own inflexibly materialistic convictions. In the confrontation, it does not change but instead defends (example: pesticides no longer effective and deleterious to health? Then revise methods with genetic engineering). Not the least of its defects is the lack of moral stamina to resist the temptation to prostitute itself to corporate greed combined with government bureaucracy. The pseudo-ideal of pure science evaporates in the competition for corporate and government funding. Obviously, Darwin and his close friends could not have foreseen much of this in the 1850s, or even 1870s. Yet choices have inexorable consequences, for which reason it is essential to ask how the choices made by those just mentioned have created the culture (or, to use a less Germanic term, the civilization) we now live in.

In establishing a new theory which promises to solve many problems, its creator may have to make bold assumptions. When Darwin found himself in this position, the most serious transgressions he committed against the established culture of the first half of the nineteenth century—which, of course, traced its heritage back through the Christian centuries to its Hellenic origins—consisted of two interlocking radical assumptions. The word transgression is used here not to prejudge the act of experimenting with radical hypotheses (which may have promise) but in awareness of how a radical hypothesis incapable of proof was deliberately and with full knowledge of its imperfections sold as virtually indisputable fact by its defenders[6] to a public then—and still today—bewildered by the vastness and complexity of evolution. So well did they accomplish this that neither their successors nor the public *attempt* to grasp the difference between supporting a flawed but conventionally accepted hypothesis and seeking the truth, however costly and inconvenient, at any price. This destructive attitude has spread like an epidemic to most areas of public life, not least in politics, today. I believe that the genesis of that attitude is to be sought in the two interlocking assumptions mentioned above.

These two fundamental assumptions were *not dictated* by the outer world of observable phenomena but arose in the inner world of human consciousness, namely: the concept of unarticulated time and the ignoring of the relation of each individual human consciousness to that of other individual beings, whether less prescient ones (animals) or arguably more prescient ones (angels or even more highly placed ones in a spiritual world). It must be remembered that, in the 1830s and 1840s and even beyond, the civilized *consensus* (shared at first by Darwin himself) was that a higher world was automatically a factor that could not simply be ignored at will. These issues of time and of consciousness, though intertwined, need to be separated for analysis.

In order to set the stage for detailed analysis some general cultural considerations must be aired. Up to and including the Greek era—with the notable exception of Hebrew culture—time was experienced as cyclical, as a constantly recurring progression of stages.[7] The similarity of this to the processes of organic nature, with its constant renewal of life in the ever recurring four seasons, is more than coincidental. It reflects the fact that early societies lived fully within a feeling of Divine Nature embodied in gods and goddesses and recurring religious festivals. In mid-fifth century B.C. all this was organized into a philosophy of four natural forces: earth, water, air and fire (see Part One, Chapter 1) that enabled and encapsulated a new stage of human consciousness—new because it rose above, without abandoning, a complete immersion in natural religion. I have elsewhere demonstrated that the intellectual achievements of the Classical philosophers and artists and their descendants, which to this day serve the world as the paradigm of civilized creativity, were intimately associated with this philosophy. That applies above all to the prologue of *De Rerum Natura* by the Roman Epicurean poet Titus Carus Lucretius, whose appeal to Nature as the benevolent goddess Venus (see translation on p. 140) expresses superbly the durable Roman equivalent of what was called in the Middle Ages, in a more intellectual form, *Natura Naturans*. This orientation exercised a profound effect on subsequent epochs of European thought, as I shall try to show in the course of this study.

The Double Helix

The cultural factors just examined became interwoven during the spread of Christianity into the western Mediterranean world, with a Hellenized (Pauline) version of the teleological aspect of the Messiah from the Hebrew sphere. Yet the slow progress of Christianization owing to Roman imperial opposition, combined with the non-reappearance of Christ, considerably reduced the teleological factor.[8] Also, the basic Four Elements tradition continuing from Hellenistic culture had some affinity to the natural religions of the Germanic and Celtic peoples who became the bulwark of medieval culture. Eventually, the Renaissance that began in Italy to some extent renewed the Four Elements orientation to cultural development. If this was somewhat shaken in the elite sphere by later philosophical and scientific questioning, it still held as the fundamental, practical basis of life: traditional agriculture based on natural fertilizers prevailed, medicine had a herbal basis, production of necessities depended on artisans, life was rhythmically organized around religious festivals keyed to the seasons, and so on. Darwin himself in his first phase, despite some training in the rudiments of scientific disciplines as they then existed, expected to retire to the country as a gentleman-cleric and breed pigeons. One could say that he had a rather naive relationship with Nature.

Despite this aspect of profound continuity of Four Elements culture, which has been traced in detail in a recent study by the broth-
ers Boehme,[9] Christianity had brought in a new element at
variance with it, that is, the idea of a culmination to human moral
development upon the return of Christ for a Last Judgment. From
this came gradually a conflicting strain of restless consciousness
willing to accept the challenge of continuous development toward
perfection—with or without the religious component. With the
Renaissance came an increasing turn toward physicality as something "out there" (that is, independent of human consciousness) to
be looked at objectively; by the end of the eighteenth century with
the dawning of separate scientific disciplines this included Natura
Dea herself (Mother Nature). In a cultural sense, this precipitated a
kind of schizophrenia in Christianity, which had spawned the idea
of progress as a teleological necessity but yet still lived (more or less)
in the balanced natural world of Four Elements orientation as
described above. An existential conflict between this latter orientation of Christian thinkers (as in the Reverend William Paley, 1743–
1803) and a new unfettered investigation of the idea of *physical* progression in the history of nature (for example, in Jean Lamarck,
1744–1824) became inevitable. Both of these thought-currents
rested uniquely in the destiny of Charles Darwin (as pointed out in
the previous paragraph). The intertwined claims of the Church and
of Nature reinvestigated were incompatible.

The key to understanding Darwin's double jeopardy must be
sought first in the abstract problem of chronology and second in the
by then abstract concept of theology. The battlefield was the emerging discipline of geology. James Hutton saw that the earth's crust was
formed of overlying strata of various rocks, the formation of which
could have required great stretches of time; several millions of years
were suggested. Theology had its answer ready. No need to suppose
that; each layer could have been put in place by the Creator without
much lapse. It may seem almost as if by a divine inspiration that
already in the first half of the seventeenth century, Bishop James

Usher of Dublin had prepared a formal chronology of the Old and New Testaments and come to the conclusion that the world had been created at 8 pm on Saturday, October 22, 4004 B.C.—a conclusion that retained great force throughout much of the nineteenth century. It is not necessary to recount and evaluate all the theories and struggles which arose out of this confrontation—which hardly gained the attention of the general public until much later. What is important was the opinion of Charles Lyell, the mentor of Darwin, that all *stratification* occurred by natural processes such as weather and volcanoes *and required vast time stretches.* This theory he called Uniformitarianism.

Yet it is important to make clear that the Hutton-Lyell conception of time did not of itself translate into rejection of religious belief, even though it consigned a narrow interpretation of the Bible to the shadows. Deism (the concept that a divine creator withdrew from his meticulously planned creation and allowed it to perform by itself, thus sidestepping the question of miracles) had been an option in English theology since the seventeenth century. A normative version of this kind of rationalism devoted to the intricacies of design in nature had appeared in 1802 in the *Natural Theology* of William Paley. In a sense this work, which had a lasting influence on Darwin, himself an intended man of the cloth, is a summation of European Enlightenment just before religion and the newly forming world of observational science started, not so slowly, down the path of divorce.

A strong impetus to tread that path was given in 1815 when an obscure English surveyor and canal engineer, William Smith, published the first geological map of England. On this, the various fossilized remains were clearly seen to belong to the system of stratification by which the rocks themselves were laid down. Thus it could be concluded that the existence of life went back as far as the lowest stratum and, furthermore, in a way that suggested incremental changes in form. Yet, while carrying this message, the finds, being only *disjecta membra* of once living beings, were not easy to understand until the discipline of comparative anatomy was established by Baron Georges

Cuvier. While it was obviously a great advantage for other researchers to have some definite knowledge of the skeletal frame of vanished animals in aid of species classification, it must not be forgotten that at best there was only an incomplete corpse on which to base conclusions. Unavoidable as this was—and is—it amounted to an impenetrable veil over actual processes of organic life, even now at best inferable from DNA—in effect necessitating and at the same time encouraging speculation. That speculation is, compared to the material factuality of geological data, the source of an endemic practice which in time ceased to be regarded as speculative theory, that is, it accorded to materialistic interpretations of *past life* the same factuality as that of geological data.

The Cultural Climate Darwin Entered

The foregoing section summarizes the principal facets of contemporary theories about nature that applied to the problems Darwin dealt with when he undertook to understand and explain the data and experiences he had collected on his South American voyage and the researches he was making into contemporary breeding practices. His thinking also came to be influenced by Malthusian speculation about growth of human population in relation to food availability (an economic-social problem rather than a species problem) and the emerging practice and theory of unfettered capitalism. The latter was in turn embedded in the ruthless exploitation—including direct enslavement—of peoples less technologically advanced than the European nations vying for colonies they could control unilaterally. This behavior was, of course, supported by a new entrepreneurism in technology. The English were at the forefront of all of this. In short, the peaceful rural life Darwin envisioned was fading as an illusion.

At the same time, there were also in more agrarian countries intellectual movements such as German idealism, some of whose adherents were, nevertheless, quite alert to scientific problems

(Novalis was a mining engineer as well as a poet; Goethe was a passionate and informed critic of Newtonian color theory and a pioneer in the field of animal morphology as well as a writer about profound spiritual themes) and transcendentalism (New England).

Not much of that seems to have been on Darwin's horizon as he sequestered himself in his country home and struggled to produce a theory. If this resulted in a view of reality perhaps best described as (unintentionally) agnostic (a word not yet invented at that time), he was not alone in this: a similar development had occurred in France in the Revolution and was continued by Auguste Comte. Nor did he much affect the course of cultural history until his first book became known in the 1860s. At that time his interpretation—with its breathtakingly bold claim of exclusive validity—began to overtake and soon outrun all that had been going on while he worked. This is dramatically illustrated by the term "Romantics" which came to characterize as dreamers those who had proposed a different set of values than those proclaimed in the new harsh world of Darwinian survival of the fittest.

There are many indications that, in the span of years under consideration here, the Four Elements frame of reference as renewed in the Renaissance had begun to unravel. Artistic sensitivity—a quality of much Enlightenment science—is inherent in that frame of reference. Thus, the history of architecture and interior decoration at this time is a sure warrant for its disintegration. The styles based on Classical inspiration were faltering already by the later eighteenth century when the Gothic Revival began. The last gasp of originality in this tradition is evident in the First Empire style of furniture in Napoleonic France, with its coordinates in the Regency and Federal styles in the Anglo-American sphere, and then the Biedermeyer style in Germany. After this came a flood of arbitrary revivals of earlier styles, often strangely hybridized. Darwin himself does not appear to have had any interest in artistic matters. Yet a literary work of the same period gives expression to the crisis in European spiritual values so profoundly that it seems almost to have been minted for the kindly old gentleman that is the public image of Darwin. Goethe created—prophetically of course—in Dr. Faust the prototype of the intellectual of the modern age who is tempted by Mephistopheles to exchange his soul for the secret key to the universe. A moot but not inconsequential question arises out of this picture. Would the aged Charles Darwin—loving husband and father, thoughtful and considerate colleague, lover of English country life—if he could have foreseen what Neo-Darwinian microbiologists are doing in his name to living nature in our time, have recognized himself in this prototype?

Darwin's First Assumption

That question is, of course, unanswerable but it brings up a problem that *is* highly pertinent. It seems that the farther the historical Darwin recedes in time, the more a mythical Darwin, the model and unassailable idol of modern scientific method, inhibits critical inquiry. The public is aware of only two positions on this: orthodox natural selection or creationist, the latter cast as "unscientific" or even shameful. Who knows (or cares) about the foibles, the contradictions, the prejudices of the founder—as if those had anything to do with the validity of the theory which, like a golden goose, is producing abundant (but toxic) golden eggs? At mid-twentieth century this was still not quite the case and two thoroughly researched and careful studies: Himmelfarb and Eiseley (see Bibliography), from quite different directions converge on the problems mentioned above. But in the public perception today these have evanesced. Even from the scientific reporter in *Time* magazine (March 11, 2002) one gets a sloppy—even uninformed—and rather patronizing put-down of some Intelligent Design adherents who are taking it into their own hands to break the iron grip Neo-Darwinism has on public education. This is condemned on the grounds that it "deprives" students of the benefits of learning Natural Selection (no thought that this works both ways!). A false assurance that current official science actually *is* what it is supposed to be: *impartial and open-minded*, has settled over the public understanding of education like a pall.

To approach the dilemma of the Intelligent Design adherents and the *Time* reporter, we must examine the quality of thought of the founder of evolutionary biology (whom the reporter, in sympathy for his being attacked, calls "poor Darwin.") That is, we must look at the nineteenth-century man, not the later mythical hero.

What actually *is* natural selection as an *idea*? If it were an idea which could be transmuted into an *ideal*, offering something new and inspiring without shattering the foundations of a millennia-old cultural tradition—instead of becoming, as it has, a doctrinaire dogma—we would not be stumbling over the language problem at the very beginning. Why did Darwin choose these particular words? It seems that he saw a satisfactory departure point for his theorizing in the grand "prolepticly" evolutionary scale of being, that is, of nature, in Paley's work,[10] which, however, had the defect for Darwin of accepting as the usual source of energy for this a Divine Creator. As it was still daring to dispense altogether with "supernatural" (a "loaded" word in our times) causation, Darwin needed to find (we might suggest) a seemingly neutral expression. "Natural Selection" was selected, as if by a higher power meddling in human affairs.[11] As it turned out, "deceptive" would describe the term chosen more accurately than "neutral."

How *does* the word "selection" serve Darwin's purpose? First of all, by using the noun form of the verbal concept he de-emphasizes the transitive quality of the verb. Attention is subtly drawn away from that by focusing on the *results*, in this case the traits being studied. Of course, in the background must be some agent (*ago* = do) but its identity is left unspecified. Since the "selected" traits make sense, are meaningful on some level, the *logical* implication is that some intelligent force (being) did the selecting. Otherwise we should expect a jumble, a heap of unrelated fragments, to have resulted. It is exactly this expectation that is denied. We are to believe that the meaningful selection of traits *selected itself,* that is, to have come about spontaneously. And not once, but repeatedly, while the previous selection still existed to be acted on by the same chance processes. Taxed with this abstraction, Darwin admitted that the term was meant not literally but as a metaphor for the "aggregate action or product of many natural laws" (see note 11)—not to be thought of as an "active power." Far from being a clarification, this simply re-states the original proposition with another noun form of a different transitive verb, the transitive quality of which is again denied. The logical impasse remains. Unanswered is our burning question: how do natural "laws" (a term that in human affairs always implicates a law-giver) that control highly specific activities such as rain-making or blowing earth around produce any results other than rain or displaced earth? To make sense, would we not have to make the critical assumption of a *pre-existing* organic world capable of *reacting selectively* to those lawful but not "active powers"? This dense mental muddle is ignored or trivialized to this day by Darwinians. Thus the grammatical and logical absurdities inherent in this use of the word "selection," concealed in a new but equally meaningless terminology, remain unknown and unsuspected by the general public.

However, we have still to examine the even more critical role of the adjective "natural" in this expression. Actually, to do this two conflicting concepts that play a strong part in Darwinism: "natural" and "machine," need to be treated simultaneously, but since that is impossible I shall begin with the former. Just as "machine" leads forward to the cultural determinant of our time, technology, "natural" leads us back to the pre-Darwinian cultural situation.

In qualifying "selection" with "natural," Darwin sidestepped the intellectual task of deciding what *aspect* of *nature* he was referring to, for the adjectival form conceals the problem. Did he mean *natura naturans*, the active, creative principle in visible nature (as when flowers grow in the spring) or did he mean *natura naturata* (for these terms see note 32), the summer product, the fruit and its seed? To have faced this problem squarely would have threatened his assumption that there is no "supernatural" (divine or metaphysical) side of nature, traditionally an inalienable part of human consciousness. The price for this default—admittedly he did not see it as that, and his followers one by one fell in line with that view—was that the resulting confusion remained built into his theory. When he started his work in the late 1830s, the view of nature as an intelligent active force was part of the popular culture which drew on the unequivocal support of such pantheistic poets as Wordsworth and Coleridge[12] and painters of the Sublime, such as Turner. And, of course, this includes the practical world of agriculture and medicine. Notice especially the homeopathy of Samuel Hahneman which kept its position in much of Europe throughout the twentieth century and even in America until the 1930s. Technology as well as crafts were still basically embedded in an undisplaced if never discussed Four Elements view of the world, which occasionally emerged quite specifically on a folklore level.[13] In fact, the influence of this orientation cannot really be said to have diminished to the point of virtual ineffectuality until Darwinism was largely accepted, that is, when "his work had destroyed the man-centered *romantic* [italics mine] evolutionism of the progressionists"[14] The promising achievements in tradition-oriented culture during the fateful half-century between the 1830s and 1880s were thus quite overshadowed in the twentieth century by one word (romantic) which suggests that Darwin's speculations about *biological* evolution had mercifully brought to an end a spurious and backward view of *cultural* reality. According to the unspoken implication of that, Darwinism is to be lifted up and above the stream of *cultural* evolution—that is, the evolution of human consciousness from one stage of understanding to another—as exempt from radical, rational scrutiny. I will define exactly what I mean by this shortly.

The review by Frederick Crews (note 4) exemplifies this. He is so inwardly fortified by, so convinced of the necessity, the rightness, the inevitability of Natural Selection—and above all what has been made of it—that he basically cannot grasp (and this shows through his choice of words) that other people are equally fortified by *their* orientation to reality, by their own integral, ineluctable destiny, to reject Darwin's approach. By putting all this in the context of current political and cultural "conservative" and "liberal" tendencies, he manages to place Darwinism at center stage *and* associate the various objectors with motives which do not necessarily motivate them. And especially since that particular dichotomy did not—or did only remotely—exist in Darwin's unpolitical formative years, it cannot be apposite to a judgment of the quality of his thinking; and this after is all the fulcrum of the argument.

The problem seems to lie in the modern intellectual assumption that thinking is produced by chemical reactions in the brain; in this sense it is included in any manifestations of "intelligence and foresight"—to use Crews' expression—owed to "our staggeringly complex neural circuitry." From the humanistic point of view this is a *staggeringly simplistic* assumption, the immediate result of which, as demonstrated above, is to view the Darwin debate as a clash of circuitries, with only certain ones (like Crews') being programmed for gratitude to Natural Selection (which is personified here, if not deified) for making the bold experiment of human brain circuitry.

But from the point of view of a Four Elements functional psychology, which I have tried to work out in my study of Greek sculpture (*GSFE*), human beings are individual entities, virtual species as it were, who make use—with varying degrees of consciousness—of three faculties which permeate the entire body from interconnected organ-locations. The brain is only one of these, but has a coordinating function as well as being the organ of ratiocination. A person thinks, feels and wills at the same time, although not in equal proportions since a sequence factor is involved. Consciousness can be described as saturated with a fluctuating mixture of these not normally separable functions, as when one says "I feel that..." to express an opinion tentatively (or politely). The actual thought occurs in the brain while the hesitation expressed in the word "feel"—traditionally associated with breathing—shades the meaning of the thought. In the controversy discussed in the previous paragraph, willing—the third stage of Dilthey's progression and the most mysterious human faculty of all, associated with the metabolic system—has almost totally absorbed an earlier moment or stage in which thinking was more prominent. The gut tightens when one defends a belief. Where is true objectivity? We speak in this case of commitment. Thus, a committed Neo-Darwinist *wills* to doubt the scientific acumen of all who distance themselves from Richard Dawkins' theories. Can we never rise above this? Can we not go back to what Darwin actually did or did not do to the nineteenth-century phase of the evolution of human consciousness, to see whether and how much of his work is still useful? The last thing that can help here is to talk patronizingly about "poor Darwin," since his virtues as well as his faults are not in question.[15]

Words can be treacherous, so if there is to be a scrutiny in the sense referred to on p. 159, I must first define how I am using the word "rational." Surely not least in the still current usage of being in accord with common sense: we do not deliberately defy the law of self-preservation by knowingly stepping in the path of an oncoming vehicle if we are of sound mind. On a higher level, I have no problem with the eighteenth-century philosophical conception of rationalism, that "reason is a source of knowledge in itself, superior to and independent of, sense perception" (Webster's). I write these lines by grace of the benefits bestowed by the authors of the American Constitution, who were informed by the Enlightenment or Masonic understanding of deity. But there have been times and places since then—and no doubt still to come—when to write in this vein would have earned a sojourn in a psychiatric ward, or, worse, a Gulag. But even to point out that the *scientific* assumptions of the Soviet regime were identical with what is the basis of the modernist, more specifically Darwinian, western conception of rationalism is, to say the least, politically incorrect. In fact, seriously to reject a world view ruled by Natural Selection and its consequences is still regarded by the mainstream as irrational. If we have intractable problems, their origin lies in somebody other than Darwin (Crews gives a list, in the wrong chronological order). By a weird inversion, traditional rationality is now radical; it is, in fact, irrational. For if anything still cannot be handily explained on the basis of Natural Selection, it *will* be understood with more research. It must be clear by now that a "radical, rational" scrutiny of Darwinism as the fountain head of modern "naturalism" can take place only on the basis of the fruits of centuries of metaphysical experience rather than by questioning individual facets of materialistic science.

My first consideration is, accordingly, that for the advancement of his method Darwin in effect eliminated metaphysics (Aristotle's word is equivalent to supernatural without the stigma) *from the beginning*, notwithstanding his pattern of tergiversation about a Creator, and that the various specialized sciences, acting singly, came to accept this first as highly convenient, then as an article of faith. Even though the world of real people has continued to exist on an increasingly tattered remnant of the metaphysical tradition—its loss mourned by such culturally prominent personalities as Prince Charles and Vaclav Havel[16]—Darwin's legacy has been converted into a force so powerful that most of the world is not even aware that its only real contestant: Four Elements science, even exists. Many, including moral leaders of that tattered remnant, are willing to rebel but have been unable to get their objections heard in a world dominated by an imperious scientific dogma.

* * * * *

Part of this problem is no direct fault of Darwin at all but rather a kind of cultural temptation posed by the unique relationship of Western Europe to the machine. In referring to the Renaissance revival of interest in the Greco-Roman heritage, I am fully aware that what already characterized European culture in respect to machines has no analogy in the ancient world—*even though that does not affect the organic aspect of the revival.* To return now to Darwin's rather theoretical materialism. That can be seen as not totally out of keeping with various complicated currents of thought in his working years that might seem to justify a radical theory of matter. Particularly in this category were developments in geology, to which I shall turn later; but also others arising out of the "Scientific Revolution" of the seventeenth century were by mid-nineteenth century synthesized into insights about the "sub-natural" (invisible inner) aspect of the elements of the Greeks, such as electromagnetic field theory or the laws of thermodynamics and conservation of energy.[17] This concentration on the inner dynamics of the outer world pushed hard in the direction of materiality without yet being a scientific world view (*Weltanschauung*, a word not then invented). To understand how Darwin(ism) actually took charge of this push, the relation of the machine to materialism must be approached by pursuing several strands of thought.

Materialism or Mechanism

First of all, Darwin's *direct* relation to the machine in his two major works is so tenuous as almost not to exist, but still is as ambiguous as other matters already mentioned. He presents his ideas on the level he calls "organisms." He seldom shows awareness of the mechanical world that was springing up all around him. The most pointed reference to that world that I was able to find in *Origins* occurs in Chapter IV: "she (Nature) can act on every internal organ, on every shade of constitutional difference, on the whole machinery of life." At another point, in discussing eyes, he used, with feigned reluctance but very tendentiously, the analogy of the telescope (but not mentioning the camera which was already revolutionizing, among other things, the art of portraiture).[18] But when it suited his purpose he quoted Helmholz: "whose judgment no one will dispute, after describing in the strongest terms the wonderful powers of the human eye, [Helmholz] adds these remarkable words: 'That which we have discovered in the way of inexactness and imperfection in the optical machine [the eye] and in the image on the retina, is as nothing in comparison with the incongruities we have just come across in the domain of the sensations.'" [19] In view of Darwin's general avoidance of the theme it seems quite remarkable that "Many of Darwin's defenders and more of his critics, both among his contemporaries and afterward, took his theory to be materialistic or mechanistic." [20] To be sure, the use of the machine analogy (man-computer) is now embedded in the crassest terms in Neo-Darwinism, as I have shown, from which other disciplines take their cue. Yet the two terms "materialistic or mechanistic" used in the sentence just quoted are not synonymous and must be unraveled separately.

Materialism is the broader term, so that its origin must be sought first. I discount any real materialism in the ancient world. The tentative atomism of Demokritos-Epicurus seems more an unpromising ethical thrust than a threat to Empedokles' Four Elements science, which in its turn soon enough became engulfed in (Christian) theology with its entirely different priorities. Yet it was out of medieval Christian theology that the first deadly attack on Four Elements orientation came in the form of nominalism. That this became the impetus to western materialistic science is very well known. But the materialistic *bias* arising out of the denial of superexistent *types* of living beings, welcome to a reductionist view of the history of science as release from bondage to Platonism, required a long time to permeate western civilization. This slow release, in fact, took place against much resistance, at various times and in various places. It can be studied advantageously in the history of western painting, from the gold backgrounds of medieval art to the new interest in the physical appearance of the sky and of interior décor in Flemish religious scenes, and so on. Gradually, from the early fifteenth century on, there developed a kind of cultural acceptance of ever-increasing emphasis on material aspects of life—particularly as these were enhanced by the burgeoning inventions on the crafts level, where an incredible degree of complexity had been reached by the time of Darwin's beginnings.[21] However, everything about his life and works proclaims that there was no scientific-materialistic *Weltanschauung* governing human thinking until his disciples and followers had digested and interpreted his extraordinary books as offering a new universal principle for the re-making of human consciousness. *Only* biology could grant that principle because, after all, cultural activity can exist only on the basis of biological activity. Thus, the only accurate designation for what had existed previously is *cultural materialism*.

Cultural Materialism

Cultural Materialism was in its inception a barely perceptible turning away from the experience of an all-embracing spiritual world as the source and arbiter of life (consciousness). It was a turning toward a dawning sense of the immediacy of one's own physical (material) surroundings as conveyed by the senses. In this event the spiritual world comes in from a distant heaven, as it were, and, in order to hold on to its reality, artists began to depict it in terms of the everyday reality of their own time. The definable station on this route may perhaps be the fresco program of Giotto di Bordone (1267–1337) in the Arena chapel in Padua of 1305, in which the birth of Jesus is depicted as taking place in a house in a medieval Italian town peopled by reasonably substantial (volumetric) contemporary townsfolk. Art historians recognize this as the beginning of a new age called Proto-Renaissance. Northern European artists responded to this impulse somewhat belatedly by inventing a new technique using oil-based paints in their interior biblical scenes so as to use light effects to enhance the realism of figures and objects depicted.

However, perhaps even more indicative of a new age is the work of Italian sculptors in the early decades of the fifteenth century, most particularly by Donatello, whose statue of St. Mark (see Pl. II b) in Florence (1413) successfully re-introduced, either by intuition or re-invention, the principle of contrapposto (literally in this case oppos-ing position of left and right sides of the body). I have shown in *GSFE* that the original discovery of this principle by Greek artists of the fifth century B.C. as they studied the consequences of shifting bodily weight from one leg to the other (Pl. II a), was not only their greatest achievement. It also indicated a sea-change in conscious-ness in all the creativity of the Greeks which made them the van-guard of future world culture.

During a long medieval hiatus when the significance of contrap-posto was forgotten, it existed only as a decorative enhancement. Its rediscovery by Donatello again marks the revolutionizing of the con-sciousness of a foregoing (medieval) age in the same way that the Greeks had led into a new age of balancing the physical and the (pre-viously overweening) spiritual sides of life. That the Florentines understood their special relation to Greco-Roman antiquity perfectly is shown by their use of the word Renaissance. It is to this by no means anti-spiritual attitude permeating the founding period of what we think of as the modern era, that I refer when I characterize this study as a humanistic approach to the phenomenon of Darwinism.

There was obviously much in contemporary European culture to create a certain favorable climate for Darwin's single-minded con-centration on the physical products of evolution. Yet the relatively rapid acceptance of his ideas may obscure the likelihood that indi-vidual physical sciences on their own would have had no driving incentive to abolish metaphysics entirely, Lyell's hesitant attitude being a case in point. The decision to see nature as restricted to only a material manifestation had to come from biology in order to be inclusive enough. And, it must be noted again, Darwin himself ter-giversated to the end about this. Subconsciously, at least, he was aware of the magnitude of what he was doing. But once the die was cast, there was no going back. Cultural materialism with its open-minded attitude toward the world was abruptly transformed into scientific materialism (my term for atheistic/agnostic materialism endorsed and practiced on a research basis by all disciplines, regardless of the life style of the researcher).

In recent years archeologists began to study the "material culture" of early peoples in aid of social history. This has its own justification as a branch of cultural history but "material culture" is quite distinct from "cultural materialism" in the ancient world, as my discussion of Lucretius will show. Early peoples had very elaborate spiritual conceptions of reality based on group dynamics managed by specially designated persons, for example, priestesses or priests or even divine kings, expert in white magic. Their entirely workable concept of nature became refined by experience and finally reduced to intellectual order by the Greeks (see Part One). However, the perception of civilization as group dynamics did not change basically even for the Greeks, for the great cultural innovations they created were always deeply linked to the welfare of the respective city-states—even though they had importance far beyond that. Individualism in the modern sense was hardly more than a promise even in the Hellenistic metropoleis, and soon became absorbed into Roman statism, with which early Christian idealism also eventually blended.

The purpose of the preceding discussion is not only to clarify my conception of materialism, but to lay the ground for a pertinent suggestion. I surmise that the limitation of the development of ancient technics came not so much from external causes like the existence of legal slave labor (which, after all, has continued to exist in one form or another right into the industrial revolution). Instead, technology was the prerogative of the ancient state for its own (from our point of view, limited) purposes, so that there was little or no movement toward technology as a matter of private entrepreneurship.

Clearly, then, there could be no major upswing in the field of mechanics until the new conception of individualism I have postulated as a result of nominalism took hold of segments, at least, of European mentality. Then, despite the continuing claims of states

on their citizens, private initiative began to produce striking technological innovations such as the printing press, which in turn began
to affect the relation of the state and society, and the weight-driven
clock, which opened new vistas of the nature of time. It was perhaps
inevitable that the analogy of an ordered, clock-like universe would
suggest itself—and then be extended to living beings: first, the animal-machine and then *l'Homme-machine*. Nevertheless, that direction of thought was utterly alien to the Renaissance revival of
interest in the Four Elements paradigm of Nature which, as we have
seen, had no fundamental stake in technology. Thus, at first, the
prevailing tendency was to see the incredible intricacy of what the
eighteenth century was calling the organic "machine" (above all, the
universe) as a vindication of the wisdom of the Creator; in that light,
the theoretical speculations by Julien Offray de LaMettrie, a physi-
cian, and his supporters that organic processes were understandable
as mechanical self-starting assemblages, were angrily denounced in
the citadel of Reason that was France at that time. Despite the tem-
porary subsidence of anything that extreme (this airy departure
from Four Elements medical tradition must indeed have seemed
shocking), variations of the man-machine analogy gradually
entered western biology and ultimately sustained the illogical reversal of spirit and matter as mechanistic causality.

This, then, was the first major spiritual crisis of the present era,
the first head-on assault on the definition of Greco-Renaissance logi-
cality that governs this study. An analogy is treated as a metaphor
and then, in a daring leap, the metaphor is proclaimed to be an equation. In retrospect, it would be difficult to imagine the grammatical
and logical perversity, to say nothing of the moral insolence, of this
irresponsible meddling with causality, did we not know that two
hundred years later Neo-Darwinists (and others) would be touting a
similar position[22] on the same analogy. To be sure, at no time has this
been put forward with malevolence, but the popular acquiescence in
it—as if common sense were shrouded in a fog—has led to disastrous results in the natural world. No further discussion of this

incredible crisis would be useful without attempting to dispel the mental fog just referred to—and to which I have already alluded in my comments about rationalism (p. 162). In fact that word itself *constitutes* the mental fog, so that its historical position must be investigated at this juncture.

Rationalism and Logic

The triumph of a scientific attitude deeply—and one might well say, even petulantly—committed to a materialistic, secular approach to the phenomena it investigates and attempts to explain, was largely in place by about 1875. Its triumph was so complete and overwhelming that whatever preceded its methodology and style seemed subject to historical amnesia. Thus, in the fairly detailed survey, *The Story of Nineteenth Century Science* by Henry S. Williams, written as early as 1900, Four Elements science of nature is not mentioned, either by name or in concepts, although he treats Goethe and Erasmus Darwin as poetic forerunners of the mutability of species.

Indeed, already the terms *Naturwissenschaft* (Science) and *Geisteswissenschaft* (in this context translatable as Humanities) had become inalienably separated, although each was committed to the total abnegation of non-physical reality *as a method*, regardless of personal or private reservations. It is therefore not surprising that current scholarship in ancient studies seems virtually incapable of imagining that there is any difference between the terms rational(ism) and logic.

Thus, the former term is freely applied to Greek philosophical thinking of all periods, even though it is admitted [23] that there is no Greek word that really translates it; "logos" is offered as a starting point, but the briefest glance at the spiritual connotations of this word early and late would indicate that something totally different from the concept "rationalism" is in play. That term is essentially a creation of the seventeenth-eighteenth centuries, both in theology and science, as in Descartes and Spinoza, reflecting the cultural struggle between reason, as then defined, and experience, as empiricism. The fact is that this struggle was never really resolved, but rather simply absorbed into materialistic science as an attitude which denies or ignores any concepts not approved by that "science," particularly anything remotely metaphysical (such as a type of consciousness *not produced* by brain physiology). At least, in my experience, that is how rationalism is accepted by the world at large (if one wants to use it in any other way, it is necessary to redefine it, as I have tried to do on p. 162). One result of accepting the universal validity of materialistic science is that the (obviously) unreflective use of the "rationalistic standard" in discussions of ancient culture produces anachronistic interpretations that "muddy" the historical waters. Equally inaccurate are the soaring divagations brought about by the term "irrational" which *inevitably* has connotations of psychiatry for the ultra-modern mind—connotations which could not have existed even in the eighteenth century, let alone antiquity.

An example of the relentless anachronism in modern scholarship—egregious in this case, since the scholar is noted for carefully examining Greek terms—occurs in the statement "…the Milesians used their primal substance as the basis for a cosmology (*kosmos* = order) in which the world was seen as a *perfectly functioning machine*" (italics mine).[24] Apart from the fact that the word "cosmology" with all its systematic connotations for us does not exist in the ancient Greek language, and that the Pythagorean word *kosmos* itself in the sense of "universe" did not actually come into use by philosophers (e.g., Parmenides, Empedokles) until the first half of the fifth century and thus not in connection with the Milesians, the most serious confusion in the quoted passage is that the idea of the universe as a functioning machine did not exist until the late seventeenth or more likely eighteenth century. I take this kind of cultural benightedness broadcast to generations of students as a perfect illustration of how profoundly the "rationality of science" has been beaten into the modern mind—active in whatever discipline—as the last and final template of all reality. The fact that

that template is an arrogant nineteenth-century fixation that after a few years lost its relevance to the human condition in *all* fields of research and scholarship is totally hidden from contemporary consciousness. The result is that this consciousness goes on blithely remaking history and the world in its own image. Since 1900 at the latest, the world has moved backward into ever more insensate chaos while preening itself as liberator from the chains of tradition. The arts have reacted to—or predicted—this situation as one might expect, with a succession of iconoclastic movements from cubism to minimalism to the desperate mimeticism which characterizes the most recent art and architecture (this is not to prejudge the aesthetic value of any particular work of art in the twentieth century). A mid-century scholarly equivalent of this is the trendy concept of the Greeks and the Irrational,[25] a formulation which should make anyone who has grasped what I am saying here shudder.

With what tools, then, should we approach the achievement of the Greek philosophers? I believe that the modern template of reason, so drenched with overtones from the French and American Revolutions and above all with its abstraction: "rationality," should be abandoned, so that attention can be focused on what the Greeks really *did* contribute to world history, namely, the discipline of logic, which is coeval with, and implicit in Four Elements philosophy. This discipline is described in incisive terms by the authors of *Anaxagoras and the Birth of Physics*[26]: "it seems that there evolved, in the West at least, a fairly uniform concept of reason [the authors mean "logical analysis" as evident from the preceding sentences] intuitively understood and used in everyday life. This intuitive concept first underwent careful review and development at the hands of Greek thinkers around the time of Anaxagoras. What they began to do was to lay down rules in an explicit, formal manner as rules of logical thought. There followed a period of development that culminated with Aristotle's famed treatises on formal logic, which served to summarize and extend two centuries of painstakingly wrought advances, some of which can be seen being forged in the probing studies of logic found in Plato's dialogues." The authors go on to say that Anaxagoras assiduously combined these rules with careful observation of natural phenomena and insisted that "all observations be fitted into a logical framework...he...(was the first to demand) that observation and logic join hands in natural philosophy, and that neither take precedence over the other, and that where they seem to conflict they must be conjoined, harmonized, and even compromised, without either of them ever being abandoned."

Such, then, is the basic methodology of Four Elements science. To compare this with the methods of Darwin and his successors, as criticized in the present study and also by many others, is to understand what I mean by saying that the noble tradition of Greek culture, which had endured in some form and was even renewed in the Romantic movement, was overwhelmed and buried in the "rationalism" of Darwinian and modern science. Yet, it is fair to ask how this term came into being. Its root is, of course, the Latin *ratio*, but the explanation for this is not that the Romans invented the later concept. What they did was to add to a word already heavily freighted with meanings and nuances the task of expressing their relation to Greek philosophy. The Romans themselves understood that they were not a race of original philosophers, and they early and late looked to the high culture of Greece for their supramundane values. As far as philosophy was concerned, they basically chose among the various competing Hellenistic systems, particularly Stoicism and Epicureanism. Just how slavishly these were followed can be judged from the case of one of Rome's most brilliant intellectuals, Lucretius. The theory behind each of these systems came to be referred to as their *ratio (e.g., ratio Stoicorum)*. By extension the word could mean the weighing of factors in the choice, the application of reason, or reason itself (as translated in dictionaries of Latin). What is clear, however, is that this is not reason in the modern sense, but the application of logical principles, the only guide to intellectual life that existed in the Hellenic world to which Rome was heir. The further demonstration of my conclusion is that the adjectival form *rationalis* was rare, while the abstraction *rationalitas* was late and even rarer and apparently used only in connection with religious matters. But these abstractions were preserved or recreated later in the Latin that remained the mode of learned converse in Europe even into the nineteenth century.

Placed against logical criteria, that is, those intellectually defensible by the standards of an Anaxagoras, Natural Selection totally and egregiously fails the test. The fact that objections based on that failure—starting at once and continuing to the present day—were and are simply brushed off is in itself incomprehensible on normal historical grounds. It is not my intention to approach this here on a metaphysical level, but I believe that the proximate cause is the legacy of those French theorists of the late seventeenth-eighteenth centuries who proposed that living beings functioned like machines and were, in fact, in a bold flight of fancy, machines. I have demonstrated that there is no preparation for this in previous cultures. Here is a first portentous triumph of biological illogic: living beings in their highest form, human beings, who *invented* mechanisms ("cunningly devised" is the flavor of the Greek word *mechane*) as an extension or facilitation of human limb activity, suddenly, and insanely, call themselves a machine with a self-starting mechanism, all of which is utterly alien to the organic milieu into which they were *born* as helpless infants, and by which they were *nourished*. Of course, outrage at this claim did ensue, but by the time of Darwin the concept was beginning to seem plausible or "rational" in the sense of a *ratio machinarum* (though such a perversion of common sense is not to be attributed to the Romans, for whom a *machina* was a mere artifice and often a deliberately deceptive one at that).

The references to the mechanical sphere I assembled from *The Origin of Species* (p. 163) allow only the inference that its author cannot have been totally unaware of that new trend of thought as he created his idea of Natural Selection. But he did not formally subscribe to it or apparently even realize that others would see something machine-like in the way his conception functioned. They perceived that because, in fact, camouflaged though it is, Natural Selection is the second triumph of biological illogic—this time not theoretical and with disastrous results for civilization.

The events of the early nineteenth century make it clear that an explanation for the existence of species needed to be attempted. Of the various contemporaries who could have, might have or even did assail this task, Darwin's circumstances gave him the best chance of winning recognition. It is world destiny that he chose to be guided not by the time-honored, strict and harsh taskmaster, logic, but chose the easy and convenient tempter, rationality, that offers quick short-term results and a technique for shelving the hard questions indefinitely.

Mechanism and the Enigma of the Will

Not only the medical sphere of LaMettrie was affected. The Europe of the "Scientific Revolution" had already become so obsessed with mechanics that the workings of the machine became synonymous with rationality in astronomy. The latter was built on Newton's genius for abstract mathematics in the conversion of Kepler's Laws to a mechanistic system that seemed to explain everything, quite without Kepler's respect for the supernatural. Yet Newton himself was plagued by doubts about his too easy success, and Kant and LaPlace in the end decided that all their efforts to mechanize the universe with exact mathematics had produced only some probabilities that never really clarified anything. Even Diderot ended in perplexity. However, none of this seems to have made any difference to the rock-solid faith of mechanistically-inclined contemporaries in their methods.

In any case, it would be difficult at best to project more than a kind of default-atheism on the most hard-core mechanistic-materialists of the late eighteenth and early nineteenth centuries, who seemed to be concerned with means more than ends, and certainly not with Nature in its entirety. To obviate anachronism, I would call this proto-atheism to distinguish it from the militant, programmatic Dawkins-Hawking atheism of the twentieth century. Moreover, as if on Hegelian cue, in the late eighteenth century the spiritually pro-active Romantic movement set in. I would prefer to call it the reaffirmed Four Elements movement in order to rectify the cultural slight imposed on it by (current) scientific materialism under the misconception that the "Romantics" really had nothing to offer but an emotional, literature-based dilettantism. Yet that attitude has become a convention, thoughtlessly transmitted from one generation to the next. On this basis, besides the Pantheist English poets, William Paley should also be included in the Romantic category, as are, of course, the German Idealists.

The preceding picture displays a humanist's understanding of the challenges and temptations facing Charles Darwin as he tried to make sense of his data. What is immediately striking in his major works is his—one might almost say bewildered—suggestibility. On the one hand, one sees his almost poetic sensitivity to the beauty and complexity of living beings, his conventional use of the terms organic and inorganic, and his frequent references to the Creator and to the activity of Nature (with the pronoun "she"). On the other hand, one notes his ready adoption of Malthusian speculation and geological theories. Yet, as in the English garden compared with the continental, there is no *clarté*, no coming to terms of the idylls of nature with the grim sub-plot of the merciless struggle for existence that is intended to explain how the sense-world that surrounds us came about. Yet what I would most strongly emphasize is that his own theory did *not* come about by simply taking over the far too easy " machine-thinking" of the continental rationalists. The accidental, random quality of the harsh struggle of organisms to survive and propagate is at total odds with the *designed and programmed*, precision-mandated functioning of a machine. Although the cold, impersonal quality of Natural Selection may *remind* one of a machine, it was left to his followers to confuse this issue, whereas it is totally *wrong* to call *his* theory mechanistic. But while he thereby escaped the riddle of the French "rationalists" as to how or why a Creator produced the marvelous cosmic machine, he sacrificed the intelligence of their position and further muddled the problem by offering no solution at all. Even though the title of his great opus has as its *key* word "origin" (which was, after all, the issue between the machine school and the renewed Four Elements school), the reader finds the word *used* (once again a linguistic contortion) to represent a modality of undirected evolution with no ultimate decision about anything else, as if modality and causation were unrelated problems. In fact, the author specifically avows his ignorance about the factor the word "origin" would normally suggest.[27]

However, another factor of profound importance to all the theories I have been describing is the matter of will. In the case of the machine advocates, they either shunt the problem back to a remote deity or (knowingly) defy it. To my knowledge, in the case of Darwin, only Eiseley[28] has commented (and then only in passing) that no struggle (to survive) can take place unless something *wills* to put up the struggle. By treating organisms essentially as will-less objects acted upon by outside conditions (that is, natural forces: see p. 158) Darwin forfeited the opportunity to notice that he was dealing with an evolution of *consciousness,* not merely of matter. This obtuseness is not a symptom of Darwin's age (though it is of ours), for the role of will in the cosmos was a serious issue in his contemporary scene (Schopenhauer). To point out that Darwin, to his discredit, simply ignored and left unresolved some of the most vital issues of his contemporary world (and still of ours) to promote his own only superficially plausible theory, drawn—and misapplied—from another thought realm, is to call attention to a not easily explained but dramatic pull toward a scientific fundamentalism that uncritically welcomed Darwin's ideas in the half-century (1830–1880), when modernism came to birth. Warning bells, to be discussed later, sounded then and have continued to do so, but are continually drowned in the harsh sounds of a world literally drugged by the environmental and social results of that kind of science. Certainly there are many signs of disaffection, but it seems that the broad public in the West is only slowly, if at all, identifying the culprit as the totally illogical epistemology which has just been examined.

Darwin's Second Assumption

It is my belief that the intellectual failure in this crisis would not be so difficult to reverse were not also another entirely obvious, but quite ignored, pernicious factor involved. This factor affects the emotional and volitional faculties of sentient beings right into the metabolic and nervous systems. Previously I examined that part of Darwin's hypothesis that deals with living or fossil complexes, that is, spatial phenomena. The other part is best introduced in the words of Eiseley (his p. 200): "Both [referring also to Lamarck] recognized that vast intervals of time were involved in the process of organic change. Each visualized the process as continuous, not saltatory. Each saw clearly that it was the exceedingly slow tempo of evolution as contrasted with the development of the individual which gave the illusion of total organic stability. Both saw life as branching and ramifying into a diversity of habitats and becoming by degrees ecologically adapted."

Near the beginning of his Chapter X (on geology) Darwin himself expressed wonderment at the suggestion of recent geological research about chronology: the idea that the formation of the earth's crust must have required a million or more years to take place. Indeed, he cited a paper by Mr. Croll, who tried to bring this down to human comprehension by imagining a strip of paper eighty-five feet long divided into inches, with each inch representing a hundred years; then Darwin undertook to understand a century in terms of domestic breeding results. In citing that paper, his consciousness touched for a brief moment, at least, on the practice of reckoning geological time in *years*.

But that is all; for his purposes it was a heaven-sent gift that the new uniformitarian geology was going in this direction, for only the vast intervals of time just mentioned—taken from a different, be it noted a basically anorganic, discipline—could give his theory the remotest chance of being taken seriously. Who could have expected him not to embrace the opportunity or bother much whether it was a legitimate borrowing? For very few except the Biblical creationists at that time doubted that legitimacy in principle. In fact, from that time on, evolutionary theory has had a carte blanche to extrapolate on a chemical/mathematical basis enormous periods of time for the permutations recorded in geological strata and, accordingly, for the fossil remains connected with them. On this latter point Darwin benefited decisively from an opportune discovery of an English contemporary, William Smith, as noted on p. 153. Yet this interlocking idea of spatial and temporal factors is far from being the simple matter it is assumed, without further discussion, to be.

Darwin's wonderment deserves to be considered from a humanistic point of view—even without bringing up the philosophy of time, which has engaged the attention of western intellectuals since St. Augustine—that is, to ask what vistas stood before him. His vision was seemingly to imagine the evolution of organic beings in lockstep with geological formations, and governed by the same will-less, climatically determined breakdown and accidental re-formation of the matter that makes up the physical substance of the earth visible to the human senses. But both he and the geologists seem *unconsciously* to have equated the concept "year" with the concept of mathematical powers as belonging to the same logical category. However understandable this confusion, it is simply a fact that "year" is an organic *rhythmical* ongoing happening measured by solar or lunar observation. Numeration based on this (60 as a unit) has been in place since the Sumerians. By contrast, round numbers expressed in high potencies result from an abstract (mathematical) mental operation, ultimately going back to Islamic mathematics. To judge whether, or how much, the two can be combined requires either actual human experience, as from observable organic (such as dendrological) phenomena, or from annals or artistic creations of past cultures, or else very careful concepts. This is where the strict discipline of a true science must define itself. Can one honestly *conceive* of a million springs, summers and autumns in a straight line with no fatal upsets or catastrophes in a stable cosmic setting—and even in Darwin's lifetime this became *many* millions and soon billions? There is nothing at all factual about this: it is instead an *imagination* and obviously a very powerful one.

And if a single year which we can *experience* is not only rhythmic but invariably produces vibrant and often very speedy life processes, did not Darwin's extremely imaginative, hence unprovable, assumption about time, that life painfully slowly and randomly creates itself out of inert chemicals, contradict human experience at the source, and thus divert western thought into a mass of abstractions far more dangerous and damaging than his other largely linguistic absurdities? Exactly because it is by its nature unprovable in human experience, he and his followers have spared no efforts to find "massive evidence" to prove abstractly that this *particular* imagination must be the *only* key to human origins. This Darwinistic "goal" embodies the very same tendentious attitude which Neo-Darwinists see as a discrediting fault in their opponents. It is also the beginning of the organized madness of scientific materialism. By ignoring or suppressing the whole question of organic rhythms in which every researcher lives—and by which *all* evolutionary processes must have taken place, human thinking is released from all restraints and can soar in fanciful realms of time and space. It can ignore the obvious consideration that any thoughtful and careful investigation of nature must not only account for the factor of rhythm, but has also to take into account seriously not just the physical substance earth, but also water, air and warmth as equal, indispensable principles. In the Greek model it would be counterproductive to suppose that, in an evolutionary sense, they have less priority than what is most condensed and solid ("earth")and are merely convenient modalities.

It is characteristic of mid-nineteenth century mentality that the assumption of vast stretches of time was already in place as the purest speculation long before the discovery of radioactivity, which is presumed to justify or even improve on the idea. Yet this is actually a further non-sequitur. Whatever the ultimate explanation for the terrible destructive power that human ingenuity has been able to wrest from the element earth, and whenever and however it became a property of matter, radioactivity is not proof of something else but a profound mystery which stands in a mind-numbing adversarial position to the organic rhythm of life with its creative relationship to organisms. On the divine or even human scale it immediately raises the metaphysical question of the nature of evil. No biology that is worth its support by society can afford to clothe itself in scientific anonymity and simply use radioactivity to extrapolate mathematical estimates of time[29] which stagger the human power of imagination. Darwin himself often pointed out that there are vast areas of ignorance about nature, and would surely have agreed that this is one of them. The vagaries of the mid-nineteenth century situation seem to invite comparison with a very early thinker who in various respects prefigured it.

The Cultural Phenomenon in a Longer Historical Perspective

I

LUCRETIUS, DARWIN AND MATERIALISM

In contemplating the respective roles of Titus Lucretius Carus (first half of 1st century B.C.) and Charles Robert Darwin (1800-1882) as guiding spirits in the shaping of Western civilization, I have found that the definitions of materialism as a changing concept worked out in relation to *The Origin of Species* have equal value in understanding, or at least locating on a cultural grid, the *De Rerum Natura*, variously translated as On the Nature of Things, On the Nature of the Universe, and even The Way Things Are. For, in fact, the categories of Cultural Materialism and Scientific Materialism do not fit even roughly the work of Lucretius, since the conditions making these possible did not yet exist in his age.

Nevertheless, on the basis of the ancient theory of atoms he embraced, Lucretius is routinely classified as a materialist: another case of historical anachronism. Yet it cannot be overlooked that, in the Hellenistic world—in which a theory of atoms was pressed into service by Epicurus and then given brilliant poetic form by Lucretius—there *was* a certain disenchantment with the prevailing religious and philosophical view of the world in spiritual terms. This disenchantment affected only a portion of the elite circles to which Lucretius obviously belonged, and in no way represented the wave of the future. In fact, the so-called materialism of Epicurus/ Lucretius is simply one more of those Hellenistic harbingers of the modern world (like one-point perspective) that *almost* emerged— but never really developed in the ongoing stream of a society less deeply concerned with the physical than the spiritual aspects of a Four Elements world.

The parallel is, however, intriguing on various counts. Indeed, one can have the feeling that Lucretius was already dimly sensing some of the outlines of scientific atheism in terms of what was then available, viz., the theory of atomism that had been introduced per- haps about mid-fifth century B.C. by Leukippus and Demokritos. Unfortunately, very little of their work is directly documented and it is known most fully through the twice-filtered version of Lucretius: the heart of this doctrine is the speculation that reality is not what the senses deliver, but rather an unseen curtain of falling atoms which—in ways to be discussed—underlies visible phenomena. Stated thus baldly, the similarity with modern atomic reductionism cannot be overlooked.

Why then, could Lucretius not reach the vision of scientific athe- ism that is the proud hallmark of Neo-Darwinism? The answer is what disproves the prevailing positivist assumption that an evolution of consciousness is not a real factor in history. In fact, the culture of

the Greco-Roman world was so saturated with philosophical thinking that any tendencies toward imbalance or one-sidedness were controlled by an intellectual "instinct" to see things, above all human
problems, as a complete whole. Hence the title "The Way (All)
Things Are." Thus, Lucretius, like his Greek master, was concerned
with not just the physics of the universe (atoms), including such
things as meteorology and geology, but also the origin and processes
of nature, the senses, life and mind of human beings, the problem of
(free)will, and the development of society. The fact that he involves
himself in hopeless contradictions, as I shall show, is not so much a
personal shortcoming as the inevitable result of the Epicurean
attempt to break out of the "temper of the times" and explain the
world in a manner now referred to (ironically if not comically) as
"naturalistic," that is, with no trace of intentionality or guidance by a
consciousness higher—and wiser(!)—than that of human consciousness. It is exactly on this point that Lucretius, just like his much
later colleague Darwin, is most contradictory and self-deluded.

This contradiction is upfront and explosive. In his epic treatment
of a didactic theme he begins with the customary invocation of the
divine being who will inspire him, choosing that goddess who is
uniquely suited to his native land, Venus. For her—in effect treated
here as a goddess of fertility—he creates one of the loveliest passages
in Latin literature. In his description of the beauty and fertility of
the land, which is, of course, his own beloved Italia, he creates such a
magical picture of the higher guiding power in the natural processes
of living creatures that it can easily serve as a definition of *natura
naturans*. In effect, Lucretius—constrained as he was by the temper
of his times—could not *malgré lui* dispense with a goddess who is
the *soul* of Four Elements Nature, even though she is technically
among all the gods sidelined to the far reaches of the universe by
Epicurus. What Lucretius, like Epicurus, *did* dispense with is Ath-
ena/Minerva, who must by contrast embody the divine *spirit* behind
Four Elements philosophy, inspiring the wisdom in its contrap-
posto-understanding of balance that never veers too far to the left or

right. In his turn, Darwin in these terms eliminated not only wisdom, in the form of metaphysics, but also soul, in the form of Natural Selection; the result is modern rationalism.

The Venus of the poem is, typologically, an ingenuous forerunner, a harbinger, of the exquisite relief on the *Ara Pacis Augustae* (Fig. 2, p. 140) showing a voluptuous seated female with an infant in each arm, a figure representing the breezes on either side and various domestic animals underneath. Moreover, since Lucretius' poem is totally a-political, there can be no suspicion of propaganda undertones as in the relief. However much the invocation may be a literary convention, it also shows his intuition in the soul region of his consciousness of the "way things *really* work." True poetry does not lie. In it he participates in the universal understanding of Nature in ancient Mediterranean society.

Yet this does not give him sufficient comfort. Even before the close of the invocation he has turned to his real intention in composing the poem. He deplores the present state of corruption and decadence around him and—in another instinctive, if not admirable human reaction—he does not engage in changing those conditions by taking part, as does his patron, Memmius, in public life (although he had the social status to do so). Instead, he proposes to demonstrate, by an exposition of Epicurean philosophy, that the world is so constituted that both ambition and fear of death are pointless in an ambience in which only matter, in the form of falling atoms, has reality. With one stroke he eliminates the traditional fertility goddess of the invocation. Or does he? Does he simply succumb to the magic power of words? One of his problems, as he himself immediately admitted, was that putting Greek ideas into the Latin language was a formidable task. There is no direct Latin equivalent to atom (*atomos.* uncut, indivisible) used by Demokritos to designate the ultimately smallest element. The choices of translation open to Lucretius allowed him to bend the argument to suit the occasion: now *materies,* meaning perhaps "undifferentiated matter"; now *genitalia corpora rebus reddunda in ratione,* "generative bodies for restoration of (depleted) things as required or according to plan"; and now *semina rerum*, the "seeds" of things. Other variants are listed by Hugh de Queben (on his p. 13) in his notes to Lucy Hutchinson's translation.

Outfitted with such extraordinary versatility, the "atoms" of Lucretius maintain the kingdoms of nature in the style to which they were accustomed under Venus; indeed, they not only see to the renewal and healthy functioning of living things, they evidently also *created* them in the first place. Since, according to Lucretius' first axiom "Nothing can be created by divine power out of nothing," the implication is that the *genitalia corpora* are uncreated and eternal. And the further implication from the argument in Book I is that all the wonderful variety of species was (in some manner not explained) designed and created once and for all, since Lucretius claims (l. 588) that the species are invariable. It is noteworthy, of course, that this opinion persisted until Darwin—and it is easy to see why. For even Darwinists still only *hope* the opposite, and Lucretius (like Darwin) could not fundamentally escape the universal human experience that Nature proceeds in wonderfully orderly ways to perform its miracles for the human community. Since these are not performed *by* any human agency, they require logically the assumption of higher guiding powers. It was obviously thinkable for Epicurus to remove the gods to their own private Valhalla away from all contact with the world while simply transferring, quite arbitrarily and for private reasons (to banish the fear of suffering and death), their erstwhile divine functions into indefinable "atoms." Thinkable but implausible—and this must be the reason that the Hellenistic and Roman world took little note of it beyond admiring the poetic cachet with which Lucretius managed to enliven a series of dull abstractions. One might ask of him, why not let Venus be and find a better theme for your poetic genius? Or did some awful personal suffering (as in Darwin's case the loss of a child, or perhaps a debilitating disease) guide you into it? Alas, we know nothing about you except your epic.

II

Lucretius and the Later World

And yet how could we be more grateful that you did just what you did? For you left us a precious, even if unfortunately unfinished, account of a singular episode in the history of Greek philosophy, which—by a seemingly special dispensation of world destiny in the form of a single (unfortunately imperfect) manuscript—was preserved from total oblivion until it began to be noticed in the sixteenth century by scholars such as Giordano Bruno, and then a whole series of thinkers. They were intrigued by the Epicurean visions of a universe unbounded in time and space which you painstakingly recorded. Given the state of physics in the third century B.C. when Epicurus pieced together his teaching from recent philosophical speculation, any remote similarity his highly imaginative vision of the universe has to current mathematically derived cosmogony has to be fortuitous. Nevertheless, the problem of harmonizing the world of living nature with the raw astrophysical data that have accumulated since your age cannot be resolved *with* those data any more than you could without them; so obviously the problem lies with the atomic obsession that your Master precipitated.

Where did this obsession come from? The mists of time conceal the answer, leaving us to speculate. What we do know is that the so-called "Ionian School" of philosophers tried to understand the nature of the universe as basically deriving from respectively water, air or fire. No agreement came on this. The next thinker, Anaxagoras, working probably in the second quarter of the fifth century B.C. (when Greek sculptors were struggling to grasp counterpoise) abandoned the safe ground of sense perceptible elements and *imagined* an infinite number of invisible, identical tiny parts described as *homoiomereia* as the basis of the world's constitution. Yet Anaxagoras stayed on basically logical ground by considering these particles to be organic and endowed by the master-intelligence governing the universe: *nous* (mind) with a kind of functional intelligence. Relative chronology of events is unknown, but the "atoms" of Demokritos *counter* this view with infinite particles that are totally inorganic and presumably have weight, making them fall eternally and aimlessly in a void, with chance collisions eventually producing the visible universe in which, nevertheless, there exists some vague kind of psychic quality. This is one of the many logical contradictions involved in atomism. In sum, we can deduce that, if the collective mind of humanity works somewhat in a Hegelian manner, the final *integration* by Empedokles of the thinking of the Ionian "school" of philosophers as the Four Elements theory was bound to call forth a *disintegrative* theory (this happened also to contrapposto). Indeed, if one has the full ramifications of the Four Elements theory in mind and then tries to imagine the universe as consisting of *nothing* except a rain of falling invisible particles (atoms), it becomes clear that the entire picture of an Empedoklean balanced, divinely harmonious microcosmos-macrocosmos (corresponding to the perfecting of contrapposto by Polykleitos: *GSFE*, Ch V) is literally washed away. The concept of falling is, indeed, the key to the Demokritan system; for the first time in world history, it is denied that things rise as well as fall: see Lucretius Book II, l.184ff. The fact that *things* fall but *life* rises, the fundamental idea in Empedoklean-Aristotelian thinking, is totally ignored by the Atomists of every era.

What made possible both the philosophy of the Four Elements (think of a cross with four equal arms resting in balance on the ground) and the atomic theory of Demokritos (think of a steady downpour) was the discovery of gravity by Greek sculptors at the beginning of the Classical era. They achieved this artistically by abandoning the old stance in which figures stood bolt-upright (drawn upward by levity) as they discovered by slow increments that the skeletal frame is partially drawn down by gravity when weight is shifted to one leg only (Pl. II a). Thereafter, the two possibilities of dealing with this double principle *intellectually* (as unity and multiplicity)—

which the artists presumably did intuitively—were put in place by philosophers during the first half of the fifth century B.C.

The epic of Lucretius gives us invaluable information—seemingly never consulted by historians of science—about the competition between these two (levity-gravity or gravity alone). By the beginning of the Hellenistic period, the philosophy of the Four Elements, as represented by Aristotle, had won the day (probably there had never been a real struggle, since that philosophy was based on the cultural *experience* of most Greeks). It was at that point that Epicurus—not himself recognized as a scientific investigator but rather as a moral philosopher—revived atomic speculation apparently for the specific reason that it spared him the trouble of dealing with the philosophical implications of the levity-gravity problem. The atomic theory eliminates levity and with it the intangible substance of life itself. The negativity of this viewpoint suited him and his followers. Assuming that death is the *complete* extinction of life, why fear it, why not just enjoy whatever *is* right now?

This reasoning, which we today increasingly recognize as irresponsible (aesthetic hedonism) appealed most to a leisure class to which both Epicurus and Lucretius certainly belonged. But it did not make much headway in the ancient world. It had an immediate opponent in the Stoics—who must have regarded it as trivial—to say nothing of the Four Elements school. It is precisely at this point that the evidence of Lucretius is of prime importance: working more than two centuries later than his Master, he still feels very much under the necessity of *defending* atomism—against whom? Not other minor philosophical schools, but against the great thinkers of the Four Elements school, and the defense is almost absurdly weak.

The foregoing discussion allows me to explain my initial remark that Lucretius is not a materialist in the modern sense of the word. It is clear that, after the universe had been explained on the basis of fire, air and water, or a combination of those with "earth," no philosopher set about to derive *everything* from "earth," for that can be done only on the basis of a one-sided application of chemistry. That branch of science began to emerge only very slowly in the Late Hellenistic period in the form of alchemy. Alchemy required many centuries of application and experimentation to emerge into the kind of earth-material exclusivity that has dominated thinking since the earlier nineteenth century in the discipline of chemistry. The atomic school of antiquity started at the other end, seeing earth matter as a final coagulated result, not the beginning, of a universe of abstract atoms in a mindless void. The supreme irony is that this dead "picture" is the creation of a living mind.

My conclusion is, therefore, that it is really anachronistic to call Lucretius a materialist. The only accurate category for ancient atomism is its own name, to distinguish it from modern atomism, which *is* truly materialistic in the fullest sense of that word.

To summarize: Lucretius/Epicurus had, apart from minor overlaps, one significant thing in common with Charles Darwin: the extraordinary—and bizarre—intention to explain the organic world entirely in terms of its inorganic substratum. If the cultural climate deterred Lucretius from reaching that goal, it had become more propitious by Darwin's time. If the latter was uncertain whether he had reached that goal, his followers were not. Their influence has crept into every corner and crevice of civilization. Beginning with this one critical cognitive issue, only a new enlightenment in the inner lives of individuals, one by one, can challenge the negativity that has engulfed modern society.

Personal Aperçu: my first serious encounter with Lucretius took place more than half a century ago (1946) in a Latin graduate course on his poem. At that point I had already undergone the usual academic rite of initiation of losing the religious faith in which I had been brought up, so that the atomic prepossessions of the poet seemed neither unusual to me nor did they much interest me. Rather, what at once leapt out of the pages—and still does— was the ardor of his description of the teeming life of the Italian countryside and his deep appreciation of the higher laws eternally governing that rich life. Later, I would see that all this, like so many of his imaginary cosmic explanations, owed its poetic strength and vitality to a kind of skewed or out-of-focus borrowing from the Four Elements orientation of his surrounding (cultural) world— which can be seen again and again in his arguments (for example, Book V, ll.235-305).

The Cultural Consequences of Darwinism

With Darwin's (briefly wondered-about) capitulation to illogic in the assumption of planless time—an assumption he made not for its own sake out of a long-felt need or orientation, but solely for the sake of rescuing his theory of planless evolution—he signed the death sentence for the fundamental principle of Greek science: the human context as criterion of knowledge. This principle is scorned by modern anthropology as anthropocentrism; yet in modern terms this criterion implies a quest for unassailable balance, that is, balance between quality and quantity. In ordinary practical life, even now, for example, in commercial products, attention *has* to be paid to this. Yet in science, quality had already lost any status as objective (which had a devastating effect on color science, for example) and Darwin's time conception finished off the criterion just mentioned as a cultural determinant. The door was flung open to uncontrollable imaginations, released to infinity, of what mankind actually experiences as finite time and space. Yet, by definition such speculations totally elude the modern scientific ideal of observation and repeatability: hence the fallibility of radioactive-mathematical computation of time. Disregard of the priority of *perceived* reality became the hallmark of the modernist scientific establishment. The burden of accountability for consequences was cast aside. Technology arose to facilitate this world view: irresponsible acceleration, gigantism, miniaturization, delusions of never-ending growth, spread unchecked into all areas of human life, not least into the economic and military spheres.

The very core of human reality, respect for organic rhythm, was so readily surrendered by the intellectually elite that one is tempted to think of a pact on Darwin's part with an unknown, sinister Faustian guiding power which he mistook for Baconian methodology. The result has not been the optimistic vistas of unlimited progress envisioned by his deluded late Victorian supporters, but rather the disruption, pollution and perversion of every earth organism and natural process—including inner and outer human organs—like a silent killer growing exponentially as mishap is piled on misstep. Thus we now see the evolutionary stability of planet Earth itself—still intact when the voyage of the *Beagle* took place—threatening to disintegrate and self-destruct.

The effect Darwinism has had on scientific research and on social theory has been the subject of endless debate. However, any attempt to see his unique effect on world history from the *humanistic* standpoint must consider the character and destiny of the man, as Gertrud Himmelfarb has meritoriously done,[30] as essential for judging his contribution. Here two speculations may be of interest. It would seem that, before he became infatuated with Natural Selection, his life was normal in regard to health; thereafter he was subject to mysterious, inexplicable disabling symptoms that actually made continuation of his work problematical. A humanistic evaluation of this might ask whether this is a price he paid for his commanding role in modern cultural history. Did he experience proleptically the disruption of organic processuality that I have already referred to—simply by wrestling incessantly to bring forth, to give birth to—his theory? With Natural Selection he brought a powerful idea to the fore with which humanity would sooner or later have to deal: its own physical relation to the species on which it depends to exist. But his solution was so flawed as to be dangerous. Is there something so perverse in mankind that it must learn everything the hard way, the wrong way first? It would not be difficult to demonstrate this. In this sense the reporter's epithet of "poor Darwin" is more appropriate than he realized.

In order to make that suggestion more plausible, I must put it in the broadest possible context. I propose that Darwin inadvertently completed the de-sanctification of the universe begun, also inadvertently, by Newton. Whereas the latter did this by over-mathematicizing (in the Platonic sense) celestial relationships, the former did it by misleading word usage—disingenuous and ultimately dishonest—in the first of the assumptions discussed above. Regardless of how it happened, these towering figures are responsible for annulling the First Commandment, on which Judaeo-Christian culture rests. Yet this might have remained theoretical, in fact, probably could not have even taken place, without Darwin's second assumption. His treatment of time, as I have shown, directly chaoticizes will-forces at the same time that it surreptitiously clears the way for the most revolutionary shift in consciousness since the fifth century B.C.—and one far more dangerous for the planetary future. This association with will-forces directly characterizes the final stage foreseen by Wilhelm Dilthey in the formation of a real, that is, successful *Weltanschauung* (world view: see *GSFE,* Ch.I).

If that analysis has any validity, it can be put to a test. Did that vast universe which exists in the collective mind of humanity, at the least, respond to this life-threatening challenge, as it were, to its orderly continuation?　I believe so, and with a subtlety which cannot be explained away on a positivistic basis: that is, *not* as a reactive resurgence by the mainstream religions, which simply did not happen in the nineteenth century, and hardly later except in the charismatic movement. It would be more accurate to say that religious formalism (despite the papal bull against modernity and the courageous but rejected struggle of Teilhard de Chardin) has made its peace with Darwinism.

In this sense, it is also necessary to point out that Darwinian formalism is, but does not recognize itself as, a form of religion or cult,[31] with its anathemas and high priests whose task it is to keep the wavering, of whom there have always been many, in line. It could and would take little notice of the two impulses which I now mention as being apposite to any cultural history of the nineteenth century. The first is spiritualism which, in the most critical years of Darwin's formulation of his theory, appeared in the United States (in 1848). It opposed (not consciously) the definition he was making of Nature by proclaiming, on the basis of purely physical phenomena, that human consciousness continues after death and can make itself known by audible or visible codes. One might call this a benign form of cultural materialism, yet with totally real non-materialistic implications for human life and orientation. On this basis it flourished, and even to some extent still exists as a non-intellectual protest against scientific materialism (which reacted with parapsychology). I do not know any external reason for its sudden appearance. In any case, it frontally—if blindly—attacks Darwin's first assumption.

The second response of world-consciousness to Darwinism directly addresses the ignoring—and/or denaturalization into mechanics—of rhythm in the history of the universe that has become the hallmark of our age. I refer here to the phenomenon of Theosophy, which was officially established in the United States in 1875, and then moved on to international headquarters in Adyar, India with many branches elsewhere, particularly in London.

Although theosophical spirituality is explicit in the traditions of both East and West, the form represented by the Russian aristocrat, Helena Blavatsky, was more than a simple revival of ancient Hindu wisdom. Her own relation to it was admittedly revelatory, but there was clearly intelligence behind it aiming to provide a cosmogony that counteracted the doctrine of planless evolution forming in England. To be sure, she posited (in *The Secret Doctrine* of 1888) very high numbers of years for cosmic development, but the numbers are not open-ended. Instead, they were exactly apportioned to interlocking, rhythmically repetitive, septenary cycles, themselves embedded in recurring stages of non-time (duration). "Years" in this context are clearly a qualitative metaphysical concept—not an homogeneous linear thrust.

Historically, Blavatsky's Theosophy led to a resurgence of the Western tradition of theosophy. This took place in the movement separated off in Germany by Rudolf Steiner in 1912 (Anthroposophy), wherein the predominantly meditative quality of the Eastern version was penetrated by full recognition of not only the benefits but also the tragic dangers of scientific materialism. Out of this attitude many practical impulses in various fields of human endeavor, both scientific and cultural, have resulted. This is the most Hellenic-based of all the movements opposing unregenerate Darwinism (see Part One).

The Cultural Phenomenon

For clarity, the term "phenomenon" should be examined before prefixing the adjective "cultural." Here, not the modern general omnibus usage is implied, but rather the careful Greek sense of the *appearance* of something to the senses (or the mind), that is, as opposed to the changing aspects of that something, or to the real and ultimate being of that something. That ultimate being might not—but can—be coincident with its appearance. As an example of the latter case, one may take the very polished taxonomy of species achieved by Linnaeus as an expression of the Scale of Being in a perfected form of harmonious balance; this would be akin to the harmonious balance in Mozart's music. The ultimate eighteenth-century ideal in both cases seems coincident with ultra-mundane reality (that is, what the "inner eye" can see or the "inner ear" can hear). This coincidence may explain the confidence of many Enlightenment thinkers in an intelligible universe. But their experience of clarity could not be found by Kant, who felt obliged to banish the conviction of reality in the appearance or the perception of the "something" mentioned above to a categorically unknowable status (*Ding-an-sich*). This recalls the resignation of the Stoics and looks forward to the *néant* of Sartre.

Goethe and Darwin show us at opposite poles what the nineteenth century made of this crisis.

Both looked at the natural world around them—exactly the same world so beautifully classified by Linnaeus and explained by Paley. Both lived and breathed in the natural rhythms so universally expressed by Mozart that they are understandable to primitive tribes. For Goethe these rhythms became the basis for a serious intellectual field: physiological morphology. However, beginning with Darwin's ascription of all change to Natural Selection, that version of morphology is only minimally appreciated in the scientific world. Yet it offers much promise for a Four-Elements theory of evolution. In any case, life-sustaining rhythms play no part in the time-theory of Darwin. One may look in vain for any discussion of them in Darwinistic literature. From this fact, contradictions, out of the reach of traditional logic, created by the various assumptions discussed in this study, become transparent.

Yet perhaps still not transparent enough. It may therefore be useful to review once more Darwin's relation to the time-honored rules of thought. In Chapter IV he defines Natural Selection as "the preservation of favorable individual differences and variations and the destruction of those which are injurious." This is also called Survival of the Fittest. To objections that this is tantamount to personifying or even deifying Natural Selection, he replies somewhat testily that this is a metaphorical expression. In Chapter III he had already defined Natural Selection as "the principle by which each slight variation, if useful, is preserved." Yet he finds an even more accurate principle to be the term, Survival of the Fittest. This latter term is then related to The Struggle for Existence, an even larger principle underlying the entire natural world. But given that there are severe limitations to the appropriateness of the term "struggle," he will use also this in a metaphorical sense.

In these two passages the groundwork for a structure of evolutionary theory is laid, and he has disposed of objections. But has he really disposed of them? My answer to that has been given in the previous pages but can be approached in a different way. In the first place, a metaphor is a literary device, not a scientific principle. This can be demonstrated by exposing his reasoning in one of his examples at the beginning of Chapter IV. Almost with a sigh, one feels, he once more defends Natural Selection by comparing it to the will-less reactions of chemical elements among themselves and of objects attracted to each other by gravity. He thereby sidesteps the real objection of his critics, which might be summarized in the following way: living beings cannot be forced into the straight-jacket of a Nature that Darwin explicitly equates with the aggregate effects of blind "laws" he has just mentioned. In fact, he himself is not entirely comfortable with this, and so he makes a stunning concession: "In the literal sense of the word, no doubt, Natural Selection is a false term." This proves my point—and complicates the next phase of his reasoning.

Second, in both passages, Darwin insistently and—in this case—literally, not metaphorically, equates, fuses, totally identifies Natural Selection with Survival of the Fittest. In the literal sense, then, this duplicate expression must also be false (and we shall see that it is indeed so). I have pointed out that the word "natural" brings with it a cloud of historical, cultural and metaphysical connotations. How can these—forcibly combined with a neutral (and meaningless) verbal form—be the exact equivalent of Survival of the Fittest, a recent idea misapplied from a non-scientific sphere— and, in any case, in itself an oxymoron. The word "fittest" with its connotations of individual or group, bodily or sexual or social or environmental—and no doubt other—advantages that have to be conjectured at best from *disjecta membra* out of an infinite, unknowable past, requires so much interpretation that it becomes too vague to support the intended word order, as has long been contended. In fact, survival would be the definition of fitness, not vice versa. Thus, any identity of the two phrases is limited to their illogic. To these Darwin added the "Struggle for Existence," a term he admitted was so broad that it too could be used only metaphorically. In my opinion, Darwin's thought processes do not support further analysis.

My urgent question arising from the above is: how could this linguistic abracadabra pass as a basis for real science, enchanting several generations of scientists before *real* (and at that muted) questioning arose? The proximate cause is, of course, that Darwin left aside, in effect disqualifying, metaphysics—hence, research by the strict standards of an Anaxagoras (see p. 172) in advance as a control on thinking: ultimately it was this that allowed his will-drenched trains of thought to carry so much conviction. However, his very Englishness is also part of the answer. He belonged to a country which for centuries has cultivated the word and its sounds as no other (with the possible exception of France), probing in an incomparable literary tradition its mysterious, almost magical power to include or exclude, lighten or darken, persuade or dissuade, clarify or distort concepts with an uncanny certitude. Language and "accent" are at the heart of the unique phenomenon of English class consciousness. I have personally found it easy to succumb to the charm of Darwin's inchoate formulations on the sheer strength of his will to convince by his modesty, self-deprecation and ready supply of homely as well as exotic examples. By the same token, it seems almost impolite to resist his linguistic salesmanship. As I have tried to show, and others have noted, it requires much effort to "stay awake" and find out what (highly deceptive) debris has to be cleared away to see how much of his industrious scholarship could be of value to the world at large. This would be part of understanding what contemporary cultural factors have played into the Darwinian phenomenon.

Natura Naturans and Sex

In the wake of Darwinism a kind of Second Expulsion from the Garden of Eden took place. The phenomenon of sexual drive, around which human society had always organized itself in an extremely controlled way, was rather suddenly seen in a new way. The veil of (often prurient) privacy surrounding it was stripped away by the proclamation that man was, after all, just an animal. This allowed a dark, often personally or socially destructive, side of this subject to become the focus of scientific, social and artistic speculation. It is hardly necessary to point out the dramatic cultural changes, not all bad, to which this has led.

A deeper explanation for this is not far to seek. The cultural "revolution" implicit in Darwin's assumptions took human consciousness away from the conventional, light-filled, profoundly impressive and deeply mysterious, visible phenomena of nature, long celebrated in art, poetry, dance and ritual (Dea Natura, Earth Mother). It redirected consciousness to the literally dark, hidden interior of *natura naturata* (not *naturans,* which eludes capture by materialistic research): atoms, molecules, microbes, DNA strands, genes—all conventional names for microscopic (or invisible) forces. What these forces really are can only be speculated about, since attempts to manipulate them may produce results quite unlike in type or scope what is expected. In the heady desert air outside the former Garden of Eden, researchers industriously probe to replicate by sheer manipulation of chemicals the wonders wrought by Dea Natura, who they have been taught does not exist. Yet, despite the fact that this current cultural perception has led to an increasingly destructive snare of grotesque abstractions, *natura naturans*[32]—in the fully traditional sense of the expression—patiently continues to maintain whatever viability and future hopes for the world still survive in our deteriorating infrastructure.

Given the cultural climate of Darwin's formative years, he can be both excused for not understanding or thinking about the dark side of sex but *also* blamed for ignoring the human *experience* of sexual rhythms, and for not considering their complex implications for the *original* and endlessly continuing appearance of the organisms whose variable traits he so assiduously studied in domestic breeding. In his private life, the experience of sexual rhythms in the human species must have been an indispensable necessity as he fathered numerous offspring. Not a scintilla of this seems to have carried over into the pallid, endlessly impersonal system of Natural Selection proposed as the *only* reasonable explanation for the rich organic tapestry of the beautiful rural world surrounding him. If anything was to be extrapolated into untold eons, how could it not be what he actually knew to be the *real* processes of the natural world? In his succession, the prophets of hard science have applied his abstract reasoning to their explanation of the moment of origin of the universe—as the explosive encounter of clouds of inert chemicals—and this at the same time as *they* knew in their private lives the same thing Darwin did: no conception takes place without the dynamic coition of two polar living forces. The higher in the scale of being, the more this takes the form of a rhythmical crescendo culminating in an (explosive) orgasm. The Greek creation myth of Gaia and Ouranos takes some account of this; the scientists leave only the explosion. The wonder and mystery of life remain intact in the first account, which can indeed be called a provocative fairy tale in the best cultural sense. The second account is a heartless tale with no point at all.

"Who Killed Cock Robin?"

To evaluate the word "provocative," we should again recall the powerful role played in the earliest known societies by stone statuettes that were almost exclusively female ("steatopygous"). These emphasize the female role in the maintenance of culture, very possibly actually matriarchal, in some Neolithic societies. From these, massive echoes followed in all ancient Mediterranean societies in the form of cults of goddesses (e.g., Isis) and continued—very specifically, for example, in reverence for the Madonna—well into the Renaissance. Obviously, all of this reflects an understanding of the feminine role—not only in a physiological sense but also in the far wider and equally important sense of keeping a balance in the emotional, and even intellectual, development of culture.

Yet with the "scientific revolution" of the seventeenth century, the latter aspect of this equation began to be marginalized. The sense for women's potential as cultural determinents (for instance, Beatrice) became so buried in the debris of "progress" framed exclusively in masculine terms, that only recently have the contributions of a few brave women who defied the conventions begun to come to light. The Early to Mid-Victorian career of Darwin falls right at the first beginning of a showdown on this situation which, as every one knows, is still going on. Thus, in a sense, it is not so much a fault as an historical circumstance that Darwin's ideas and the actions of those who have carried them to their present grim culmination, have taken a crudely, totally one-sided masculine form: simplistically linear and construction-oriented (an example of the effect of this on nature may be found in the traditional attitude of the US Army Corps of Engineers toward ecological factors).

History also makes clear that there were men in Darwin's time, the much scorned and maligned "Romantics," who did *not* approach the new problem of evolution by blithely ignoring the basic rhythmic basis of all life (even, and especially, including their own). I have already referred to the sensitivity of the Romantic poets toward Nature's wholeness. Does this exist in the same universe as Natural Selection? Yes, the same universe is there, but Darwin decapitated Nature, discarding *natura naturans* and leaving its corpse, *natura naturata,* as its own creator and provider, a poor accidental *thing* consisting of earth only—and yet, in defiance of all logic, soon to be thought of as somehow mysteriously constructed as a machine (a/c-d/c alternation might qualify as its rhythm; but where is the switch to turn it on?). Vital to this concept is the iron-clad "law" that absolutely nobody, absolutely nothing in the universe ever foresaw or designed this complicated *thing*. It has become heresy to doubt that the law of probability constantly operated favorably for the emergence of a highly intelligent machine that can analyze itself (even a few "mistakes" don't matter in the course of billions of years; probability perhaps even "learns" from them).

Perhaps another picture might come closer to the reality of current molecular biology. We have said that Natural Selection decapitated living nature, thus making it impossible to grasp how *life* truly works—for by then it is already dead and gone. What could still be done is what Darwin's followers have done. They detach the head, as it were, from the body and then peer into the detached body and discover a wonder-work of interlocking organs, which on inspection with electronic devices, is seen to consist of DNA strands and countless cells, each a universe of its own. The question arises: what could possibly coordinate all this to make the incredibly complicated thinking, feeling and willing of human beings function with its exquisite delicacy? Aristotle said the heart, but that cannot be because a seventeenth century physiologist decided that the heart is just a mechanical pump (the ready-to-hand masculine predilection for a machine model, but surprisingly noone until recently thought to ask whether this is even possible hydrostatically). So they peer into the detached head with its innumerable neuron connections and discover a brain of even greater complexity, if that is possible, than the body. Again, the handy machine model: "a switchboard" that would be the envy of all industrial designers, for it created itself (but unfortunately in unthinkably long eons) and operates itself so long as consciousness exists.

Unfortunately, no one can define what consciousness is or where it comes from, but that is a detail certainly solvable by future research. This picture of man: the accidental master and manager of the planet, if not, the universe, seems to me a fairly accurate, if highly generalized, statement of the way current science, as authorized by materialistic biology, proceeds. Up to a point it can defend itself because it is half right; but being only half right, and arrogant and aggressive as well, has been a formula for disaster. Historical reality has its way of dealing with stubborn stasis. New words have been added to the scientific vocabulary in recent years that reject that model, words like ecology, organicism and holism. What can holism mean if not putting back together the parts of organic theory that belong together—but have been separated or altogether denied?

"All the King's horses and all the King's men can't put Humpty Dumpty together again."

Can this be done? The "decapitation" trope refers, of course, to what goes on in the minds of Darwinists and, by extension, in those of their credulous and uncritical public (most of us, including humanists, at one stage or another). It refers to a picture of Nature which is false, because it leaves out half of world reality (the feminine, rhythmic, creative half) and misleading, because it clothes itself disingenuously at best, deceitfully at worst, with the soothing words and symbols of a former (and still valid) world view of Nature that it by definition rejects. This has enabled it to escape scrutiny and, when challenged, to lay the blame on something else.

But the trope also refers to a continuous wounding and desecration of outer nature—and accordingly of our own nature. Thus by being constantly told that human beings are nothing but higher animals, these human animals literally desecrate Nature who feeds them. This process has gone so far that probably not one single cell or organ of living beings on the planet has escaped pollution— pollution so omnipresent and insidious that there is no way in sight to restore the comparatively pristine conditions prevailing in pre-Darwinian times. The natural balance of the planet, flexible as it was, has been so violently and recklessly disrupted that even the public is beginning to notice that a real crisis is upon us. Even holistic methods, helpful as they are, will not stay this—unless minds and hearts abandon Darwin's illusions and go over to Four Elements science. And this will be very hard to accomplish, given the diehard resistance of the current sick model. Indeed, it would mean recreating culture on a different pattern in which, for example, the basic polar contrast of gravity-levity would revolutionize the conception of the universe and everything in it. A hint of levity is given in the concept of "negative gravity," which science is not keen to explore because it is incomprehensible to materialistic thinking.

Conclusion

The ideas of Darwin represent *in toto* a phenomenon of history, as do the personal ideas of every human being who has ever lived. Yet few such phenomena have experienced the immediate public attention and—what is often deleterious when it does happen— the overwhelming, largely uncritical acceptance by vast numbers of people as did Darwin's. I emphasize uncritical because, by passing from a personal phenomenon to a mountainous factor in public life, it became a *cultural* phenomenon. Thereby reputations were invested in it, often involving money and prestige, and then monetary advantages for various enterprises. Hence, on the scientific level, efforts to see it critically diminished as it became disreputable to question the phenomenon, and no amount of effort was (and is) spared to make the theory appear plausible. These justifications are often presented truculently as "scientific facts". Although it is obviously up to every individual to decide whether any real substance is behind the phenomenon of Darwinism, or to what extent it is an ill-fated illusion, it is fair to note that since at least the mid-twentieth century increasing numbers of people all over the world[33] have noted that something is desperately wrong and are taking steps, often at great cost to themselves, to correct the symptoms of irrational, ultimately destructive, thinking that has spread to all realms of life. In my view, as I have tried to show, what is wrong can be traced back to Darwin's charming and apparently harmless—even reassuring—expression "Natural Selection" that nevertheless harbors the bitter taste of intellectual confusion and dishonesty.

Afterword: The Permanence of the Philosophy of the Four Elements

From at least the era of the first World War, the doctrine and practice of scientific materialism has so thoroughly obliterated previous views of the nature of reality—on the assumption that they were wrong or even childish—that few people of the present day have any idea of what the *concept* of the four elements really is (and even less interest in it). Nevertheless, that concept is ineradicably bound up with the emergence of the present dogma of science. Despite the fact that few contemporaries realize this—or would give it their attention if they did—that influence is, in one form or another, struggling back into major importance for considerable segments of humanity. I refer to those who, out of disillusionment with the arid self-satisfaction of materialistic science, are seeking a more logical way of coping with reality.

Seen as a historical process, the emergence of materialistic science can be described as a slow reduction of the four *principles* of the Greeks: combustion, rarefaction, liquefaction and condensation in tandem with miscibility, and working on the basis of polarities. This system is explicit or implicit in the scientific writings of Aristotle, and enhanced in medieval alchemy by the three principles of mercury, salt and sulphur. The reduction of these nonphysical principles, generally referred to as fire, air, water, and earth, to multiple physical *substances* was actually a predictable outgrowth of the restless curiosity and experiments associated with alchemy of the Baroque period—the age also of physical exploration. Thus it can hardly be surprising that the first chemist in the modern sense, Robert Boyle, was both, as it were, the last Christian alchemist and the first skeptical chemist—a characterization that with slight modifications fits also his contemporary in astronomy, Isaac Newton. The stations in this seemingly irresistible direction of European intellectual history have been discussed by G. and H. Böhme (their pp. 131–142): it appears that, even by the time of Lavoisier's Table of Chemical Elements (1789), profound confusion between *principle* and *substance* had set in and that, by the early nineteenth century, a reversion to the Demokritan concept of indeterminate *atoms* preserved by Lucretius provided a new direction. For John Dalton's acceptance of it, in order to establish the atomic weight of the separate substances for their more exact identification, led to the discovery of ever more "elements" (again, I stress, *not* what Aristotle meant by element) and ultimately to the twentieth century Table of Atomic Weights. All of these, whether solid, liquid or gaseous, were treated as if belonging to the earth category of the Greeks, since purely quantitative methods were used to identify them. And more such methods were found, for example, in the discovery of the spectroscope (in the fateful year of 1859) with which the dark lines of the spectrum of each element serve as a "fingerprint" even as far away as other planets. It is not surprising, then, that the next step in studying so many discrete substances was to dismantle the substances themselves into ever smaller parts (starting with molecules and electrons). This had to wait for the later part of the nineteenth century and remains theoretical in the sense that these are simply names for processes and forces that—despite massive efforts—defy a convincing physical explanation.

What proved the most difficult in establishing a purely materialistic re-interpretation of the Four Elements system was fire or warmth, as G. and H. Böhme point out. The idea of the Law of the Conservation of Energy formed in the minds of several thinkers in the 1840s, particularly of J. P. Joule and Robert Mayer, and the corollary Law of Dissipation of Energy (Entropy) in 1852 (while Darwin was still mulling over Natural Selection). However, it was not until considerably later that Lord Kelvin and Hermann Helmholtz took fire out of the realm of theory into practical application. But it is, in fact, on the (Greek) element of fire that modernist *theory* is bound to founder. In the case of the other three elements (earth, water and air), analyzed as substances rather than taken as the principles of condensation, liquefaction and rarefaction, there is indeed something sufficiently tangible that scientists, starting with Boyle, could transpose it into the so-called three aggregate states of matter,[34] at the price, of course, of the logical impasse this transposition creates in regard to the definition of matter. That impasse might be summed up in the unanswered question: how can the varied functions and qualities manifested in these three states truly be one and the same *substance*? And where do the external dynamics that create these differing states come from if *nothing* exists except the matter that is being acted upon? Thought to the end, this means that either condensation, liquefaction and rarefaction *create* the matter they act on, or else that matter creates the external processes that act upon it. *This is exactly the same impasse generated, but not honestly faced, by Darwin when he abolished Natura Naturans.* In terms of logical thinking, one simply cannot have it both ways, any more than one can simultaneously strike out in both directions at a crossroads. Even the most accomplished sophistry cannot eliminate the necessity for animate beings to make choices.

Actually, of course, mainstream modernist science has no patience with criticisms of the basic choice it made well over a century ago, especially when criticism presents itself as a deeply logical, hence philosophical question.[35] The short-term gain in ignoring that problem has become paramount, even though that would not have been a widely approved attitude as recently as the first half of the nineteenth century. Even the fact that each short-term gain leaves a troubling problem has no lasting effect on methodology, because the modernist attitude has become an ideology declared to be the only "rational" view of reality.

It is worth examining the expression "aggregate states of matter." I have wondered where it came from but no scientific source seems to offer any enlightenment. However, what may well be the earliest form of this expression appeared before it had, or conceivably could have had, its current meaning. The English Divine and early naturalist

John Ray (1627–1705) in his volumes on birds, fish and insects speaks of "those vast aggregates of air, water and earth."[36] At that date he could only have been thinking of the traditional meaning of those elements. But in serendipitously prefixing the rather ponderous adjective "aggregate," which implies massing things together, he literally and uncannily predicted the formulation of a modern scientist commenting on the Greek view of the four elements with its vectors of hot-cold and wet-dry (see note 35): "as more understanding emerged it was realized that *mass* (italics mine) is more important in differentiating substances than these qualities." Unmistakably in Ray's phrase, the genius of the English language, like a sensitive antenna, was picking up the *direction* of scientific thought (note that his working life was almost exactly contemporary with that of Robert Doyle). Because of the rather dramatic effect of Ray's phrase it possibly insinuated itself into the scientific jargon of materialism almost immediately, but I have not been able to trace it specifically.

To recur now to the problem presented by fire (heat): while the concept of mass implying density is thinkable in relation to the three states of matter discussed above, it is far less easy to see how it could be applied to heat, as duly noted by G. and H.Böhme. Attempts, not widely accepted (see note 35), have been made to apply it to the (basically mysterious) phenomenon of plasma, discussed in connection with color in Part One (p. 102). While this delivers a neat concept of Four Aggregate States of Matter, it seems only to compound the logical difficulty in the modernist ideal of a single, irreducible definition of all reality. To define heat in this way simply throws into high relief the Greek recognition that heat operates both in the visible world and also in a non-material state as a spiritual entity (see Ill. 11). That view is possible only on condition of the all-important assumption of a macrocosmic-microcosmic relationship as the basis of all life. This is that feature of Four Elements philosophy and science which is now least understood and most forgotten, even though, as I have pointed out in Part One (p. 25) it is the one which actually underlies the differentiation of categories through which we still understand the world. Nevertheless, scientific materialism sees life as an accidental (but functional) accumulation of chemicals on a lifeless planet in a lifeless universe (as schoolchildren can learn from etiquettes in the Hayden Planetarium in New York City).

As a *cultural formula*, the materialist view is even more anarchistic than that of the mechanists of the eighteenth century, who still retained enough of the macro/microcosmic conviction to see machine-man as an analogue to an admirable cosmic machine, both being of the same essence. But the enhancement of machine-man into the computerized-man of modern medicine (that is, of Neo-Darwinist microbiology) leaves that wretched self-created creature with its implants and interchangeable organs, passive but still clinging to life in a meaningless cosmos, empty of anything but clumps of chemicals that work by mysteriously invariable laws. Yet in a last attempt to find hope in this situation, scientists make routine attempts to pick up radio signals of intelligent life somewhere out there. But this is how rational people think nowadays.

The core of the problem lies not so much in the non-alignability of fire (heat) with the aggregates as in the extraordinary fact that a version of the fifth element, ether, continued to be recognized all through the deconstruction of the other elements. It was not discarded until quantum physics replaced classical physics in the early twentieth century.[37] The significance of that event again lies not so much in the displacement of ether as in the corresponding awareness by physicists of the dilemma of good and evil in their manipulation of matter in its subatomic state: heat of a previously unimaginable destructivity was the result. No longer can science be neutral, value-free. The "fall-out" on the biological sphere, having unmistakably both a physical and a metaphysical component, henceforth haunts the contemporary world. Yet the materialistic template remains intact as the world sinks into violence and terror, with total extinction a daily possibility.

Recurring to the compensatory act of world consciousness discussed in connection with Natural Selection (p. 192), one can also point out that, contemporary with the early development of quantum physics, Rudolf Steiner reconstituted not only Four Elements theory, but also the Fifth Element in terms of the *Four Ethers,* which are identified in Part One, Chapter 4 of this book.[38] This is the final evidence of the transmutability of the Four Elements theory suggested by G. and H. Böhme (their p. 142) as the reason for its longevity. Only a theory grounded in physics *and* metaphysics can make sense of the lethal subatomic forces discovered by scientific materialism. One may argue as to whether that discovery had a teleological meaning (for example, the realization of freedom of will). What is not arguable is that humanity now faces an existential crisis in cognitional methods, about which it is largely in denial.

Nevertheless, it is only fair—and optimistic—to notice that an increasingly widespread rejection of many of the assumptions and results of materialistic science has taken place among the educated public, particularly since about 1990. Yet it is unfortunate that relatively few of these, for example the leaders in organic farming and in the new medical holism, are aware of the deep epistemological crisis presented in this book. The only relatively noticeable movement working in awareness of this aspect of the crisis is centered in Middle European countries under the name of "Goetheanistic Science." While this designation is accurate, it is also carries a suggestion of being culturally parochial—which at least partially explains why it is virtually unknown elsewhere. I have consistently used the historically indispensible and much more neutral and cosmopolitan term "Four Elements Science" in the hope of making clear that its research subjects include such factors as the combating of the industrial pollution of water by a study of the rhythmic movements possible in the element water (Theodor Schwenk), and are thus *vital* to human life everywhere.

Notes

1. The American Humanist Association was founded in 1941. It advertises itself as promoting a progressive philosophy that, without supernaturalism, affirms our ability and responsibility to lead ethical lives. In a similar vein, but possibly less intellectually oriented and more proactive, the Council for Secular Humanism was founded in 1980 by Paul Kurtz. To my mind there is a certain irony in the fact that both the Christian Fundamentalists and the Secular Humanists seem now to be deeply involved in politics, on the extreme right and extreme left respectively, seeking to win hearts and minds to a moral and political order of their own crafting.

Working from the standpoint of organized religious bodies, the Fundamentalists tax the Humanists with imitating religious structure in secular form, much to the annoyance of the Humanists. In fact, this charge is more appropriately leveled at the Neo-Darwinists, as I have shown in note 31, to whom the Humanists presumably do not object.

To explain its pedigree, the Secular Humanism web page (under History) offers—among other things—some generalizations about Greek philosophy so broad as to be meaningless in the context. In regard to Protagoras, there is enough misapprehension in general to justify citing here the careful and judicious study by G.B. Kerferd *The Sophistic Movement* Cambridge, 1981 as a corrective. Moreover, I consider it totally anachronistic to call Aristotle a "Naturalist" in the usual modern sense (see my note 30 on the corruption of this word).

Despite its almost truculent allegiance to the materialistic world view, Secular Humanism espouses many of the great ideals that emerged over the centuries from the Judeo-Christian experience, both within and outside formal religious bodies. The same flagrant inconsistency in regard to the ancient spiritual tradition of Buddhism exists in the attitude of those "Mahatmas" who inspired Lenin and his lifelong defender, Helena Roerich, to the unrelenting and uncompromising occult atheistic materialism of Bolshevism (see Sergei O. Prokofieff *The East in the Light of the West Part I Agni Yoga* (translated from Russian) London 1988, pp. 133-145.

2. *Faith in a Seed*, ed. B.P. Dean, Island Press 1993, pp. 3-17.

3. This does not prevent the hard sciences from accepting the lead of biology in their speculations, which are often sensationalized in the media.

4. "Saving Us from Darwinism," Parts I-II in *NYRev* October 4 and 18, 2002.

5. Cf. especially "Fossil Man and Human Evolution" in *Yearbook of Anthropology* 1955, pp.61-78.

6. The recognized triumvirate who represented and defended *The Origin of Species* on the public and professional level were Joseph Hooker, Thomas Huxley and Sir Charles Lyell. The first two acknowledged that the theory was unproved and probably unprovable but, in effect, insisted that it had to be valid. Gertrude Himmelfarb writes, p. 265:

> "Thus Huxley managed to recover at the end what he had pretended to forfeit in the beginning. The working hypothesis turned out to be indistinguishable from an established theory, the 'test of observation and experiment' was discounted in advance, and the verdict of posterity was assured from the start."

The attitude of Lyell (on whose pioneering geological theories Darwin was *totally* dependent), however, was ambiguous to the end, never convinced that Natural Selection could explain the human species. The defection of the two most distinguished thinkers connected with Darwin: Lyell and Wallace, which should have been a signal to "go back to the drawing board" on the process of evolution, was ignored in their day and is still banished to the outer darkness by mainstream Darwinians.*

The idea of an evolution (as opposed to special creation) of living, or once living, beings was being discussed and debated before *The Origin of Species*. It was such a serious matter that a careful weighing of possibilities to explain it should have taken precedence over all else. But Darwin's spectacular and implausible generalization was forced on the world by his disciples and has mired modern thinking in hostile, defensive postures (e.g., the "two cultures syndrome"). The only real solution is to go back to the pre-Darwinian cultural launching pad and begin anew the weighing of possibilities on another basis (this cannot, of course, mean ignoring all the data that have accumulated since then).

Will twenty-first century science be awake and energetic enough to evaluate its habits, for example its fixation on creationism, and try to think of form as something created and inhabited by a being that needs it? Such a scenario does not preclude later adaptations to suit changes in outer circumstances, but it does lead directly to the core-problem systematically avoided by Darwinism, what is the *real* nature of a being—including *us*—that needs to inhabit a form unique to itself? And hence to a reinstatement of metaphysics as an indispensable factor of reality *however hard it may be to deal with it*. This is not some remote problem of ontology to be shunted off to modern philosophers who are constricted by an

---

* In the same way they ignore or marginalize the most creative thinker of the twentieth century, Rudolf Steiner. Exclusion based on convenience is no more a virtue in philosophy than in science.

atheistic science. Darwin *made* it a problem of science, and the resulting failed model of science that is draining the life-blood of the present cultural era cannot count on having forever the authority to ban metaphysics to solitary confinement. When that ban is lifted, the traditional concept of *wisdom* as something higher than human intelligence—a distinction Darwin himself incongruously applied to Natural Selection—must begin to melt the icy, self-circumscribed and hence intellectually provincial, axioms of current reductionism—a process now complicated by the phenomenon of "junk science."

7. A full scale discussion of this factor can be found in my study *GSFE*, Chapter III. However, the present study has enabled me to see the philosophical nihilism of Darwin's time concept. Here, as generally, one can trust the instinct of artists to ferret out, in visual form, the unspoken consequences of the intellectual assumptions of their age. First of all, the invention of the camera in the 1830s led to the possibility of endlessly repeatable, mechanically produced, hence identical, mirror images. Second, this consequence parallels—if it did not actually suggest—the demand in the biological sciences for the possibility of endlessly repeatable identical results of any experiment, even though *living* organic processes might be involved.

The first effect of the camera on artists was to require a rethinking of priorities: the hand-to-brush-to canvas aesthetic could be replaced by a purely intellectual reckoning with the technical factors of the machine to produce the desired results. The ultimate conclusion from this situation was reached by Andy Warhol. Using the endlessly repeatable option of camera images as a theme, he created serial images of objects and people, for example, soup cans, the Mona Lisa, and Marilyn Monroe. Particularly in the latter two cases, he thereby mocked the uniqueness of the subject. Before such a composition the viewer is trapped in a meaningless time warp that is indifferent to a development in the past and gives no intimation of a future outcome. In fact, one experiences emotionally something like the kind of abstract, nonorganic time designated by scientists as that type of "year" that recedes endlessly into the past and advances endlessly into the future—an idea arbitrarily postulated as necessary by Darwinian theory (to avoid metaphysical "contamination").

8. What remained of this is nevertheless important: the substitution of the birth of Christ for the founding of Rome as the basis of civil time measurement in years.

9. G. Böhme & H. Böhme, *passim*.

10. Cf. Eiseley, p.184: " 'The thought of each age,' remarked Sir William Thistleton-Dyer on the occasion of the Darwin-Wallace Celebration in

1908, 'is the foundation of that which follows. Darwin was an admirer of Paley, a member of his own College. He swept in the whole of Paley's teleology, simply dispensing with its supernatural explanation.'"

11. Some of the more technical defects of the word were pointed out to Darwin by critics, and even colleagues, but in the end he retained it. Cf. Himmelfarb, p. 322.

12. Cf. Wordsworth "Nature and the Poet": "Or merely silent Nature's breathing life" and Coleridge: "To Nature."

13. As late as the end of the eighteenth century Erasmus Darwin unabashedly couched his thoughts about industrial development and evolution in the language of the four elements (cf. "Men in the Moon" *NYRev* December 19, 2002, p. 47). The Four Elements (and Seasons) were a beloved theme in European arts from the Renaissance to the Neo-Classical.

14. Eiseley, p.195. Even artistic movements have been affected by this word. Thus, Impressionism may owe some of its popularity to its presumed scientific objectivity in the use of color.

15. One of his virtues that has been sadly and ruthlessly ignored by materialistic psychology and medicine was his belief that animals are ensouled: see *The Expression of Emotions in Man and Animal* (1889). Ironically, however, what has become of his conception of nature as a whole has undoubtedly contributed to the ease with which the original Descartian concept of *animal-machine* was, and still is, maintained in massive and sadistic animal experimentation that was criticized from the very beginning as unscientific, not to say inhuman.

16. Prince Charles "Reith Lecture 2000"; Vaclav Havel *The Art of the Impossible* Knopf 1997, p. 98; pp. 238-39. In these and many other speeches Havel refers directly or indirectly to the vital importance of the metaphysical standpoint and its rejection in contemporary scientific practice.

17. *Dictionary of the History of Ideas* Studies of Selected Pivotal Ideas (Scribners) Vol. IV 1973, 364.

18. *The Origin*, p. 87.

19. *Ibid.*, p. 96.

20. Himmelfarb, p. 342.

21. Robert S. Woodbury *Studies in the History of Machine Tools* M.I.T. Press 1972 studied chronologically the machine tools that made possible the mechanization of western culture. For example, even the wheel-cutting machine of 1672 used for clock gears looks formidable to the uninitiated.

Between 1800-1850 the refinements had been created to make possible rapid industrialization.

22. Richard Dawkins *The Blind Watchmaker* New York 1986. We now have, of course, man-computer and even computer-man.

23. By David Furley writing in the *History of Ideas* Vol.V, pp.50-51 under the rubric "Rationality among the Greeks and Romans."

24. J. J. Pollitt *Art and Experience in Classical Greece* Cambridge University Press 1972, p.5. Parmenides may have been the first to use the term *kosmogonia* formally. In any case, that very word tells us that the origin of the planet was being thought of as a birth—certainly quite literally organic as in the myths and utterly devoid of any relation to machines, which did not then exist in our sense. Even the atomists, if Lucretius (in his Book I) is a reliable witness, did not have any choice but to impute some kind of natural creativity to the uncreated and immortal atoms.

25. E. R. Dodds *The Greeks and the Irrational* Berkeley 1951. A much more sensitive approach to certain factors in Greek culture that do not conform to modern ideas of rationality is offered by Gertrud Kantorovicz in *The Inner Nature of Greek Art* Amherst MA 1992 (translation).

26. D. E. Gershenson and D. E. Greenberg New York 1964, p. 7.

27. *The Origin,* Chapter VIII, p. 119: "I may here premise that I have nothing to do with the origin of mental powers any more than I have with that of life itself."

28. Eiseley, p. 200: "The struggle for existence, the *willingness* of the organism to struggle, a fact which Darwin does not attempt to explain...." (italics are in the quotation).

29. Physical or physically derived spatial units constitute a different problem.

30. See, for example, Norman Macbeth *Darwin Retried: An Appeal to Reason,* Boston 1971. This is an investigation by a trial lawyer who thoroughly researched the underpinnings of Darwin's thought as practiced in twentieth century scientific circles. His results, virtually unknown to the general public, show that Darwin's verbal obscurities have been transformed into various equally illogical verbal meanderings. This quality is extremely in evidence in the present enhanced form that calls itself "methodological naturalism." The first word is virtually an academic buzzword sometimes employed in the field of education, where method may seem more important than content. More literally, it describes a "branch of logic dealing with the principles of procedure" (Webster). Applied to a theory that dismissed at the outset any concern with philosophy, of which logic is a branch, the word is an inappropriate and pompous substitute for "methodical" (which, in any case, should be taken for granted in biological studies).

But it sounds impressive in the popular media. Even more disingenuous is the second word of the expression "naturalism." This is nothing more than a warmed-up, simplified substitute for "Natural Selection," which raises hackles in some quarters, and also sounds less threatening and more comforting to the public. People are increasingly distressed and alarmed by the anti-natural environment they are forced to live in, as witness the current perplexity of the supermarket shopper who hopes to find in products labeled "natural" some relief from endemic artificial ingredients. But alas, there is no certainty what the label means, for the dominant form of biology has destroyed any common-sense understanding of the concept "nature"—and natural and naturalism. The vast, ubiquitous chemical "flavor industry" is an egregious case of this in practice.

In any event, the use of "naturalism" to describe Natural Selection, unfortunately common since the nineteenth century, has always been sloppy and has, as I have suggested, an unwitting but distinctly diabolical effect. In earlier theology and philosophy, naturalism referred to attempts to explain nature without invoking a deity, but not *denying* the existence of a deity, since, of course, the living quality of nature was not put in question. This is an extreme example of what I mean by the term cultural materialism (a turn toward the physical world at the expense, but not denial, of metaphysical factors). With Natural Selection, however, begins—somewhat uncertainly but unmistakably in the thinking of Darwin himself—the intensification of cultural materialism into a programmatic denial of the existence of a deity (I designate this as scientific atheism), so that the badge of atheism is proudly worn (but perhaps nowadays mostly not openly in America). This was so controversial in Late Victorian times that Huxley *invented* the term agnostic to spare the public's worst fears. I sense that there is still some confusion about this even in the minds of scientists. Actually, agnosticism was the position taken by the founder of positivism (Comte) much earlier, but without giving it that name. Again, positivism is confused with scientific atheism; and when "naturalism" is thrown into the mix the muddle becomes dense. Naturalism, by any historical standards, does not refer to the decapitated Nature of Darwinism (see p. 199) but to an intact, if superannuated, holistic Nature. Moreover, since the Late Victorian period, the public is much more familiar with its use in the arts, especially theater and painting, to describe realism, so that it has acquired a certain cultural cachet. Altogether, its continued co-option by Darwinians amounts to pure disinformation. An accurate *translation* of Methodological Naturalism would be Atheistic Materialism. Would the self-satisfied author of "15 Answers to Creationist Nonsense" (an arrogant title in itself) in the *Scientific American* for July, 2002 have dared to advertise his wares* by that name in this popular journal in the United States where 95% of the population is said to believe in God—even though Natural Selection has been proclaimed for 150 years as the sole "rational" solution to the riddle of existence? Surely that majority does not understand what the issues are. For example, it does not want to be identified with those benighted Baptist *creationists* and it does not realize that *anybody* who might disagree on any grounds with Neo-Darwinist dogma is considered a creationist.

It would be an act of profound honesty for a word as compromised as "naturalism" to be dropped from the scientific vocabulary.

It is indeed difficult to reconstruct in one's imagination the sense of release from traditional restraints that early Darwinism exercised on avant garde intellectuals in the heady 80s and 90s of the nineteenth century, given what has become of that impulse: a sclerotic, intolerant, programmatic thought-pattern, oblivious to all other world views. In the cultural perspective it will eventually be marginalized by a corrective view of reality, but will leave its deep wound on the world.

31. One may cite the revelatory quality of its inception on the *Beagle*, the mythic scientific infallibility gradually accorded its founder, the Koran-like status of *The Origin*, the disciples who launched the doctrine and the latter's gradual hardening into rock-firm dogma with no accommodation for any dissent, the aggressive hold on public education through domination of teacher training, as well as manipulation of school boards through public pronouncements about protecting children from hearing views that are not the "scientific truth."

32. The introduction of the terms *natura naturans* and *natura naturata* is attributed as probable to the Islamic philosopher Averroes (1126-1198) by Wilhelm Windelband *A History of Philosophy* (trans. J. H. Tufts) Macmillan 1919, pp. 335-6, 338, who also comments on its continued use in German scholastic thought (via Eckhart) and Renaissance thought (via Giordano Bruno). In the original philosophical sense, the terms referred to the deity "as productive or generative essence" *(naturans)* which becomes "real or actual only by knowing and unfolding itself in God" *and* the "produced" world which is the result of that unfolding *(naturata)*.

* As to be expected, his answers show that he is not listening to the intent of the "nonsensical" objection but simply lecturing about data that the objector probably already knows. Mr. Rennie is angry that the "massive evidence" always hauled out by Neo-Darwinists fails to persuade the critics. Observed facts are one thing; interpretations are quite another.

Despite the obvious importance of this *concept* in the unfolding struggle between nominalism and realism beginning in the 11th century, I have not found these *terms* as such discussed in modern, that is, post-Darwinian histories (or even encyclopedias) of philosophy other than Windelband. Even continuation of the general sense (of the terms referred to above) is not necessarily made clear by others. The explanation for this seems to be the same as that suggested by Nicolai Hartmann in note 17 of Chapter I: "The historian of philosophy can recognize in his array of texts *only* those insights that he himself has already worked out in the sense of a systematic philosophy." In this case it is, of course, the positivistic bias of everything post-Darwinian that is at fault. To improve on this situation I offer the following insights of my own.

While Averroes' definition of nature was indeed to have a long and lasting effect, more so than has hitherto been realized as I am attempting to show in this book, the actual concepts from which it must have stemmed—pretty much *expressis verbis*—take us back to the 5th century A.D and undoubtedly much further than that. In effect, it was a commonplace of ancient philosophy (see below).

It seems hardly adventurous to suggest that Averroes was drawing rather directly on the translation of Dionysios the Areopagite by Eruigina rather than on his favorite philosopher, Aristotle. As cited by Dermot Moran in *The Philosophy of John Scottus Eruigina* Cambridge 1989, p. 249, that Carolingian thinker used the term *natura creatrix* as part of the "ineffable nature of God" (I, 460c). "And in Book III, 621a he explains that 'by that name, nature, is usually signified not only the created universe (*creata universitas*) but also that which creates it (*ipsius creatrix*)'." Despite the all too easy—and common—conclusion from passages like this that Eruigina is basically a Neo-Platonic pantheist, Moran (p. 101) argues that the discussion of the nature of human intellect ("nousology") puts the Godhead (or One) beyond being and non-being and is thus not at all equivalent to helpless absorption of that intellect in the Godhead. He adds that this prefigures in essence the German Idealists, who actually interpreted Eruigina in this sense.

In this interpretation, the relation to the terms used by Averroes that I have proposed seems confirmed. That author's terms were *also* sometimes interpreted as a kind of pantheism (for example by Spinoza (see *The Encyclopedia of Philosophy* Macmillan 1967 vol. 6, 33), yet inspired a quite different direction of thought in the very thinkers (Eckhart, Cusano, etc. into the Renaissance) whom Moran sees as influenced by Eruigina. And the Gothic architects of France, no less than its Realist philosophers, appear in this way as suppliants of the goddess Natura, from Suger's original impulse (see Erwin Panofsky, *Mean-*

ing in the Visual Arts Anchor 1955, Ch. 3 "Abbot Suger of St. Denis") to the fern-like outlines of Gothic cathedrals and the glory of the flora and fauna of their surfaces. Moreover, the suppleness and playfulness of French decorative arts through the Renaissance and beyond seem always inspired by the essence of *natura naturans*. The last original style in this French stream is Art Nouveau, mechanized in Art Deco, still a Parisian phenomenon.

Reversing the time factor and looking back to the Greco-Roman milieu, we find the Böhmes (their page 13) using Averroes' terms (without explanation of their source) as taken-for-granted truisms to describe the ancient outlook: "Die Elemente sind immer beides zugleich: Gegebenes und Hervorgebrachtes, *physei* und *thesei*, natura naturans und natura naturata, Signifikat und Signifikant, continens und contentum, also das von Natur her Zusammenhaltende und das an Natur von Menschen Zusammengehaltene, das Gemaesse und das Gemessene, die umfassende Grenze und das (von uns) Begrenzte." (The [four] elements are always two things at once: the conditions provided and the product, *physei* and *thesei (nature's gift and human contrivance)*, creative nature and its creations, the meaning and the sign, the context and its parts, in effect, what nature holds together and what in nature is held together by human agency, the appropriate scale and what is measured, the limits around us and the limits we set). In contemplating this list of inseparable relationships, we see that Darwinistic biology has managed to do the unthinkable: strike down the first member of each equation as a cumbersome hindrance rather than as a condition of thinking.

In the longest possible view, then, Averroes' brilliantly pithy formulation (achieved by exploiting medieval Latin to create a "philosophical epigram" that has "Newtonian" elegance and simplicity on the biological level) *is* literally, on the one hand, the crossing point between Greco-Roman and Medieval/Renaissance humanistic spirituality. What was preserved and organized by Eruigina in great detail and intuited as an orientation to new conditions and obstacles to human consciousness was summed up by Averroes (how self-evident his formulation is as a *pattern* of thought in antiquity is shown by its inclusion in the list of the Böhmes' above). That orientation was still the macrocosmic and microcosmic elements. Eruigina, for example, got his knowledge of the Four Elements doctrine from Martianus and from Gregory of Nyssa (Moran, pp. 39, 51).

Nevertheless, increasing experience shows that elegant simplicity in any branch of human thinking is only a passing lifting of a veil, a fortunate byproduct and certainly not the most intelligent goal. For there is always a "rub", which in the case of the Elements doctrine was the atomic theory.

Without that rub there could not have been the real search for truth in the ancient world or the era of *natura* inspiration. This may help us to recall that, on the other side, Averroes' formula *also* rested at the crossing-point of the Islamic and European thought-worlds. It could not have meant exactly—or even remotely—the same thing to both. The former was bounded by certain scientific aspects of Aristotle and a native inclination to abstraction. This can be literally seen not only in the abstraction of floral patterns in Islamic textiles but very specifically in the context being discussed here by comparing the heavily sectioned palm-fan arch decoration of the capilla of the mosque in Cordoba (tenth century) with the gracefully spiraled leaves of the decoration of capitals in the choir of St. Denis (twelfth century). There is no doubt in my mind that the inspiration of *natura naturans* is present in each. However, lacking the full Hellenic tradition with its acidic potential of atomism, the Islamic world found itself in no position to accept the full implications of *natura* thinking and went its own way artistically and philosophically without leading up to a Renaissance, a fact that is now painfully evident to much of the Islamic world itself in the current Near Eastern crisis. The deficiency—if it is seen as that—cannot be "corrected" by the "deformed Social Darwinism" (George Soros' term) that is being thrust on it by Western capitalism.

33. The first attempt known to me to understand evolution using Steiner's principles, that is, seeing it as a devolution, not descent, of species from a spiritual prototype, was published in 1931 by the biologist, Hermann Poppelbaum: *Tier und Mensch,* revised in 1960 as *Man and Animal* (London). An extremely ambitious attempt to include Steiner's cosmology in a description of the devolution of the human prototype was made by Günther Wachsmuth in 1953: *Werdegang der Menschheit* (Dornach). A somewhat similar broadly based study of cosmological physical/spiritual circumstances in which life was created was made by Ernst Lehrs in 1951: *Man or Matter* (revised 1958 London). A revolt against Darwinian materialism occurred also in the thinking of the noted Swiss biologist Adolf Portmann working mid-20th century in the Basel humanistic tradition: *Biologie und Geist* (republished 2001).Two recent non-Darwinian studies of evolutionary principles are by Erich M. Kranich, *Thinking beyond Darwin: The Idea of the Type as the Key to Vertebrate Evolution* (translation, Lindisfarne Books 1999) and Jos Verhulst *Developmental Dynamics in Humans and Other Primates: Discovering Evolutionary Principles through Comparative Morphology* (translation, Adonis Press 2003).

34. *Hawley's Condensed Chemical Dictionary* New York 1993, s.v. matter.

35. Cf., for example, *Encyclopedia of Physics* II Macmillan 1996 s.v. matter. Notice also my remark about the present position of philosophy as a discipline

(p. 25). What presents itself as a "philosophy of science" is a result of the fact that that discipline did not or could not resist the materialistic choice mentioned above, but instead basically supports and is an integral part of the modernist stream.

36. *Creation* I 1704, 114.

37. A careful recent discussion of this matter is to be found in the article "Die Aetherische Welt Grenzerfahrungen in Sinneswahrnehmungen und Naturerkenntnis": by Thomas Schmidt in *Die Drei* (periodical, Frankfurt am Main) 04/2000.

38. There is a remarkable parallel, in the respective contributions to a truly metaphysical understanding of reality, in the researches of Rudolf Steiner (1861-1925) and of Arthur M. Young (1900-1995). Each began his life with a profound interest in current physical science (in Steiner's case, also philosophy) and proceeded from there to explore with scientific acumen the realms beyond the physical (excluded by official science from the category of reality). Each arrived at a new understanding of the processual factor in the four elements (see p. 35 here and the ubiquitous diagrams of four levels expanded to seven in Young's basic study entitled *The Reflexive Universe,* Anodos 1976). In Young's treatment of Darwin he saw the weakness of materialistic evolution (Natural Selection) as the lack of a concept for soul in animals and spirit in human beings, which puts it out of phase with advances in quantum physics. In his treatment of cultural evolution he depended to some extent on Sinnett and Blavatsky but does not refer to Steiner, whose infinitely richer understanding of this and all subjects may possibly have intimidated him. Nevertheless, the prodigious and incredibly broad originality of Arthur M. Young, the inventor of the Bell helicopter, puts him far above other Anglo-Saxon scientific theorists (especially molecular biologists) and his pragmatic orientation may ultimately give him pride of place if there is ever a real cultural renewal in that trans-Atlantic cultural sphere.

SELECTED BIBLIOGRAPHY
(and abbreviations)

Benson, J.L. *GCTFE Greek Color Theory and the Four Elements* Libraries of the University of Massachusetts at Amherst 2000 see website at: http/www.library.umass.edu/benson/jbgc.html

Benson, J.L *GSFE Greek Sculpture and the Four Elements* Libraries of the University of Massachusetts at Amherst 2000 see website at: http/www.library.umass.edu/jbgs.html

Boehme, G. and Boehme, H. *Eine Kulturgeschichte der Elemente Feuer Wasser Erde Luft* Munich 1996

Bouma, P.J. *Physical Aspects of Colour.* An Introduction to the Scientific Study of Colour Science and Colour Stimuli Eindhoven 1947

Buschor, Ernst *On the Meaning of Greek Statues* Amherst 1980

Darwin, Charles *The Origin of Species by means of Natural Selection* W. Benton Publisher Encyclopaedia Britannica 1952

Diehls, Hermann *Die Fragmente der Vorsokratiker* Bd. I Berlin 1964

Dodds, E.R. *The Greeks and the Irrational* Berkeley 1951

Eiseley, Loren *Darwin's Century* Anchor Books 1961

Farrington, B. *Greek Science* Penguin Books 1959

GA Gesamtausgabe referring to the complete works of Rudolf Steiner as published by the Rudolf-Steiner-Nachlassverwaltung (ongoing) Dornach, Switzerland

Hamprecht, Bodo Various articles on the physics of light in *Das Goetheanum* (Dornach, Switzerland) 1985-1995

Himmelfarb, Gertrude *Darwin and the Darwinian Revolution* Anchor Books 1957, 1962

Keils, E. *Plato and Greek Painting* Leiden 1978

Kirk, G.S. *The Nature of Greek Myths* Penguin Books 1974

Lucy Hamilton's Translation of Lucretius De rerum natura Edited by Hugh de Queben University of Michigan Press Ann Arbor, Michigan 1996

Marti, Ernst *The Four Ethers* Contributions to Rudolf Steiner's Science of the Ethers Schaumburg Publications Roselle, Illinois 1984 (translation of 1974 German text)

Matthei, Rupprecht *Goethe's Color Theory* Arranged and Translated by Rupprecht Matthei Van Nostrand 1971 (translation of 1979 German text)

NYRev New York Review of Books 1755 Broadway New York NY

Ott, G. and Proskauer, H. *Johann Wolfgang von Goethe Farbenlehre* 3 vols. with introduction and commentaries of Rudolf Steiner Stuttgart 1980

Pollitt, J.J. *Art and Experience in Classical Greece* Cambridge 1972

Raske, Hilda *Das Farbenwort* Rudolf Steiner's Malerei und Farbenkunst im Ersten Goetheanum Stuttgart 1983 (also published as *The Language of Color in the First Goetheanum* Walter Keller Verlag, Dornach n.d.)

Schwenk, Theodor *Sensitive Chaos* London 1965

Schlepperges, H. "Antike und Mittelalter" in *Historische Anthropologie* Vol. I Freiburg l978

Sigerist, H. *A History of Medicine* Vol.II Oxford 1961

Steiner, Rudolf *Colour* Three Lectures given in Dornach 6th-8th May,1921 with Extracts from the Notebooks Translated by John Salter Rudolf Steiner Press London 1970

Vertosick, Frank T. Jr. *The Genius Within.* I have been able to consult only the review in the *Smithsonian* (magazine) of Nov. 2002, pp. 134-35

West, M.L. *Early Greek Philosophy and the Orient* Oxford 1971

Wright, M.R. *Empedokles The Extant Fragments* New Haven 1981

LIST OF ILLUSTRATIONS

END PLATES:

I. Black figure hydria with charioteer

II. a) Doryphoros; b) St. Mark

III. a) Black figure skyphos with gods; b) saturated yellow; c) Goethe's color circle

IV. a) dark spectrum; b) light spectrum

TEXT FIGURES:

1. Author's sketch of the Warka Vase p. 21

2. Line drawing of *Tellus with Breezes* p. 140

TEXT ILLUSTRATIONS: *PASSIM* IN PART ONE

Twenty diagrammatic schemata designed, with several exceptions, by the author, to visualize verbal explanations.

CREDITS

Cover illustration and Plate IIIa: Greek, Theseus Painter, *Black figure skyphos with Herakles, Athena and Hermes.* Clay and black glaze with added red and white; ca. 500 B.C.E. Nancy Everett Dwight Fund. Mount Holyoke College Art Museum, South Hadley, Massachusetts.

Plate I: Black figure amphora c. 550 B.C.E. Terracotta. 15 x 10 x 6 3/4 in. (38.1 x 25.4 x 17.1 cm) Smith College Museum of Art, Northampton, Massachusetts. Purchased 1920

Plate II a: marble statue of Doryphoros (Spear-Bearer) Roman copy of 5th century B.C. Greek work, Naples Archaeological Museum. H. Gardner, *Handbook of Greek Sculpture* London 1911

Plate II b: marble statue of St. Mark by Donatello Florence, dated 1413 A.D. A.G. Myer, *Donatello* Leipzig 1904

Plates III b, c and IV* FOTOGRAPHIE für Wissenschaft und Technik Hans-Georg Hetzel Grellingerstr. 25 CH 4052 Basel, Switzerland

Lines 1-42 of Book I from *Lucy Hutchinson's Translation of Lucretius De rerum natura.* Edited by Hugh de Queben The University of Michigan Press Permissions, University of Michigan Press, Ann Arbor, Michigan; original publisher: Gerald Duckworth & Co.Ltd London, England

Text figure 1: author's sketch of alabaster vessel in Iraq Museum, Baghdad, third quarter of 4th millennium B.C. See p. 28, note 12.

Text figure 2: line drawing of Tellus (earth goddess) with Breezes from the Ara Pacis, Rome: S. *Reinach Repertoire des Reliefs Grecs et Romains* Vol. IV p. 236 fig. 1 Paris 1909

Credit for the help of individuals and institutions given me in the creation of my internet book *GCTFE* of which *The Inner Nature of Color* is an offshoot, has been duly recorded in the preface of that book. Readers who want the full background of Part One of the present book are directed there. Here I will mention my deep indebtedness only to several persons who have literally made the publication of the present book possible: Branko Furst, M.D., who assisted me with advice and technical assistance in so many ways; Christopher Bamford, who over the years has supported me with his belief in the viability of my ideas; and always, Linda Benson.

*I take responsibility for the format of Pl. IV since it was not feasible to submit this to H. G. Hetzel to control the exact placement and proportions of the component parts.

Black figure hydria with charioteer

PLATE I

a) Doryphoros   b) St. Mark

PLATE II

a) Black figure skyphos with gods

b) saturated yellow

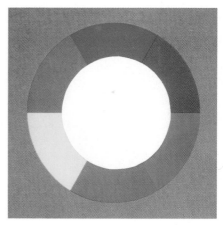

c) Goethe's color circle

PLATE III

a) dark spectrum

b) light spectrum

PLATE IV